WHOLE BRAIN TEACHING *for*
Challenging Kids

(and the rest of your class, too!)

CHRIS BIFFLE

Director, Whole Brain Teachers of America

Also by Christopher Biffle

A Guided Tour of Five Works by Plato (McGraw-Hill)

A Guided Tour of Descartes' Meditations on First Philosophy (McGraw-Hill)

A Guided Tour of Aristotle's Nicomachean Ethics (McGraw-Hill)

Landscape of Wisdom: An Introduction to Philosophy (McGraw-Hill)

Castle of the Pearl: A Guide to Self Knowledge (HarperCollins)

A Journey Through Your Childhood (Tarcher)

The Garden in the Snowy Mountains: Self Exploration With Jesus As Your Guide (HarperCollins)

WholeBrain
T E A C H I N G
A WORLD LEADER IN BRAIN BASED LEARNING

Book design: Lucinda Geist

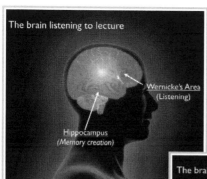

The brain listening to lecture

Wernicke's Area (Listening)

Hippocampus (Memory creation)

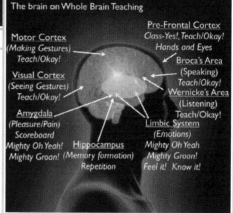

The brain on Whole Brain Teaching

Pre-Frontal Cortex
Class-Yes!, Teach/Okay!
Hands and Eyes

Motor Cortex
(Making Gestures)
Teach/Okay!

Broca's Area
(Speaking)
Teach/Okay!

Visual Cortex
(Seeing Gestures)
Teach/Okay!

Wernicke's Area
(Listening)
Teach/Okay!

Amygdala
(Pleasure/Pain)
Scoreboard
Mighty Oh Yeah!
Mighty Groan!

Hippocampus
(Memory formation)
Repetition

Limbic System
(Emotions)
Mighty Oh Yeah
Mighty Groan!
Feel it! Know it!

The Big Seven

1. **Class-Yes** involves the prefrontal cortex, the reasoning center of the brain. Think of this area as a "light switch" that must be turned on for the rest of the brain to process information.

2. **Five Classroom Rules** when rehearsed and used in class, the five rules involve the prefrontal cortex, Broca's area, Wernicke's area, the limbic system, hippocampus, visual cortex and motor cortex.

3. **Teach-Okay** is the most powerful of Whole Brain Teaching's learning activities. Students have their prefrontal cortex involved, activate Broca's area as they speak, Wernicke's area as they listen, the visual and the motor cortex as they see and make gestures. This whole brain activity powerfully stimulates the hippocampus to form long term memories.

4. **The Scoreboard** keys directly into the limbic system's emotions and the amygdala which registers pleasure (Mighty Oh Yeah!) and pain (Mighty Groan!) as students accumulate rewards and penalties.

5. **Hands and Eyes** focuses all mental activity on seeing and hearing the teacher's lesson.

6. **Switch** helps students fully develop both their speaking (Broca's area) and their listening (Wernicke's area) abilities.

7. **Mirror** activiates the visual and motor cortex, as well as mirror neurons in other brain areas which are central to learning.

Contents

First Words .... **viii**

1   Introduction **1**

2   The Origin of Whole Brain Teaching **4**
25 years of failure and then bingo... the light goes on!

3   Seven Common Teaching Mistakes **9**
How we make our jobs much, much harder

4   Charting Progress **14**
*You can't tell where you're going, without a
chart of where you've been*

5   The Brain On Whole Brain Teaching **18**
A short course in brain science

6   Class-Yes **27**
Instantly, magically, gain your kids' attention

7   Five, Powerful Classroom Rules **31**
Including the ultimate, no loophole rule!

8   Teach-Okay **44**
Transforming your students into eager teachers

9   Teach-Okay (Part 2) **54**

10   Teach-Okay (Part 3) **59**

11   The Scoreboard **62**
     Motivating your class to work hard

12   Mirror, Hands and Eyes.. **77**
     Two powerful student engagers

13   Daily Classroom Procedures **85**
     Eliminating challenging behavior during transitions

14   Scoreboard Levels **95**
     A year-long classroom management system

15   The Super Improvers Team................................... **98**
     Rewarding student improvement

16   Improving State Test Scores with
     The Super Improvers Team **107**
     Climbing a ladder of stars

17   Practice Cards **114**
     Targeting individual behavior problems

18   More Ways To Use Practice Cards.......................... **119**
     Rewards and in-class practice

19   The Guff Counter.. **124**
     What to do when students talk back

20   The Independents... **130**
     Watch in amazement as rebel allies turn against each other!

21   The Bull's Eye Game.. **134**
     One on one with challenging students

22   The Agreement Bridge.......................................**139**
     Collaborative problem solving with your toughest kids

23   Whole Brain Teaching and Critical Thinking.............. **153**
     Open ended questions lead to Higher Order
     Thinking Skills (HOTS!)

24 **More Critical Thinking: The Illustrious Brain Toys** **157**
What's more fun than a dozen mind games?

25 **Smart Cards** **162**
Low tech technology for instantly assessing comprehension

26 **Leadership Training and the Self Managing Class** **169**
The Gold Treasure at rainbow's end... is closer than you think

27 **Whole Brain Teaching Review** **172**
All about Everything (and more!)

28 **Whole Brain Teaching and Learning Research** **178**
by Angela Macias and Brian Macias

29 **Additional Research** **190**

30 BONUS CHAPTER:
Designing Your WBT Model Classroom **194**

31 BONUS CHAPTER:
The Five Step WBT Lesson Template **218**

32 BONUS CHAPTER:
11 Day Writing Lesson Plan **229**

APPENDIX

Mind Sports **256**

Rehearsing Procedures **264**

Notes to Parents **267**

Free Whole Brain Teaching E-Books **269**

Free Whole Brain Teaching Videos **272**

Classroom Rules Signs **275**

BIBLIOGRAPHY **280**

This book is dedicated to la mujer de mi alma,
Deidre

First Words

Whole Brain Teaching (WBT) is used by instructors in every state of the Union and in 30 countries around the world. In California alone, 6,000 educators representing over 250,000 students have attended free WBT conferences. Whole Brain Teaching videos on the internet have received over 3,000,000 views. More than 10,00,000 pages of free eBooks have been downloaded from our website, WholeBrainTeaching.com. WBT is one of the world's fastest growing, education reform movements.

For me, the roots of Whole Brain Teaching can be traced back 40 years to Harry Berger's "Introduction to Literature" seminar at University of California at Santa Cruz. Harry's genius was that he asked the right questions in the right order. He led me where I didn't know I needed to go.

I've had many great teachers since those long ago days. Two of the best, Chris Rekstad and Jay Vanderfin, began as my students. They took my college level teaching system and, with stunning creativity, adapted it to their elementary school classrooms.

Chris, Jay and I were blessed to have other great instructors join us. From the very beginning, Andrea Schindler, Angela Macias and Roxie Barrett polished Whole Brain Teaching strategies that we all went on to present to thousands of teachers across America. After Jason Pedersen, our brilliant programmer, created our website, WholeBrainTeaching.com, we were joined by a remarkable group of educators: Jeff Battle (North Carolina), Jackie Pedersen (Utah), Susan Floyd and Stacie Glass (Missouri), Nancy Stoltenberg (California), Deb Weigel (Arizona), Dave Brobeck and

Lindsey Roush (Ohio), Kate Bowski (Delaware), Liann Nutini (Canada), Sarah Meador (Illinois), Jasselle Cruz (Pennsylvania) and Farrah Shipley (Texas). W.B. Yeats said that his glory was his friends. Poor Yeats. He never knew anyone who matched the wondrous gifts of my colleagues.

My greatest lessons have been taught to me by three divine muses, my daughters Persephone and Saskia and *corazon de mi corazon, mi querida*, Deidre.

CHAPTER 1

Introduction

Year after year, good teachers leave teaching because they are tired of warring with disruptive kids. Too many classrooms are battle zones between kids who want freedom and teachers who want order. Every evening, thousands of our colleagues go home frustrated, disillusioned, defeated. We enter teaching because we want students to be successful and we are daily beaten down by the kids who most need our help.

This is the dark, painful truth in our hearts: *we can't teach classes that won't listen.*

We know yelling and scolding doesn't work. If students' behavior could be controlled by angry adults, then kids from troubled families would be exceedingly polite. It's impossible to help our classes control their emotions by blowing our stack.

Schools are dangerous places. According to the National Center for Education statistics, in 2007 there were "1.5 million victims of nonfatal crimes at school, including 826,800 thefts and 684,100 violent crimes." Children were more likely to be crime victims in school, than outside of school. Over 260,000 teachers in the U.S. were subject to threats of injury by students. Three times more elementary school teachers reported being physically attacked than middle school instructors.

We know the behavior of challenging kids cannot be improved by heavier and heavier doses of punishment. Challenging kids are rebels; punishment makes them more rebellious. No sane adult wants to punish kids; we punish *because we don't know what else to do.* Most challenging kids genuinely want to be part of the classroom environment; this is why they work so hard, and continuously, to get everyone's attention.

Isn't it obvious what every pupil wants? Kids want to laugh and play games. Our system, Whole Brain Teaching (WBT), produces classrooms that are full of *orderly* fun. Students follow our rules because we make our rules fun to follow. Kids teach their neighbors because they delight in playing teacher. Students work hard with their classmates to gain a few minutes of free time, because we have created structures that make this hard work more entertaining than zoning out.

WBT is more like a large, lively game than a traditional elementary school classroom management system. Just as in all games, there are penalties as well as rewards... but like "going to jail" in Monopoly®, even our penalties are entertaining.

Here is Whole Brain Teaching's secret, which I learned after a quarter of a century of failed experiments: *if a student's whole brain is involved in learning, there isn't any mental area left over for challenging behavior.*

It doesn't matter what state you live in. It makes no difference if you teach in the inner city or miles from the nearest paved road. The guerilla warfare between bands of rebel students and solitary instructors is the same on every front. Disruptive kids break rules, distract classmates, bond with other rebels, retreat into walled silence, are nourished by resisting their instructor's best intentions... *because their brains demand activity which the classroom does not provide.* The brain has no off switch... and is constantly learning either positive or negative behaviors. Don't think your challenging kids are not learning; they are studiously acquiring, from each other, the arts of rebellion. Instead of the intricacies of math and the nuances of written expression, your rebels are mastering the rhetoric of intimidation and performing independent studies in chaos creation. We must involve our students' whole brains in peaceable learning or lose them to their own dark entertainments.

If you have kids who won't stay in their seats, or who talk out of turn, or who turn in sloppy work (when they turn in work at all), or who are openly rebellious, or who are locked in their shell, or who disrupt class with clownish antics, or who know exactly how to push your buttons, or who are a danger to themselves and/or others, then please read this book with a large hanky. When you are finished, you'll be sobbing tears of joy.

Tens of thousands of teachers use our techniques daily... and give us rave reviews. Many, perhaps even the majority, of our instructors work in poverty level schools. Recent news reports indicated that San Bernardino, an initial source of hundreds of our seminar participants, ranked last among U.S. cities in high school graduation rate and first in murder rate. If you have kids whose parents are drug addicts, or who walk to school through gang infested neighborhoods, or who are always ready to fight, so do we. Whole Brain Teachers are experiencing success in schools that are as challenging as any in America.

All our conferences are free. We have given away over 10,000,000 pages of teaching materials. We are not a business. Whole Brain Teaching is a grass roots education reform movement. If you haven't done so yet, visit our website, WholeBrainTeaching.com, and access our free eBooks and videos.

In this book, you'll find a set of detailed instructions for teaching challenging kids. You'll also learn what other Whole Brain Teachers across the country have discovered; our program makes a remarkable difference not only for your rebels, but also for your wonderful loyalists.

CHAPTER 2

The Origin of Whole Brain Teaching

*25 years of failure and then bingo...
the light goes on!*

As you'll soon learn, Whole Brain Teaching techniques work superbly, *if you practice them daily*. As Rafe Esquith, 2002 National Outstanding Teacher of the Year, said, "there are no shortcuts to excellence." There are no shortcuts to being an excellent guitarist, dancer, scientist. There are no shortcuts to being an excellent teacher, one of the noblest and most difficult callings on earth. But, unfortunately, you can work really hard, using the wrong techniques, and get nowhere. If you don't do the right steps, you'll never dance the cha-cha.

I practiced hideously wrong steps for 25 years.

I speak to you as a determined failure.

In 1970 in Watsonville, California, I helped establish Children's House, one of the first federally funded preschools for the children of migrant workers in the United States. We had a budget for food and nothing else. We had no books, paper, pencils, crayons, toys, nothing. Our supervisor told us that part of our job was to beg merchants to donate teaching supplies.

I was fresh out of college, had no teaching experience and worked from 7 AM to 7 PM. You read that right. Twelve hour shifts. Thirty-five kids, some of them weren't potty trained, and we not only ran classes, but made all the snacks and lunches! That's 105 meals a day. So, from the very beginning, I understood what it meant to struggle in a difficult teaching environment.

I spent my next two decades teaching in a barrio community college. Though my core subject turned out to be introduction to philosophy, at one time or another I taught or tutored: history, English, algebra, trigonometry, calculus, history of art, history of architecture, computer programming, music, and science... in addition I've spent many seasons coaching volleyball and basketball.

Though I had lots of wonderful, hard working students, I had many who were drug addicts, alcoholics, hard core gang bangers, students just out of prison, or heading, despite my best efforts, back into prison. I've jumped in to stop more than one fight, taken kids to rehab, and visited them in mental wards. I've spent thousands of hours counseling students who where rape or incest victims, substance abusers, or simply so ruined by their upbringing that they had lost all hope.

Reading scores at my college indicated that our average student was two years behind grade level; even worse, 25% of our students read at the eighth grade or below.

I spent two and a half decades searching, day after day, class after class, for an approach that would reach all my pupils, with their astounding range of problems. I failed for 25 years. I got so sick of teaching that I contemplated becoming a lawyer. Imagine that.

I remember the exact instant of my breakthrough. I had just finished lecturing about Plato's Theory of Forms, a topic I knew well. For some reason, I asked a student in the front row, a good, solid "B" student, to repeat what I had just said. She stumbled around, made little sense, finally confessed that she couldn't. I was floored. *My lecture had been so clear!* So lively, so engaging! So much better than anything I had heard in college! But if this good student couldn't repeat what she had just heard, what hope was there three weeks later when she sat down to the midterm?

So, I saw what many of us in education know instinctively; there is something dreadfully wrong with the lecture model. Our kids listen, maybe they take notes, but soon, they glaze over, zone out, are lost inside private worlds. And it doesn't matter if the students are in college or kindergarten.

Here is the First Great Law of Whole Brain Teaching:

The longer we talk, the more students we lose.

John Medina, director of the Brain Center for Applied Learning Research at Seattle Pacific University and author of *Brain Rules*, confirms the problem with lecturing. First noting that his students began to tune out after only 10 minutes of his energetic presentations, he explored research on attention patterns. "Peer reviewed studies confirm my informal inquiry. Before the first quarter hour is over in a typical presentation, people usually have checked out. If keeping someone's interest in a lecture were a business, it would have an 80 percent failure rate."

After realizing that my lectures were ineffective, I began to think about my "discussions." Oh, how I loved lively discussions. But wait a minute. How many students actually took part? I realized that if I had seven students, one here, one there, two over there, one right here, two more back there, involved in talking about philosophy I felt like we had a wonderful time sharing ideas. Seven students out of 35! What were the rest doing? Far too many were in their seats but out to lunch.

Goodness gracious. Lecture and discussion didn't work!

What to do?

I began trying strange new teaching devices that came to me early in the morning or late on sleepless nights. I tried techniques in class that I had never heard of. Most failed. But a few, right of the box, were strangely successful. I remember the first year I hit my stride, sometime around 1995; teachers in neighboring classes pounded on the walls... I mean it, pounded on the walls because they were angry at how much noise my students were making. Hey. It's not noise. It's 35 kids going nuts over Descartes!

And then I had another breakthrough.

I was coaching a middle school girls club basketball team. Great girls who, if given the chance, could display remarkably unpleasant attitudes. I started using the same techniques that had worked in philosophy *on the basketball court. And the girls loved it. They ripped through practices. They stared at me, listening to every word I said, with manic, breathless intensity.*

"Wait a second, this is amazing!," I thought to myself after a particularly fun, hysterically intense practice. I had techniques that worked no matter whether I was teaching Aristotle or the art of zone defense. I began to get excited. After all, at that point I had been teaching 25 years … maybe I had found something that worked. Forget law school! Perhaps I could be a teacher!

I called two of my former students, Chris Rekstad and Jay Vanderfin, who had gone on to become elementary school instructors. I asked them to try some of my strategies. Chris taught 4th grade; Jay taught kindergarten. I'm not saying my approach was an instant success for them. In fact, it is only because of the creative tweaking of Chris and Jay that the system you are about to explore works on a wide range of teaching problems.

But after a few weeks, Chris and Jay began to see dramatic changes in their students. They found ways to use my college approach with elementary school kids. Two thirds of Jay's kindergarten students could hardly speak English… but they loved the new strategies.

Okay.

Maybe we'd discovered something. A classroom learning system that worked kindergarten through 14th grade… no matter whether we taught the alphabet, lay-ups or the epistemology of Kant.

Chris, Jay and I had 80 meetings over the course of a year and pounded out the core of a program that tens of thousands of instructors are now using. In the last 12 years, our free seminars have grown astoundingly. We started in 1999 with a meeting of 30 desperate teachers in my living room. In February, 2010, over 900 educators registered for our free conference in Hemet, California, making our seminar one of the largest in the United States.

Several years ago, I began to wonder why so many instructors at every grade level (including special education teachers) found remarkable success with Whole Brain Teaching. I started exploring brain research. It wasn't long before I discovered that the system that had been pounded out, semester by semester during a decade of trial and error, *worked because it was brain friendly.*

Knowing little about how the brain operated, Jay, Chris, I and a group of other instructors, were driven to unwittingly employ more and more of the brain's learning potential. We found our students were completely engaged in class when they were emotionally involved in lessons that required seeing, saying, hearing and physically moving. Error by error, we developed a core method that involves many brain activities simultaneously (much more on this later). In a remarkable number of cases, our challenging kids couldn't be challenging because their entire brains were too busy learning.

Before you explore Whole Brain Teaching's strategies, let's start with what *not* to do.

CHAPTER 3

Seven Common Teaching Mistakes

How we make our jobs much, much harder...

In the early years of the 20th century Mary Mallon worked as a cook in Oyster Bay, New York. A typhoid epidemic spread through town, and by the time it was traced back to Mary, she had disappeared.

A few years later Mary resurfaced in Manhattan, still working as a cook, still spreading typhus bacteria. And still avoiding apprehension by the authorities. It took George Soper, a sanitary engineer in the New York City Department of Health, seven years of tracking Mary through cooking jobs in sanatoriums, hospitals and private homes before he was finally able to have her quarantined for life, on North Brother Island in New York. The medical reason that Mary kept spreading typhoid was because she was immune to the disease. Fifty one cases of typhoid fever were directly attributable to Typhoid Mary, and countless more were indirectly linked to her.

Now, think about this.

Bad teaching breeds challenging students. Teachers, by their teaching choices, create environments that nourish rebel behavior.

Many teachers, let's call them typhoidians, are like Typhoid Mary, with one crucial difference. Mary was immune to the plague she spread; typhoidian teachers are prime victims of the disease they create.

The greatest mistake we make as instructors is making our classes more difficult to teach. Why would we do that? We look out at our students, too many of whom are rebellious, and we engage in behaviors that make them *even more rebellious!*

Madness!

Here are seven ways we make our challenging students more challenging.

1. When we lose our temper with difficult kids and yell at them, we don't fix our teaching problem, we make it worse. Many of our most disruptive students come from families that are filled with superbly experienced, high volume yellers. If being addressed by screaming, out of control adults made our challenging kids better, then children from crazed families would be our model pupils.

2. Confronting rebellious students when they have an audience of their peers, will make them braver, more rebellious. Our most difficult kids, given the opportunity to increase their reputation for toughness, will cunningly defy us, if they are surrounded by their classmates. I use the word "cunningly" deliberately. *Our worst students are geniuses at rebellion.* They know exactly what to say in defiance, exactly how to get up to, but not over the line. They've had a lifetime of experience and often been surrounded by skilled role models among family and friends, in being superbly, brilliantly rebellious. When teachers make the mistake of confronting disruptive students, choosing them off, in front of their peers, these highly skilled rebels, relish the spotlight. We make challenging students more challenging, we nourish their rebellion, by confronting them when they have onlookers.

3. Disorganized teachers breed chaotic classrooms. If you have mutinous students, a good way to make your problem worse is by shooting from the hip. The less class structure you have, the less structured your classes will be. Isn't that amazing? Challenging students thrive, adore, explode into wonders of rebel behavior, with loosey-goosey, "let's see, I'm not sure what we should do next" teachers. If you say one thing and do another, promise a test for Friday and then put it off until Monday, say you want X, Y and Z on an

assignment and then, "to be nice" are willing to accept Q, make promises you can't keep, or threats you can't fulfill, your classes are headed for CHALLENGING STUDENT HEAVEN! At minimum, there should be a place for everything in your classroom, and everything should always be in the same place. Jay Vanderfin told me, "every one of my kids has a box of colored pencils and they know exactly where on their desk that box should be." Everything in Jay's classroom is like that. Great teacher.

4. Teachers who don't like teaching have the most challenging students. The unhappier you are as an instructor, the unhappier your classes will make you. Even if you think you are careful to mask your job dissatisfaction, your facial expressions, that little edge in your tone of voice, your sighs and small groans, say it all.

In Dante's hell, sinners received punishments that matched their sins. Murderers, for example, boiled for eternity in rivers of hot blood. Go into class with a negative, burned out attitude toward your profession, and your students will be waiting with pitchforks.

5. The less work you do outside of class, the more work your classes will be. Outstanding instruction involves huge, truly mountainous amounts of labor, preparing, practicing, researching, thinking through, refining instructional units. If you don't pay the price before you step into the classroom, you'll pay the price as you fumble through shoddy lessons.

You don't save yourself work by taking it easy at home, or in that last summer month before school starts. If you aren't willing to invest hours of preparation in what will turn into minutes of classroom teaching, your challenging students, or worse still, far worse still, your best students will present you with the bill.

Lazy teachers create classes that could care less about what is being taught and thus, are lovely breeding grounds for rebellion.

6. If you think your disruptive students should be like you, you'll make them even more disruptive. You were a good student, you turned in your work on time, you spoke respectfully to your elders. Of course you did. At least that's how you remember it.

Your kids are round pegs that won't fit into your square hole. Face it.

The more you look for your own shining face in your class, your noble, hardworking habits, your passion for learning, the more detestable you'll find students who don't mimic your values. And of course, the more you dislike your challenging students, the more they will teach you about challenging behaviors you never imagined.

Invite students into your world; don't expect to find them already there.

7. Here is the great law that governs the universe. And the classroom.

   Grow or die.

   Plants, animals, nations, corporations, students, teachers don't survive by maintaining the status quo. We are, to quote Bob Dylan, "busy being born, or busy dying."

   If you're a seedling in a forest of tall trees and you're just holding your own, you're doomed to deathly shadows.

   If you're a nation in a world of superpowers, you must grow your economy or be swallowed.

   You're a teacher. Grow, learn, transform yourself, or die by ossification. If you're afraid to try new teaching techniques, you are petrifying yourself to death.

   Think of teaching as a seesaw. You are on one end, and your entire class of challenging students is on the other. As your growth declines, their challenging behavior skyrockets.

America, for several decades at least, has been in the middle of a national crisis. According to Justice Department and Census Bureau statistics, one in every 31 of Americans is either in jail, awaiting trial or on probation. We have the largest prison population of any nation on earth. The National Coalition for Literacy reports that one in five of our citizens is functionally illiterate. Functional illiteracy is defined as the inability to understand a map, follow written instructions or read a newspaper. According to the U.S. Census Bureau, 30% of our students are one, or more, grade levels behind. The ship of American education is not floundering in the waves, it's gurgling toward the bottom.

All teachers have the same story. If only we could get our challenging students under control, we could do some real instruction. Our nation is spending millions on teacher training, education grants, text books and multimedia, whiz bang, learning systems... *and it is all for nothing, if we can't keep challenging students from turning classrooms into zoos.*

We know how to teach reading. We know how to teach writing. We have wonderful materials for teaching math, social studies and history. But we don't know how to get our classes under control; we don't know how to keep bullying, disruptive students from changing learning environments into war zones.

Astonishingly, my Whole Brain Teaching colleagues and I have found very little in teacher training programs that addresses our most important teaching problem. Again and again teachers have told us that they weren't ready for the challenge of teaching challenging students.

The more you practice our strategies, the more power you will have as an instructor to change your students' lives, and the more power your students will have to master the learning tasks you set before them.

There are scientists in the world today who are deliberately trying to grow viruses, develop new poisons, create mutations of diseases. Many teachers are afflicted by rebellious students and engage in teaching activities that make their classrooms more toxic.

So, to sum up, if you don't want to make your challenging students more challenging then:

- control your temper
- confront challenging students when they don't have an audience
- be superbly organized
- fall in love with your profession
- work hard at teaching, when you're not in class
- understand that your students are not your clones
- grow or die

In the following, the instructor is referred to as Mrs. Maestra; we will imagine her as a wise, veteran Whole Brain Teacher. The grade is Any Grade in elementary school.

We'll begin with a simple system Mrs. Maestra uses all year to chart her progress.

CHAPTER 4

Charting Progress

You can't tell where you're going, without a chart of where you've been

To track teaching improvements, Mrs. Maestra, used a simple, but crucial measure, to make a weekly evaluation of her own performance.

Mrs. Maestra deeply understood one of the Great Truths of Whole Brain Teaching:

You cannot manage student behavior if you cannot manage your own behavior.

Mrs. Maestra understood that the two crucial features of managing her behavior were:

- controlling her emotions by controlling her tone of voice.
- consistently following through with her classroom management plan.

Mrs. Maestra knew that good cops could control their emotions and make wise decisions on a murder scene. Good soldiers could maintain self control and make wise decisions in battle. No matter how obstreperous her students, Mrs. Maestra clearly understood that her task was far easier than the difficulties facing the police or soldiers. She knew that good teachers could control their emotions and tone of voice in the face of the most mutinous student.

It was obvious to Mrs. Maestra that she couldn't manage her challenging students, if she couldn't control her reaction to them. Every week of the school year, as part of her evaluation system, Mrs. Maestra gave herself a grade 1-10 (with 10 being highest) on her ability to control her emotions by controlling her tone of voice.

It was also obvious to Mrs. Maestra that she could not manage students if she could not consistently follow her own classroom management plan. If her pupils were unruly, Mrs. Maestra would never improve them by inventing teaching strategies on the fly.

So, every week Mrs. Maestra gave herself a grade 1-10, (with 10 being highest) on her ability to consistently follow her classroom management plan. At the end of each week, Mrs. Maestra added these two grades (self control and classroom management consistency) together. This was her teaching score. Mrs. Maestra enjoyed doing this... it made the difficult job of instruction a little more entertaining, like an engaging solitaire game.

Mrs. Maestra didn't focus on managing her students as her primary classroom goal. Her primary classroom goal was managing her own behavior!

When Mrs. Maestra had a large group of rebellious students, she could still consider herself a success, a noble success, any week that her combined self evaluation score was 16.

Another part of Mrs. Maestra's evaluation system helped her chart her students' progress, their journey upward.

Here are four measures (you can substitute others if you wish) Mrs. Maestra used to evaluate each student's classroom behavior. Her model students:

- followed directions quickly
- raised their hands for permission to speak
- stayed on task
- turned in neat work

Using these measures to determine her initial average score for the behavior of all her students, Mrs. Maestra divided her class into four groups (without, of course, telling her students).

Alphas: These were Mrs. Maestra's model students; they raised their hands for permission to speak, followed directions quickly, stayed on task, and turned in neat work. Mrs. Maestra gave herself 4 points for each Alpha.

Go-Alongs: These students would usually "go along" with Mrs. Maestra; however, they sometimes fell short of being model students. Go-Alongs usually, but not always, raised their hands for permission to speak, frequently followed directions quickly, usually stayed on task, and, in general, turned in neat work. Mrs. Maestra gave herself 3 points for each Go-Along.

Fence Sitters: These students were ones that could go either way. One day they were close to being model students; the next day, Mrs. Maestra wondered what went wrong. Her Fence Sitters inconsistently raised their hands for permission to speak, often didn't stay on task, follow directions quickly or turn in neat work. Mrs. Maestra gave herself 2 points for each Fence Sitter.

Challenging Students: Mrs. Maestra's challenging students rarely, if ever, raised their hands for permission to speak, followed directions (quickly or otherwise), stayed on task, or turned in neat work. Mrs. Maestra gave herself 1 point for each of her challenging student.

New Students: Mrs. Maestra put every new student into the Fence-Sitter group.

Leaders: One of Mrs. Maestra's highest goals was to create a group of students who were above her Alphas. She wanted her very best students to strive for a difficult goal, becoming leaders of a classroom that was largely self-managing. As the year progressed, Mrs. Maestra gave herself 5 points for every Alpha that became a Leader.

Mrs. Maestra understood that it was very important to keep a weekly record of how her challenging students were performing. Rebel pupils were "long term projects." Mrs. Maestra would never know if she was getting anywhere with them, or the rest of her class, if she didn't keep careful track of where she'd been.

Every week, Mrs. Maestra totaled all the points for her kids and then divided by the total number in her class. This was her average score for the behavior of her students. Though Mrs. Maestra was very busy, she enjoyed this part of her work. Before she had used this method, Mrs. Maestra could never determine if she was, or wasn't, making progress with classroom management.

Mrs. Maestra's overarching goal in Whole Brain Teaching was to move her Alphas to Leaders, her Go-Alongs to Alphas, her Fence Sitters to Go-Alongs and her Challenging Students to Fence Sitters. She realized that if she could raise the average score for the behavior of all her students by only .1 per month, then by the end of the year *every student in her class would have moved up, on average, one level in classroom behavior.* This was Mrs. Maestra's high, but reachable, goal.

CHAPTER 5

The Brain on Whole Brain Teaching

A short course in brain science

In order to understand an overview of Whole Brain Teaching and especially its techniques for helping challenging students learn, let's make a model of your brain.

Lace your fingers together and hold your hands in front of your chest. The rather small shape your two hands make is about the size of your brain, the most complex organism in the universe. Weighing about 3 pounds, your brain contains about 100 billion neurons, brain cells that transmit information; the total length of your brain's nerve fibers is over 94,000 miles!

Now, look at your fingers laced together; your left hand represents the left hemisphere of your brain and your right hand represents the right hemisphere.

Wiggle your two little fingers; these represent your prefrontal cortex, the uniquely human brain region that controls reasoning, planning and decision making. Think of the prefrontal cortex as the brain's boss.

Now wiggle the middle fingers on both your hands. These represent the motor cortex, the brain's most reliable memory area. If you haven't been on a bike in 20 years, you can still ride one perfectly well ... because complex bike riding information is stored in your motor cortex.

Now wiggle your thumbs. Look how large they are compared to the rest of your fingers. Your thumbs represent the visual cortex at the rear of your brain. They occupy such a substantial area that some scientists call the brain the "seeing brain." The visual cortex is one of the brain's most trustworthy memory areas. You remember faces much better than names because information about how people look is stored in your visual cortex.

The back of your left hand represents the outside of your left hemisphere. Toward the front of your left hand is Broca's area, crucial in speaking. Toward the back of your left hand is Wernicke's area, important in hearing and understanding language.

Now, let's look at how these brain areas work together. Let's say you're reading aloud from this book. Information passes from your visual cortex (seeing), to Wernicke's area (language understanding), to Broca's area (speaking) and finally to the motor cortex to activate your lips, tongue and vocal chords. If you then decide to stop reading and eat a banana, you've used your prefrontal cortex in decision making.

Pull your hands apart, separate your left and right hemispheres. The base of the palm of both hands represents your limbic system, the center of your emotions. If you like, or don't like, what you're reading, your limbic system is involved. Let's say you really can't stand Whole Brain Teaching and fling this book across the room and break your spouse's bowling trophy. Oh, no! Why did you do something so irrational? Because your limbic system, your emotions, took control of your prefrontal cortex, your reason. We'll come back to that broken bowling trophy in a moment.

Now, roughly speaking, how do you learn? As I mentioned, your brain is composed of 100 billion neurons, information processing nerve fibers. Attached to each neuron, very much like branches attached to a tree trunk, are dendrites. When you learn a language, understand how to solve a math problem, figure out a complex recipe, you're growing dendrites. The more you know about a subject, the more you have repeated activities associated with a subject, the more interconnected are your neuronal dendrites. *Repetition equals dendrite growth equals learning.* Repeat that sentence over and over so that your learning produces bushy dendrites.

Let's add a few more facts about the brain before we put all this information together into an overview of Whole Brain Teaching.

Interestingly enough, your brain has no single area dedicated to memory. The hippocampus, in the region of your limbic system, processes memories and then sends that information back to the region where it originated. Let's say you want to learn how to cha-cha. You watch a video, listen to a song, sing the words, do a few steps. What learning is being acquired inside your brain? Not much, unless you watch the video over and over! More repetitions equals more dendrite growth equals more learning. Spend some time practicing the video's lessons and you will have stored the sound of cha-cha music in your auditory cortex, the look of cha-chaing in your visual cortex and the actual dance moves in your motor cortex. The more brain areas involved, the more dendrites are grown, the deeper and more lasting your learning. You can't learn to cha-cha by listening to a lecture on dance history.

Brain scientists distinguish between short term and long term memory. The capacity of short term memory is usually limited to three to seven items. If you want to remember a phone number, you repeat it over and over to yourself, holding it in short term memory. If someone tells you their address, you probably will have to write it down, because it contains more than seven items. Not only is short term memory limited in capacity, but also it is very limited in duration. According to Laura A. Freberg in *Discovering Biological Psychology,* a standard text in brain science, "Classic research by Peterson and Peterson (1959) showed that material in short-term memory was lost rapidly, in 15 to 18 seconds, but others believe that loss occurs in as little as 2 seconds." Now you know why when you make that reading assignment, a few seconds later, someone asks, "do we have any reading homework?"

Unlike short term memory, long term memory's capacity is unlimited. Putting new information into long term memory does not push old information out. If you repeat data frequently enough, it will be permanently stored in the infinite space between your ears.

Another crucial, very crucial, brain fact for teachers is that there are more connections from the limbic system to the prefrontal cortex than vice versa. Your emotions can control your reason much more easily than your reason can control your emotions. That's why you irrationally broke the bowling trophy. Plato was one of the first to understand this deep human flaw. When our lower elements, appetites and desires, control our reason, we are "upside down" and deeply unhappy. Conversely if we, like Plato's philosopher king, rule our desires (limbic system) with our reason (prefrontal cortex), no calamity can upset our internal harmony.

The prefrontal cortex, the brain's boss, does not fully mature until our early 20s. This provides an explanation why children and teenagers can act so irrationally. Growing up is often a struggle between unequal forces, a partially developed prefrontal cortex trying to guide a fully mature limbic system. The hand of a child trying to rein in the emotions of an adult.

Two more items, and then I'll bring all this together into Whole Brain Teaching's educational strategy.

If you say "ba, ba, ba" to a baby, before long you'll get a "ba, ba, ba" back. And you'll laugh. And the baby will laugh. Soon, you'll be ba-ba-baing each other. What is happening? Many brain scientist believe that you and the baby are activating special kinds of neurons, mirror neurons, scattered through your brains.

According to V.S. Ramachandran, Director of the Center for Brain and Cognition at the University of California, San Diego. "The discovery of mirror neurons in the frontal lobes of monkeys, and their potential relevance to human brain evolution... is the single most important 'unreported' (or at least, unpublicized) story of the decade. I predict that mirror neurons will do for psychology what DNA did for biology: they will provide a unifying framework and help explain a host of mental abilities that have hitherto remained mysterious and inaccessible to experiments."

Stand in front of a class of little kids, and slowly clap your hands. A few children will clap along with you. They are doing what you are doing, mirroring your behavior, activating their mirror neurons. If you think about it, you'll realize that a large amount of the learning in every grade involves mirroring the instructor's words or actions. A well organized classroom becomes increasingly well organized as children mirror each other's orderly behavior. And the flip side is true. Disruptive classroom behavior will generate more disruption, as children mirror each other's unruly actions.

Finally, surprisingly, consider the sea slug. The sea slug's nervous system is so simple that it is ideal for understanding crucial features of stimulus and response. If you turn a sea slug over and poke its flute, a hollow tube it uses to suck nutrients from the ocean, the slug immediately contracts its gills. Keep poking and the gills keep contracting ... until about the tenth poke. The response to your stimulus gradually declines until you can poke that flute all you want and you'll get nary a gill flutter. The technical term for this process is *habituation*... one of the most important concepts in education. Habituation occurs when an individual's response to a stimulus decreases after repeated stimulation. In 1970 I lived next to street car tracks. They made lots of noise for a few days. Then, I never heard them again. They must have switched to rubber wheels. The truth was that I became habituated to the noise. The racket was out there, but it didn't flutter my gills. If you are a veteran teacher, you've observed the mystery and frustration of habituation... what worked wonderfully with your class in September, bores them out of their skulls in December.

Now, let's bring all this together into an overview of Whole Brain Teaching's learning strategies.

On the journey ahead, you'll discover seven, powerful teaching techniques; we call them the Big Seven.

Here they are, briefly described for now, with relevant brain information attached.

1. **Class-Yes:** Our primary attention-getter activates the prefrontal cortex, the brain's boss. The prefrontal cortex controls decision making, planning and focus of attention. Little if any learning can take place if the prefrontal cortex is not engaged. We think of the Class-Yes as a brain switch that readies students for instruction.

2. **Teach-Okay:** Brain and learning research indicates that students learn the most when they are involved in teaching each other. By emphasizing energetic, instructional gesturing we engage, during Teach-Okay sessions, five of students' brain areas: visual cortex (seeing gestures), motor cortex (making gestures), Broca's area (ver-

balizing a lesson), Wernicke's area (hearing a lesson), and the limbic system, (giving emotional content to a lesson.)

As you will see, a key component of our Teach-Okay method is that teacher's must speak briefly, often not more than 30 seconds, before asking students to rehearse the lesson with each other. Remember that short term memory has limited capacity, three to seven items. The longer teachers talk, the more students we lose. Conversely, the more students repeat lessons to each other, especially while using descriptive gestures, the more students are engaged... and the more thoroughly lessons are embedded in long term memory.

3. **The Five Classroom Rules:** Our classroom rules (chapter 6) not only efficiently activate five areas of every student's brain (visual cortex, motor cortex, Broca's area, Wernicke's area, and limbic system) but also, because they are frequently rehearsed, involve the brain's mirror neurons. Orderly behavior creates the mirroring of orderly behavior... which causes teachers and students to mirror each other's happy faces.

4. **The Scoreboard:** We believe our Scoreboard is the fastest, most entertaining and, for limited teaching budgets, the cheapest motivational system in elementary education. Wired directly into the brain's emotional center, the limbic system, the Scoreboard replaces marbles in a jar, candy, table points, play money and other classroom reward strategies. When an instructor marks a Smiley or a Frowny on the Scoreboard, students feel a small, positive or negative, emotional jolt. By enlivening the marking routine with a "mighty oh yeah" or a "mighty groan" the reward circuitry in the limbic system is activated.

To avoid habituation, the decline in response to repeated stimulation, the Scoreboard is set up in levels, like a video game. November's Level Two Scoreboard presents challenges not dreamed of in September's Level One... and oh no! What's coming in December's Level Three?!

As you will see, the levels on the Scoreboard are precisely attuned to the problem of teaching challenging kids. The lower Scoreboard levels will unify many students (often about 80-90%) behind your leadership. The higher levels of the Scoreboard use this classroom unity as powerful peer pressure to encourage all but your most rebellious kids to participate in learning activities. But what about students who are immune to every penalty? The most challenging of the challenging? The highest two levels of the Scoreboard are designed for your most determined rebels. If children are unfazed by every punishment, then they need a system that is pure reward... and that's what the Scoreboard's top levels provide. At the highest levels of the Scoreboard, challenging kids can't fail... because there's no failure involved!

Go ahead. Go get a large hanky. When you contemplate a system that will touch the rebel hearts of your most challenging kids, *you want to sob tears of joy!*

5. **Hands and Eyes:** When we are making an important point, we want students to focus intensely on what we are saying. As employed by an experienced Whole Brain Teaching instructor, Hands and Eyes creates instant silence, eliminating all learning distractions; the prefrontal cortex takes control of brain activity focusing the visual cortex and the auditory cortex on the instructor's lesson.

6. **Switch:** Some students talk easily, often too easily! Other students fall into the role of passive listeners. In terms of brain structure, classes are often divided between those who are Brocaians (speakers) and Wernikites (listeners). By using Switch, an instructor can easily teach listening skills to the speakers and speaking skills to the listeners.

7. **Mirror:** As mentioned above, many brain scientists believe that we learn by mirroring the gestures and activities of others. They have identified mirror neurons scattered throughout the brain that are activated by mimicking the behavior we observe. Our own experience in WBT classrooms indicates that when a class mirrors our gestures and, when appropriate, repeats our words, a powerful learning bond

is created as the teacher and students' visual and motor cortex engage each other.

All of WBT's instructional strategies have been rigorously classroom tested, many for over 10 years. Based on feedback that we receive at conferences, on our website and via emails from hundreds of teachers across the country (and around the world), we have constantly refined our techniques.

Our initial, and primary, research goal was to create a system that instructors would willingly adopt. Classroom management strategies that are imposed by administrators often meet understandable resistance from instructors and therefore, have a short teaching life span. (On a side note: we believe there will be no substantial educational reform until administrators, specifically principals, roll up their sleeves, step into rebellious classes and show teachers how to instruct unruly students. We need educational leaders... not financial bean counters. WBT has provided many administrators with the tools to demonstrate effective instruction from the front of the classroom rather than criticize it from the rear.) We believe there is a direct correlation between the effectiveness of a classroom management system and an instructor's enthusiastic implementation of the system. Over the last five years, we have asked instructors at the end of our seminars to answer one question:

Compared to other teaching systems that you are familiar with, Whole Brain Teaching is:

    a. much better
    b. better
    c. about the same
    d. worse
    e. much worse

In one of the largest surveys of its kind, we have polled over 2,000 K-12 educators in California, Arizona, Texas, Montana, Louisiana, Minnesota, Missouri, Georgia, Utah, Florida, Pennsylvania, Arkansas, Tennessee, Michigan, Virginia, Vermont, New Jersey, Oregon, North Carolina,

New York and Alabama. The results have been astounding. Seventy percent of instructors rated our system "much better" and 28% rated it "better." The results are close to unanimous; 98% of educators believe WBT is superior to every other teaching system they are familiar with. We believe no other instructional strategy can match these numbers.

For a description of Whole Brain Teaching in the context of education theory, see Chapter 26, "Whole Brain Teaching and Contemporary Learning Research" by Angela Macias and Brian Macias.

Now, let's return to Mrs. Maestra and watch her start her class with the first of the Big Seven, Class-Yes.

CHAPTER 6

Class-Yes

Instantly, magically, gain your kids' attention

On the first day of the school year, Mrs. Maestra stood in the front of her class, raised her arms slightly in an embracing, but also commanding, gesture. She welcomed her students and spoke briefly about her expectations for the year.

Whenever Mrs. Maestra talked to the entire class, she generally used a special voice, loud, firm, authoritative... the voice of command. She had noted that other teachers who were respected by students used a similar voice.

Mrs. Maestra believed that one of the crucial factors in gaining students' respect had nothing to do with the teacher's size and certainly wasn't determined by their aggressiveness. Large angry teachers, if they lacked this special factor, had as much trouble with challenging students as anyone. Mrs. Maestra remembered her third grade teacher, Mrs. Takahara. Mrs. Takahara was dainty, almost elfin, but no student messed with her. She was universally respected by her classes. Mrs. Takahara's power over students came almost entirely from her tone of voice. She had a superb, self controlled, voice of command. Every year Mrs. Maestra did her best to Takahara her students.

As Mrs. Maestra spoke on the first morning to her pupils she scanned the classroom. Mrs. Maestra knew some students would be listening intently, some would be swiveling their heads around the room inspecting the new environment, some would already be zoned out. As a veteran Whole Brain Teacher, Mrs. Maestra knew for certain that a group of her pupils, from the very beginning, would not be paying attention. Mrs. Maestra was untroubled. She clearly understood Whole Brain Teaching's strategy. Her initial goal was not to immediately win over every student, but to set up a series of routines that would unite substantial numbers of her pupils behind her leadership.

Mrs. Maestra had two enormous advantages over even her most challenging kids. First, she knew that her rebels were predictable. They would engage in disruptive behavior, talking to their neighbors, speaking disrespectfully to teachers, turning in little or no work. Mrs. Maestra's father, Guantanamera, had been a fairly decent middleweight boxer. He often said, "A predictable opponent is already half defeated."

Mrs. Maestra's second enormous advantage over her challenging students was that she knew her Whole Brain Teaching plan, they didn't. Mrs. Maestra always knew what was coming next; her rebel students had no clue what was up Mrs. Maestra's sleeve. Mrs. Maestra understood that the central idea of Whole Brain Teaching was to solve the easiest classroom management problems first, uniting the most amenable students behind the teacher's leadership. Next, the instructor would organize the class so that it was not a breeding ground for challenging behavior and eventually, special techniques would isolate rebels from peer support and address the most challenging students of all, those who were immune to penalty.

Near the beginning of the first class meeting, Mrs. Maestra used her own version of a routine, a script, she had received at her first Whole Brain Teaching seminar in 1999. (Of course, Mrs. Maestra didn't read from the following dialogue. She had practiced her own version many times at home.)

SCRIPT: THE CLASS-YES

Teacher: When I say Class!, you say Yes! Class!

Students: Yes!

Teacher: However I say Class!, you say Yes! Class! Class!

Students: Yes! Yes!

Teacher: (Using a low voice) Claaaasss!

Students: (Mimicking the teacher's low voice) Yesssss!

Teacher: (Using a high voice) Classssss!

Students: (Mimicking the teacher's high voice) Yesssss!

Teacher: Classity, class!

Students: Yessity, yes!

Mrs. Maestra had taught many grades from kindergarten to college in her long career. She was never concerned that students would find the Class-Yes script babyish. Chris Biffle used Class-Yes in college. Mrs. Maestra had used it in adult education courses. The reaction of students, of every age, was always the same. When they got to the "yessity, yes!" they were grinning ... and happily responding. In the few seconds that it took Mrs. Maestra to use the Class-Yes routine, she had already begun to achieve an important goal. *A large proportion of her students were laughingly following directions.*

This is quite important, a central strategy in Whole Brain Teaching. The more educational fun we can introduce into our classrooms, the more students will learn and the fewer opportunities there will be for challenging behavior. Students perform at high intensity when they are having the most fun learning. Video games can be insanely complex, with rules and procedures that would tax a rocket scientist. Kids master the difficulty of video games because they are having so much fun they don't even notice they're learning. If you walk down the hall past WBT classrooms, one of the first things you'll notice is the amount of task focused laughter. *Kids follow our rules, because we make our rules fun to follow.*

Mrs. Maestra knew that she would use the Class-Yes routine 15-20 times an hour. Over and over again, she would need to gain her students' attention. Many of the Whole Brain Teaching procedures Mrs. Maestra used, she would have to repeat. She wasn't troubled. Mrs. Maestra never minded repeating herself. She loved the Whole Brain Teaching rule: *If repeating yourself bugs you, don't go into teaching. Teaching is repeating.*

Mrs. Maestra knew that the Class-Yes script was quite effective, but if she didn't occasionally vary the way she said "Class!" some of her students would, eventually, ignore her. Mrs. Maestra faced an apparent paradox. Her students needed consistency and variety. They needed consistency's clear structure and variety's engaging novelty. To solve this problem, Mrs. Maestra consistently used "Class!" to gain her students' attention, but occasionally varied her tone. Her voice could be high, low, funny, serious, growling, robotic, froglike, super fast, super slow, pretend angry.

Mrs. Maestra was not a clown. She didn't teach because she enjoyed her students' laughter. She taught because she enjoyed seeing her students happily learning. Mrs. Maestra found that being the leader of joyful learning was one of life's supreme pleasures. And so, though Mrs. Maestra wasn't a clown, she wasn't averse to occasionally using a robot voice or a squeaky voice to merrily engage students who might otherwise be dreaming. Mrs. Maestra was inventive and, when necessary, a free spirit. She intuitively understood what Biffle's greatest teacher, Harry Berger, Jr. at the University of California at Santa Cruz, had told him, "Teaching is a performing art."

CHAPTER 7

Five, Powerful Classroom Rules

Including the ultimate, no loophole rule!

Mrs. Maestra and other Whole Brain Teachers post a copy of their classroom rules in a prominent location near the front of the room. (Large copies of the rule signs can be found in the Appendix; full color, 8" x 10" versions are available at WholeBrainTeaching.com.)

As a Whole Brain Teacher in elementary school, Mrs. Maestra has her students rehearse rules every morning, after lunch and after every recess.

On the following pages, you'll find the rules:

Rule 1: Follow directions quickly!

Rule 2: Raise your hand for permission to speak.

**Rule 3: Raise your hand for permission
to leave your seat.**

Rule 4: Make smart choices.

Rule 5: Keep your dear teacher happy!

Mrs. Maestra used the script below to teach her students her rules. She assigned a gesture to each rule not only because this activated her students' motor cortex, the brain's most powerful area for creating and retaining memories, but also, even more importantly, because gestures made the rules entertaining, fun to rehearse (which is to say, engaged her students' limbic system).

Mrs. Maestra learned to make the following gestures by watching Chris Biffle's *Intro to Whole Brain Teaching* videos at WholeBrainTeaching.com. Of course, Mrs. Maestra didn't repeat the script below verbatim, but she enjoyed having a model to follow.

SCRIPT: CLASSROOM RULES

Teacher   Class!

Students   Yes!

Teacher   (Pointing at the board.) We're now going to review our classroom rules. Please repeat after me and make my gestures. Rule 1: Follow directions quickly! (She raises one finger ; then, moves this hand rapidly through the air.)

A few students: (Weakly, some mimicking the gesture.) Rule 1: Follow directions quickly!

Teacher: (Smiling, but firmly) Please repeat after me and make my gestures. Rule 1: Follow directions quickly! (She raises one finger; then, moves this hand rapidly through the air.)

Students: (More energy, mimicking her gesture) Rule 1: Follow directions quickly!

Teacher: (Smiling) That's fine for a start. Rule 2: Raise your hand for permission to speak! (She raises two fingers in the air; then, bringing thumb and four fingers together she makes her hand "talk.")

Students: (Laughing, mimicking her gesture) Rule 2: Raise your hand for permission to speak!

Teacher: (Smiling) Good! Rule 3! Raise your hand for permission to leave your seat! (She raises three fingers in the air; then, with two fingers "walks" the fingers through the air.)

Students: (Laughing, mimicking her gesture) Rule 3: Raise your hand for permission to leave your seat!

> **Teacher:** (Smiling) Good job! Rule 4! Make smart choices! (She raises four fingers in the air; then, she taps her temple with one finger four times.)
>
> **Students:** (Laughing, mimicking her gesture) Rule 4: Make smart choices!
>
> **Teacher:** Rule 5! (She raises five fingers in the air; she raises her fingers toward her mouth, bobs her head from one side to the other, makes a smiley gesture and grins merrily.)
>
> **Students:** (Laughing energetically, mimicking her gesture) Rule 5: Keep your dear teacher happy!

To cement this routine, Mrs. Maestra reviewed the rules with brief prompts... and, to make the rehearsal entertaining, skipped chronological order. Thus, she merely said, "Rule 1, Rule 4, Rule 2" pausing briefly so her students would repeat the entire rule ("Rule 1: Follow directions quickly!") and the gesture. By the end of this rehearsal all her students were laughing happily. What a fun class this was going to be!

(Important point: If you are starting Whole Brain Teaching in the middle of the year, don't say anything like the following, "I've learned a new teaching technique. Let's see if you're going to like it." Rebel students love to tear new teaching techniques to shreds. Instead, say something like the following, "Usually, about this time of the year, I go to a more advanced teaching technique. It's used in college... but I think you're ready for it." In other words, pretend as if you had been *planning all year* to start WBT... and now your class is finally mature enough to handle it!)

Here is Mrs. Maestra's rationale for each rule.

Rule 1: Follow directions quickly. Mrs. Maestra wanted students to follow directions quickly because she didn't want to waste a second of class time. If her students weren't following directions quickly, they could be wasting 5-10 minutes every hour in non-educational activities. Over a school year, this added up to an enormous amount of lost time. In addition,

the more slowly Mrs. Maestra's students followed directions (handing in paper, opening books, sharpening pencils, etc.) the more possibility there was for disruptive behavior.

Rule 2: Raise your hand for permission to speak. Mrs. Maestra believed that any classroom in which students could speak whenever they wished, was headed for chaos. If you agree that students need to raise their hands for permission to speak, NEVER (unless it is an emergency) answer a student who violates this rule. Smile, but say firmly, "I'll be happy to answer your question, but please raise your hand." At the start of the year, Mrs. Maestra sometimes had to say this 50 times a day (literally!) and, it occasionally seemed like an enormous hassle. However, Mrs. Maestra knew that over the school year, she was saving herself substantial grief.

Rule 3: Raise your hand for permission to leave your seat. Mrs. Maestra didn't want students wandering around her classroom, unless they were on a mission she approved of... in advance. However, Mrs. Maestra occasionally had classroom exercises where she allowed students to move around the room without asking for permission. In that case, she put a green post-it note on Rule 3 indicating that it was temporarily not in force.

Rule 4: Make smart choices. Mrs. Maestra understood that this is a fundamental rule, perhaps the fundamental rule, for all human activities. Philosophers from Socrates in 5th century B.C. Athens to Jean Paul Sartre in 20th century France disagree on almost everything, except one guiding principle: Humans should use their reason carefully...

they should make smart choices. In Mrs. Maestra's view, Rule 4 was wonderfully powerful. It covered every area of a student's world at school, at home, out with friends, on the Internet, engaged in a sport or hobby, dating, Everything. From childhood to adulthood, she knew we need to make smart choices. Mrs. Maestra found that this rule was especially powerful in covering every kind of disruptive student behavior, in class and out.

Rule 5: Keep your dear teacher happy. This rule is, like Rule 4, a general purpose rule that covers an enormous amount of student activity. Many times in Mrs. Maestra's class, a student would do something unexpected and they would argue that it was "a smart choice." Mrs. Maestra's response was, "That might be true. But what you just did breaks an important rule... it doesn't make me happy. Trust me. I'm the world's leading authority on what makes me happy." Mrs. Maestra found that Rule 5 was especially useful in covering the countless remarks students made that were hurtful, rude, sarcastic, disrespectful.

Mrs. Maestra was happily politically incorrect. She knew that it sounded egocentric to say that one of her rules was that her students should keep her happy. It appeared as if Mrs. Maestra did not have a "student centered" classroom, as if the whole show was about her and not her pupils. Mrs. Maestra preferred to call herself an "educational realist." She knew that the only kind of behavior that made her happy was when students were engaged in learning. So, if her pupils were keeping her happy, they were engaged in furthering their education. Mrs. Maestra also knew that the happier her students made her, the better she taught. She understood that Rule 5 was specifically designed for students who had little, or no, practice in speaking respectfully to adults... and who were very skilled at finding loopholes in classroom rules systems.

When Mrs. Maestra taught her class that they should keep her happy, she was simply underlining three important points. First, her students should engage in respectful behavior toward their teacher; second that she, Mrs. Maestra, was the sole arbiter of what constituted respectful behavior; third, there was no loophole in her classroom rules. A brief example: Mrs. Maestra occasionally accompanied Chris Biffle when he gave classroom management seminars for teachers at school sites. She was not surprised when Biffle pointed out that "some of my most challenging students are teachers of challenging students! They come to my free seminars, sit in the back of the room, follow directions slowly, or not at all... and think I won't do anything about it!"

On one occasion that Mrs. Maestra observed, Biffle gave the teachers a short break, saying, "When you leave the room, please push the back of your chair up against your table." Every teacher did as directed, except one. A smiling kindergarten instructor, turned her chair around and pushed the back against the table, but left the seat sticking out. When Biffle raised his eyebrows, the teacher merrily explained, "I pushed the back against the table just like you said!" The teacher, of course, was looking for and exploiting what she thought was a hole in Whole Brain Teaching's system. Mrs. Maestra laughed quietly; she knew what was coming next. Biffle said, "Unfortunately, you are violating Rule 5. Pushing your chair in that way does not make me happy. Please sit down. You're staying here with me while everyone else gets a break."

As a teacher of challenging students, Mrs. Maestra needed a never fail rule that none of her pupils could elude or even quarrel with. She had many student rebels, but not even the boldest tried to convince her that they were making her happy, when they weren't.

Mrs. Maestra knew that having rules posted on signs in the front of the classroom was useless, unless her students were continuously aware of the rules and engaged in practicing them. Instead of chastising her students for breaking a rule, she followed one of Whole Brain Teaching's greatest principles:

Don't scold, rehearse.

Thus, at the start of the school year, Mrs. Maestra had her students rehearse the rules first thing in the morning, after lunch and each recess and before leaving for home. By varying her tone of voice, the size and energy her gestures, and by occasionally allowing a student to lead the rules review, she made these sessions entertaining. In fact, when she forgot a rehearsal, her students often reminded her!

After rehearsing the rules on the first day of class, Mrs. Maestra explained the reasoning for each of her classroom rules that she had posted on the front board. She then asked the class if anyone had objections to the principles. Mrs. Maestra never found any objectors; she was very good at explaining to the class how each rule would improve their learning experience.

Finding no one had a problem with her guidelines, Mrs. Maestra said, "Great!... let's take a vote. All in favor of using these rules in our classroom, please raise your hand." Almost invariably, all her students raised their hands. (If some students didn't raise their hands, Mrs. Maestra would say, "I'm glad to see that the majority of you believe these are good rules... so, these are the ones we'll use. If anyone can think of better rules, I'll be happy to talk to them during recess.")

By using the vote, Mrs. Maestra had achieved "buy in." Occasionally during the semester, Mrs. Maestra would have a class discussion and a new vote on the rules. Frankly, she would have been happy to experiment with a rule change if the majority of the class thought it would be a good idea.

Mrs. Maestra found the rules and the "buy in" were very helpful when she had to talk one on one to her challenging students, John for example. Mrs. Maestra would discuss the rule that John was having difficulty with and then ask, "Do you think we should change this rule?... do you remember this is what we voted on?" By talking about the rule and the class support, Mrs. Maestra was often able to deflect John's rebelliousness. *The rule supported by the entire class became the subject and not Mrs. Maestra's authority as a teacher.*

When the rules, through frequent rehearsal, were thoroughly embedded in students' long term memory, Mrs. Maestra used them to consistently correct inappropriate behavior. Thus, when John blurted out the answer to a question without raising his hand, Mrs. Maestra raised two fingers and said firmly, "Rule Two!" Her class chorused, "Raise you hand for permission to speak!" When Juana started to wander around the classroom, Mrs. Maestra held up three fingers and said, "Rule Three!" The class responded, "Raise your hand for permission to leave your seat!"

Mrs. Maestra adored this part of WBT's system. It turned disruptive behavior, speaking without raising your hand, wandering around the classroom, into an occasion that reinforced classroom rules. The actions of challenging students instantly unified the class behind the teacher's leadership. Disruption *triggered class unity!*

Oh, weep tears of joy!

CHAPTER 8

Teach-Okay

Transforming students into eager teachers (Part 1)

When Mrs. Maestra felt confident that her students had mastered the Class-Yes and the Five Classroom Rules, she introduced the Teach-Okay script. In higher grades, she introduced Teach-Okay on the first day; in lower grades, K-1, she often waited until the second or even third week.

SCRIPT: TEACH-OKAY

Teacher: Class!

Students: Yes!

Teacher: When I say Teach!, you say Okay! Teach!

Students: Okay!

Teacher: However I say Teach!, you say Okay! Teach! Teach!

Students: Okay! Okay!

Teacher: (Using a high voice) Teeeeach!

Students: (Laughing and mimicking the high voice) Okaaaay!

Teacher: (Using multiple syllables) Te-ee-ee-ee-each!

Students: (Laughing and trying to use multiple syllables) O-kay–ay–ay–ay!

Teacher: Class!

Students: Yes!

Teacher: Good job! Now when I say Teach!, you say Okay! *and* turn your bodies completely toward your neighbors to teach them the Five Classroom Rules. (Pointing to signs at the front of the room) Here are the rules right here. Please use the rule gestures as you teach your neighbor. Teach!

Students: (Mumbled confusion, a few saying Okay!)

Teacher: Class!

Students: Yes!

Teacher: (Repeating her message without the slightest irritation in her voice) When I say Teach! You say Okay!, and turn your bodies completely toward your neighbors. Teach them the Five Classroom Rules. Go on, teach your neighbors! Teach!

Students: Okay! (more students respond together, many turning to their neighbors and teaching them the Five Classroom Rules)

Though Mrs. Maestra had only used three of Whole Brain Teaching's many techniques, Class-Yes, the Five Classroom Rules and Teach-Okay, she had already established a strong foundation for her teaching strategy. Over and over again during the day, she would gain her students attention by calling out "Class!", and then give them brief instructions about a lesson or the next activity. Then, she would call out "Teach!" and her students would respond "Okay!" and explain Mrs. Maestra's point to each other.

Mrs. Maestra strongly believed in the power of students teaching each other. According to Barbara Gross Davis, Assistant Vice Provost for Undergraduate Education at the University of California at Berkeley, "Students learn best when they are actively involved in the process. Researchers report that, regardless of the subject matter, students working in small groups tend to learn more of what is taught and retain it longer than when the same content is presented in other instructional formats. Students who work in collaborative groups also appear more satisfied with their classes. (Sources: Beckman, 1990; Chickering and Gamson, 1991; Collier, 1980; Cooper and Associates, 1990; Goodsell, Maher,

Tinto, and Associates, 1992; Johnson and Johnson, 1989; Johnson, Johnson, and Smith, 1991; Kohn, 1986; McKeachie, Pintrich, Lin, and Smith, 1986; Slavin, 1980, 1983; Whitman, 1988)."

Mrs. Maestra's experience corroborated the views of education experts; however, she believed the smaller the group, the more involved were her students. In teams of four, she often noted that one or even two students would not be actively engaged. For this reason, she preferred Whole Brain Teaching's focus on students working in pairs.

Teach-Okay is Whole Brain Teaching's core educational device. Our students, from kindergarten to college, need hundreds of hours of practice in speaking in coherent, well organized sentences. Teachers are some of the best models students will ever have of logically organized speech. Whenever pupils in a WBT classroom engage in the Teach-Okay script, they are receiving effective, *non-embarrassing*, practice in speaking, and therefore thinking, clearly. In the general hubbub of 30 students explaining a lesson to each other, a clamor as lively and friendly as the overlapping conversations in a school cafeteria, students can, without the humiliation of public failure, practice explaining ideas to each other.

Teach-Okay is not only a powerful language development skill for English speakers, but also for the huge number of students who do not hear English spoken at home. Learning a language is a laborious task; it takes countless hours of practice. If you have students who are having difficulty understanding your lessons, or explaining them to a neighbor, arrange the desks so that those with weaker language skills have partners with stronger language skills. The noise of many students talking at once in your class is really "good noise." It gives each pair of students the privacy they need to practice speaking and occasionally flubbing without embarrassment.

Unfortunately, of all our techniques, Teach-Okay is the most difficult for some teachers to master. It requires that we speak in clear, coherent, logical units! And, even worse, Teach-Okay requires that we speak briefly, in presentations that are no longer than most of our students can remember and repeat to their neighbors. Typically, when Mrs. Maestra used the Teach-Okay pattern, she rarely spoke for more than 30 seconds, before telling her students to "Teach."

Mrs. Maestra had timed herself and knew, speaking relatively slowly, she would speak about 50 words in 30 seconds, or the equivalent of a good sized paragraph. She walked around the room listening as her students explained her lesson to each other. When she found a few students faltering, she could without embarrassing them, in the privacy of the general conversation, make corrections. When Mrs. Maestra overheard numerous students having difficulty, she knew she had spoken too long. Thus, using Teach-Okay she had a way to continuously monitor her students' comprehension.

Many times Mrs. Maestra could instantly tell that she had to explain a point more simply because when she said "Teach!" her students paused, weren't quite sure how to begin. Mrs. Maestra loved this aspect of Teach-Okay; it was like she was looking inside each pupil's brain and getting a quick, clear picture of their understanding.

Now, here is a curious fact which I, and other Whole Brain Teachers, have discovered. Disciplining yourself to speak in units that are 30 seconds or less and then having your students repeat your message to each other, allows you to cover more material, not less. When you become adept at Teach-Okay, you will have eliminated all the non-educational chaff from your presentation, all the wandering, redundancy, stumbling, verbal fumbling about. You present a few points; your students repeat them to each other; you present a few more. In the little periods when students are talking, you take mini-breaks to organize your thoughts for your next few sentences. We call this approach micro-lecturing. Micro-lecturing is not an easy skill, especially because most teachers love to talk and talk and talk. But remember our Whole Brain Teaching rule:

The more we talk, the more students we lose.

Mrs. Maestra used Teach-Okay on a wide variety occasions. Whenever she was engaged in a transition activity, for example if she wanted her students to get out a piece of paper and number it from 1-25 to take a spelling test, she would explain what she wanted and then say "Teach!" Her students would respond "Okay!" and explain the task to a neighbor. Far from slowing down her lessons, this saved Mrs. Maestra the time it would ordinarily take to repeat simple instructions over and over as students tuned in or out. Mrs. Maestra also used Teach-Okay whenever she introduced new material. Often she would start with something as brief as the following:

Teacher:	Class!
Students:	Yes!
Teacher:	We're now going to talk about something totally new. I'm going to make three very important points. Teach!
Students:	Okay!

The words that Mrs. Maestra emphasized with her voice and gestures, in this case "totally new" and "three" would then be emphasized across the classroom. Mrs. Maestra had everyone's attention and was ready to go on to her first point.

Here are some sample lessons that I use in my courses at the beginning of each semester (after I have introduced Class-Yes, and Teach-Okay).

Biffle:	Class! Class!
Students:	Yes! Yes!
Biffle:	This course is called Introduction to Philosophy. The obvious question is "what is philosophy?" Philosophy can be defined as the search for wisdom. We gain wisdom by finding answers to the largest possible questions, like does God exist? What is happiness? Does life have a purpose? Teach!
Students:	Okay! (Students teach their neighbor what Biffle has just said.)
Biffle:	Class!
Students:	Yes!
Biffle:	Here are some more big, philosophical questions. How much can the mind know? Do humans have souls? Does Time have a beginning? Can we know anything for certain? Teach!

Students: Okay! (Students teach their neighbor what Biffle has just said.)

Biffle: Class!

Students: Yes!

Biffle: The big questions we ask in philosophy are called universal questions. This means that they apply to everyone. Universal questions are very different than the questions we often ask in daily life. In daily life we ask particular questions like "What time is it? What should I do this weekend?" In philosophy we ask universal questions like "What is time? What is life's purpose?" Teach!

Students: Okay! (Students teach their neighbor what Biffle has just said.)

Biffle: Class! Class!

Students: Yes! Yes!

Biffle: All right. Let's sum up three points I've made. One: in philosophy we search for wisdom. Two: wisdom is produced by answering large questions. Three: these large questions are called universal questions and are much larger than the questions we ask in daily life. Teach!

Students: Okay! (Students teach their neighbor what Biffle has just said.)

Here is a sample of how the same Teach-Okay pattern might be used with a kindergarten class.

Teacher: Class! Class! Class!

Students: Yes! Yes! Yes!

Teacher: Today we're going to talk about five important numbers. Teach!

Students: Okay! (Students teach their neighbor what the teacher has just said.)

Teacher: Classity, class!

Students: Yessity, yes!

Teacher: The five numbers I'm going to talk about are the five numbers we use when we begin counting. (Holding up her hand, counting on her fingers.) One, two, three, four, five! Use your fingers just like I did. Teach!

Students: Okay! (Students, many of them using their fingers, teach their neighbor what the teacher has just said.)

Teacher: Class!

Students: Yes!

Teacher: Now, I'm going to count five people. (Pointing at five students.) One, two, three, four, five. Do the same thing I did. Teach!

Students: Okay! (Students, many of them pointing at five students, teach their neighbor what the teacher has just said.)

Teacher: (Using a high, funny voice) Claaass!

Students: (Laughing, and imitating the teacher's high funny voice) Yeeess!

Teacher: Now, let's review. We are talking about the first five counting numbers. One, two, three, four, five. I have five fingers. I counted five students. One, two, three, four, five. Teach!

Students: Okay! (Students teach their neighbor what the teacher has just said.)

Here is a sample of how the Teach-Okay pattern might be used in third grade to introduce fractions. Note how emotions centered in the brain's limbic system are stimulated by the teacher's directions.

Teacher: (Using a funny, hissing voice) Classssss!

Students: (Laughing and imitating the hissing voice) Yesssss!

Teacher: Today we're going to talk about fractions! Some people are afraid of fractions. But we're not afraid of fractions because we going to make them easy as pie! Tell your neighbor how *excited* you are to learn about something that's easy as pie! Teach!

Students: Okay! (Students teach their neighbor that they are excited about learning something that is "easy as pie.")

Teacher: Class!

Students: Yes!

Teacher: (Making a gesture with her hands) Now, let's say I have a pie right here. Ummmm! Delicious pie! I cut the pie in half. And I eat half of it! Yummm! Tell your neighbor *how good it feels* to eat half a wonderful pie! Teach!

Students: Okay! (Students tell their neighbor about the wonderful feeling of eating half a delicious pie.)

Teacher: Class! Class!

Students: Yes! Yes!

Teacher: Now here is the pie. It had two parts (writing the number 2 on the board.) But now, there is only 1 part left! (writing the number 1 on the board above the 2 and drawing a line, making the fraction 1/2.) And so, we write a fraction, showing there is only 1 of 2 equal parts. Teach!

Students: Okay! (Students teach their neighbor what the teacher has just said.)

Teacher: Class! Class! Class! Class!

Students: (Laughing) Yes! Yes! Yes! Yes!

Teacher: When we have a fraction like this, 1 of 2 equal parts, we say, this is "one half." *Be very excited.* It's so simple! Teach!

Students: Okay! (Students, mimicking the teacher's excitement, teach their neighbor what the teacher has just said.)

Teacher: (Laughing) Oh, Classity, classity, classity!

Students: (Laughing) Oh, yessity, yessity, yessity!

Teacher: Let's review. We're not afraid of fractions. They're easy as pie! If I eat one of two equal parts of a pie, that is the fraction one half! Tell your neighbor how great it feels to learn about fractions! Teach!

Students: Okay! (Students tell their neighbor "how great it feels to learn about fractions.")

Using prompts like the above, it is simple to add emotional content to lessons. If you have students who "don't care," you can get them involved in your lessons by asking them to mimic your emotions. As

James Zull, Director of the University Center for Innovation in Teaching and Education at Case Western Reserve University, points out, emotional investment is key to brain growth. "There are recent experiments which show that... changes in [brain] networks can be generated simply by triggering neurons to dump 'emotion chemicals' on the firing networks. These chemicals are things like adrenaline, serotonin, and dopamine, and they are delivered to specific parts of the brain by specific neuron pathways. Thus, the concomitant frequent firing and exposure to the chemicals of emotion lead to great change in neuronal networks."

Notice several points about the sample lessons I presented. The Teach-Okay pattern can be adapted for subjects at any grade level. Using this pattern, the teacher breaks down a larger lesson into small, easy to follow points. (The current lingo for this is "chunking.") The students only have to pay attention for a short amount of time before they have the opportunity to practice what has just been taught. Every small lesson finishes with a review. Finally, the teacher, using variations on Class!, or with emotion prompts, has her students happily engaged in learning.

Now, let's say you have some students with Attention Deficit Disorder (ADD). Do you see the advantage of the Teach-Okay system? Your lessons are short, easy to understand, fairly fast paced and continuously followed up by students repeating key points to their neighbors. There are kids with ADD in some of the videos at WholeBrainTeaching.com. You won't be able to tell who they are, because everyone is on task. Truth be told, we think everyone has problems with paying attention... in traditional classrooms, students with ADD aren't able to conceal their inattentiveness as well as the rest of us!

Looking at the samples of the Teach-Okay pattern, you might see several problems. First, students are mechanically repeating what the teacher has said; second, this approach does not seem to generate questions from students and student questions should be at the core of any good teaching system; third, some students may begin talking to their neighbors about issues other than the lesson.

Here is an answer to each of these concerns.

While it is true that we want students to explain our points to their neighbors, more or less as we made them, this is only the *beginning* of our instruction. If we are talking about philosophy, counting, or fractions, we have key ideas which we need to communicate and which, more or less, we need students to be able to repeat verbatim. As teachers we have content that must be understood and we hope that our presentations are clear and simple enough that this content can be repeated by students to their neighbors with few if any mistakes. Yes, students seem to be repeating mechanically... but as you walk around the class, you'll find something intriguing, and deeply educational going on. Students will be putting your point into their own words, with their own patterns, sometimes even with their own examples. Students will be practicing the extremely important critical thinking skill of paraphrasing. When students can put your lessons into their own terms, paraphrased your content at their linguistic level, then important learning is taking place.

(In chapter 21 we'll demonstrate how the Teach-Okay pattern can be used to teach original thinking, and not just paraphrasing the teacher's lesson.)

It would seem to be the case that having students talk to their neighbor would diminish the number of questions which students ask, but we have found the opposite to be true. Our strongest, most verbal students will often ask if they and/or their neighbor are repeating the material correctly. In addition, quieter students will raise their hand and ask the teacher a question, which only the teacher and the student's partner can hear, because everyone else is busy talking to their neighbors.

It is true that given the opportunity to teach a neighbor, some students will want to chat about non-educational issues. How can Mrs. Maestra tell when her students are off task? We'll devote the next chapter to educational body language.

CHAPTER 9

Teach-Okay

(Part 2)

M rs. Maestra loved watching her students teach each other... but what she loved even more was to see them *energetically* teaching each other. Her dream, the dream of many teachers, was to see an entire class engaged in passionate instruction. Here is the script that Mrs. Maestra used to help her dream come true.

SCRIPT: TEACHING GESTURES

Teacher: Class!

Students: Yes!

Teacher: You've been doing a great, fantastic, wonderful, incredible, scrumdillylicious job at learning! Teaaaaach!

Students: (Laughing) Okaaaaay! (Students teach their neighbor what the teacher has just said.)

Teacher: Class! Class!

Students: Yes! Yes!

Teacher: From now on, when you are teaching your neighbor, I want you to use energetic body language. (The teacher uses expressive, large gestures as if she were a jolly, bombastic public speaker.) I want to see you really getting into your explanation, teaching with all your energy. And, if you are listening to your neighbor I want you to use *listening*

> gestures. (The teacher cups her hands behind her ears, makes rolling gestures that say "keep talking" and other body language someone would use if they were excited to hear more of what was being explained to them.) Now, use teaching and listening gestures as you explain teaching and listening gestures. Teach!
>
> **Students:** Okay! (Students, using teaching and listening gestures, laughingly teach their neighbor what the teacher has just said. Many students just flop their hands around meaninglessly, but the teacher can tell that they are engaged in teaching their neighbors. Later, she will demonstrate gestures which are keyed to lesson content.)

When Mrs. Maestra had trained her class to teach each other (and use gestures in their instruction) she always noted that some students were chronic listeners and others were chronic yackers. She wanted her talkers to learn listening skills and she wanted her listeners to come out of their shells and talk. Mrs. Maestra noted especially that students who needed language development, often those who spoke English as a second language, were most likely to passively listen.

Mrs. Maestra divided her class so that her top students were paired with her bottom students and her middle students with her middle students (of course, she didn't reveal the basis for the pairing to her kids.) Next, she counted off her students in ones and twos. If she had an odd number of kids in her class, one group had two ones, or she paired with the leftover student.

She then followed this script.

SCRIPT: SWITCH

Teacher: Class!

Students: Yes!

Teacher: Here is something that will be fun. In a second, I'm going to ask you to teach each other the class rules... we've been rehearsing them for awhile. I want the ones to be the teachers and use big gestures while they talk. I want the twos to be the listeners and use listening gestures while they listen. (She demonstrates that listening gestures can include holding a hand to your ear, nodding your head, silently mirroring the gestures of the speaker, rolling your hands as if to say, "tell me more!") Then, when I say "Switch!" I want you all to loudly say "Switch!" and the twos will become the teachers and the ones will be the listeners. First, let's practice saying "Switch!" very loudly. Switch!

Students: Switch!

Teacher: Not quite loud enough! Faster, a little louder! Switch!

Students: (Louder) Switch!

Teacher: Wonderful! Okay, ones teach the twos the classroom rules. Keep teaching the rules over and over until you hear me say, Switch. Teach!

Students: Okay! (Ones teach the twos for a minute or so.)

Teacher: Switch!

Students: Switch! (Twos teach the ones.)

As her students taught each other, Mrs. Maestra walked around the room and either praised or prompted each group. When both partners were gesturing, she praised them. If one or both partners were not gesturing, she prompted them by saying, "Please use gestures."

We believe teaching and listening gestures are important for several reasons. In Whole Brain Teaching classrooms, student explanations of course material are a primary educational activity. The main problem we find with this approach is that some students may use the opportunity to talk about non-course material. When students use teaching and listening gestures to instruct their neighbor, this problem is greatly reduced. The teacher simply scans the room, observes body language; she can easily see the pairs of students who have drifted off into private conversations. Private conversations do not involve our stylized teaching-listening gestures.

A second reason that teaching and listening gestures are important is that they are a particularly effective way of involving challenging students, especially highly active ones, in course material. Kids want to be unrestrained, burn with a desire to move around. Instead of controlling this impulse, which is almost impossible for some students, we encourage our highly active pupils to use their energy in teaching their neighbors. It is lovely to see classroom rebels use their manic vitality to explain fractions, the Middle Ages, or the proper use of apostrophes.

A third reason that teaching and listening gestures are important is that students are not only creating lessons that are visual but also kinesthetic. Teaching and listening gestures add to a multi-sensory educational experience; students learn by seeing and doing; the abstract becomes visual and physical.

A fourth reason teaching and listening gestures are a powerful educational tool is that they help students develop underutilized aspects of their learning repertoire. Some of our kids love to talk; some are content to listen. The "Switch!" command makes the yackers listen and the listeners yack.

Finally, we have often found that having kids teach their neighbors is an excellent energy boost for both the teacher and students. Late on an afternoon, every drowsy spirit can be awakened by passionately waving their arms about in an energetic explanation of the joys of "attacking" word problems, "digging into" the hidden meaning in a story, "exploring" the three mighty building blocks of good writing.

By using the full range of Teach-Okay techniques, Mrs. Maestra's students were continuously engaged in learning that involved seeing, saying, hearing, doing and feeling, lessons that stimulated the whole brain. She believed this created the kind of stimulating education environment, prescribed by her personal hero, Dr. Marian Cleaves Diamond of UC Berkeley, one of the world's foremost neuroanatomists.

Dr. Diamond points out, "Increases in cortical growth as a consequence of stimulating environmental input have been demonstrated at every age, including very old age. The greatest changes, however-as much as 16 percent increases-have been noted during the period when the cerebral cortex is growing most rapidly—the first ten years. By providing children with challenging experiences through enriched education and environments, those dendrites cannot help but be off to a good start!" As Mrs. Maestra watched her entire class energetically using gestures as they taught each other, she sometimes imagined she could hear a faint pulsation, the sound of thousands of neurons sprouting dendrites.

CHAPTER 10

Teach-Okay

(Part 3)

Now, let's add one more important element to the Teach-Okay pattern. Laughter.

According to Dr. Richard Restak, professor of neurology at George Washington University Medical Center in Washington, D.C. and author of *The New Brain,* "...scientists have confirmed that humor decreases stress, boosts immune defenses, relaxes muscle tension, decreases blood pressure and modulates pain." Laughing is good for us... and our students.

One of our earliest goals in Whole Brain Teaching was to find ways to create on task laughter. We didn't care much for tomfoolery... but we adored *educational* tomfoolery. We wanted the deep engagement, the merry learning community, that is created when teachers and students laugh together. The more fun we made our lessons, the more our students learned. (Don't get the idea that our WBT classes are laughing all the time... that would be crazy... and not much fun! What we want is for our classes to have a merry laugh whenever we need extra student involvement.)

You may have noticed a fair amount of educational tomfoolery in the techniques presented thus far. We have the option of using a funny voice with the Class-Yes routine. Teaching and learning gestures, in themselves, can be occasions for merriment. On the Scoreboard, described in the next chapter, we create student engagement with the

Mighty Groan and the Mighty Oh Yeah. But here is our most reliable laugh producer, the Tickler.

SCRIPT: THE TICKLER

Teacher: Class! Class! Class! Class!

Students: Yes! Yes! Yes! Yes!

Teacher: Great job. Now let's have some fun. If I clap twice and say Teach!, you clap twice and say Okay! Let's try it. (Claps twice.) Teach!

Students: (Claps twice ... with a few giggles.) Okay!

Teacher: How about this. (Claps three times very fast.) Teach!

Students: (Claps three times fast ... with more giggles.) Okay!

Teacher: Try this one! (Claps twice. Stamps twice. Pats top of head three times.) Teach!

Students: (Claps twice. Stamps twice. Pats top of head three times. Laughter. On task laughter!) Okay!

All the veteran WBT teachers I know use the Tickler whenever they say "Teach!"... but it involves no more than a few hand claps. This produces mild, but continuous, low voltage happiness in our students. Whenever we need to give our students an extra jolt of merriment, which generates more intense engagement, we use absurd Ticklers, like the last one above (Clap twice. Stamp twice. Pat top of head three times).

Adjust the Tickler to your needs; you can create instant entertainment that varies all the way from low voltage happiness to merry belly laughs. Develop your own Tickler patterns. The only rule is that the Tickler should precede "Teach!" Here are some suggestions:

- Disco dance move, then say "Teach!"
- Whirl a lariat over your head, then say "Teach!"
- Anything inspired by the Three Stooges, then say "Teach!"
- Funny arm flapping as if flying, then say "Teach!"
- Air guitar with sound effects, then say "Teach!"
- Any combination of claps, stamps, head pats, shoulder waggles, etc., then say "Teach!"

At this point, you might be thinking that Whole Brain Teaching sounds intriguing, but believe that your class is so challenging that you can't get them to follow directions... couldn't even get them to start teaching their neighbors, or stop once they had started. You're even afraid they'll have too much fun with the Tickler.

You want to know Mrs. Maestra's secret for motivating positive behavior and penalizing negative behavior.

That secret is in the next chapter.

CHAPTER 11

The Scoreboard

Motivating your class to work hard

In upper grades, after Mrs. Maestra had introduced Class-Yes, the Five Classroom Rules and Teach-Okay, she pointed her students to a diagram she had drawn on the board. (In lower grades, K-2, Mrs. Maestra often introduced the Scoreboard on the first day, and postponed the Teach-Okay until the second or third week.)

Early in her career, Mrs. Maestra tried a variety of motivational devices to keep her students on task, marbles in a jar, table points, play money, candy... but nothing was as simple, powerful, entertaining, flexible and cheap as the Scoreboard Game.

Here is the script that Mrs. Maestra mentally followed when introducing the game to her students. (Observe the use of the Tickler, as the lesson develops.)

SCRIPT: THE SCOREBOARD GAME

Teacher: Class!

Students: Yes!

Teacher: We're now going to play a game. A very fun game. The game is called Scoreboard. And all you have to do to win is, KEEP THE SCOREKEEPER HAPPY! I'm the Scorekeeper! (Claps twice.) Teach!

Students: (Claps twice.) Okay! (Students teach their neighbor what the teacher has just said.)

Teacher: Class!

Students: Yes!

Teacher: Today we will be playing the Scoreboard Game for more or less recess time. As the year goes by, we will be playing for other rewards: more or less homework, more or less video time, more or less free time in class, or best of all, more or less game time! (Claps twice.) Teach!

Students: (Claps twice.) Okay! (Students teach their neighbor what the teacher has just said.)

Teacher: Class!

Students: Yes!

Teacher: When I put a mark under the Smiley face, that means you are doing something that makes me, the Scorekeeper, happy. When I put a mark under the Frowny face, that means you are doing something that makes me, the Scorekeeper, unhappy. (Claps three times.) Teach!

Students: (Claps three times.) Okay! (Students teach their neighbor what the teacher has just said.)

Teacher: Class!

Students: Yes!

Teacher: This is a very important point. Give me an ah-ha-ha!

Students: Ah-ha-ha!

Teacher: At the beginning of the Scoreboard game, what makes me, the Scorekeeper happy is a class that follows our classroom rules. What doesn't make me happy is a class that doesn't follow our classroom rules. (Claps four times very fast.) Teach!

Students: (Claps four times very fast.) Okay! (Students teach their neighbor what the teacher has just said.)

Teacher: Class!

Students: Yes!

Teacher: Every Smiley face mark you earn is one minute *more of recess.* Every Frownie face mark you earn is one minute *less of recess.* (Claps twice.) Teach!

Students: (Claps twice.) Okay! (Students teach their neighbor what the teacher has just said.)

Teacher: Class!

Students: Yes!

Teacher: Now, here is a very big point. Note that the Scoreboard is labeled Level One. If you do very well playing this game *maybe I'll let you go to Level Two!!* (Claps three times, Stomps foot three times. Does a disco dance move.) Teach!

Students: (Laughing... claps three times, stomps foot three times, imitates the teacher's disco dance move.) Okay! (Students teach their neighbor what the teacher has just said.)

(From here forward, we'll omit the use of the Tickler... it is much more fun to use it in class, than read it in scripts!)

Mrs. Maestra, a veteran Whole Brain Teacher, had taught every grade from kindergarten to college. Depending on what she thought her students would enjoy, she substituted the following for Smiley and Frowny faces: Empress of the Universe and Earthlings, Captain and Crew, More Recess and Less Recess, Cool and Not Cool, Groovy and UnGroovy, Extra Credit and Dextra Credit, Plus and Minus. Mrs. Maestra also used a variety of rewards and penalties. Sometimes the marks stood for one more or one less: math problem, minute of free time, minute of video watched in the class, minute of music listened (or danced to!), or her favorite, minute of game time.

Note that by varying the way the Scoreboard was labeled and the rewards and penalties, Mrs. Maestra avoided the problem of habituation, her students becoming unresponsive to the Scoreboard's stimulus. Additional "de-habituators" will be listed at chapter's end. Also, note that in the Appendix, Mind Sports, contains a description of three, highly engaging, learning games, that can be used as Scoreboard rewards.

Mrs. Maestra said to her class, "Now, let's review. We're going to play a game called Scoreboard. There's only one thing you have to do win: keep the Scorekeeper happy. I'm the Scorekeeper! At the start we'll play for more or less recess. When you do or say something that makes the Scorekeeper happy, I'll occasionally increase the recess by one minute and put a mark under the Smiley Face. When you do or say something that makes the Scorekeeper unhappy, I'll often decrease recess by one minute and put a mark under the Frowny Face. Here's my reasoning. If you work hard in class, you have earned more free time, because you've done a good job of learning material I'm covering. If you don't work hard in class, you really need less recess, because you haven't done a good job of learning material I'm covering. Work hard in class, or during recess. Your choice! Tell your neighbors what I just said."

The students, hesitantly, explained what Mrs. Maestra said.

Mrs. Maestra continued, "Oh! That was too slow, and some people didn't even talk to their neighbors... or use *gestures!!!!* The Scorekeeper is unhappy!"

She then put a mark under the Frowny Face and said, "Give me a Mighty Groan!"

Her students groaned.

Mrs. Maestra exclaimed, "That was a very poor groan! Here's another Frowny Face mark. You now have lost two minutes of recess! You're not following the Scorekeeper's directions *and that never makes her happy!*"

Mrs. Maestra lifted her shoulders towards her ears and demonstrated a vigorous groan. "Now give me a groan like that *with my gesture!*"

Her students, many lifting their shoulders, groaned more energetically.

Mrs. Maestra congratulated them. She knew it was a poor strategy to give three Frownies in a row.

Mrs. Maestra understood that the groan was very important. Students laughed as they groaned… and thus they were back on her side, instead of being resentful that they had received a Frowny face.

Mrs. Maestra continued, "Now, you see it's really important for you to figure out what makes the Scorekeeper happy and unhappy. Let's practice. Do some things that you think might make the Scorekeeper unhappy. Go ahead. It's practice; I won't give you any Frownies. Just don't go crazy… but you can break what you think might be a classroom rule."

A few of her students did and said goofy things.

Mrs. Maestra continued, "Great! Excellent misbehavior! Now, do or say some things that you think would make the Scorekeeper happy."

A few students did and said things that made Mrs. Maestra happy.

Mrs. Maestra understood that rehearsing correct and incorrect behavior was an important principal of Whole Brain Teaching. Whole Brain Teachers never scolded… they rehearsed.

Mrs. Maestra concluded, "Right! Okay. *Now, we're going to review some of our classroom rules and procedures. Work hard to keep the Scorekeeper happy!*"

Here was Mrs. Maestra's plan. She already had her students several Frowny Faces "in the hole". Her next few marks would be Smiley Faces; Mrs. Maestra marked Smilies whenever most of her class followed her directions. Then she added a few more Frownies, then a few more Smilies. Mrs. Maestra knew that she should *never have 3 more frownies than smilies (or vice versa)*. If she punished too much her students would become discouraged; if she rewarded too much, her students would become lackadaisical. In Whole Brain Teaching, we call this the Plus/Minus Three rule. On the Scoreboard, the difference between reward and penalty never exceeds three points. Why? Because kids are most motivated when the game is close… and with the Plus/Minus Three rule, the Scoreboard game is always close!

Mrs. Maestra explained the Plus/Minus Three rule to her class as follows. "The difference between Smilies and Frownies will rarely, if ever, be greater than three points. If the class is three points behind, I will be looking for the smallest amount of good behavior so that I can give you a Smilie. *But be warned!* If the class is three points ahead, I will be looking for the smallest amount of negative behavior to give you a Frowny!"

Mrs. Maestra taught her students that just as they gave a "Mighty Groan," when they got a Frowny, they should give a "Mighty Oh Yeah!" when they got a Smiley. She called this having a "one second party." Students clapped their hands, thrust them toward the ceiling and shouted "Oh Yeah!" If Mrs. Maestra didn't want her class to make noise, she told them to lightly tap their pinky fingers together and have a "Mighty Whisper Oh Yeah." She sometimes called this a "quiet riot."

As Mrs. Maestra moved toward the end of the first period, she let the Smilies almost, but not quite catch, the Frownies. The Frownies were two marks ahead. Stopwatch in hand, Mrs. Maestra took her students out to the playground and they watched other students play for two minutes. This was important. It showed Mrs. Maestra's students that she was serious about administering penalties.

The next few days that Mrs. Maestra played the game, her class came closer to winning increased recess. Often they came out even and earned their normal recess... but it was always nip and tuck. (Oh, you're two minutes behind!... Wow, you were three minutes ahead but now you lost a minute... Mighty Groan!) She usually put students "in the hole" at the start of the day with a few quick Frownies. She found her class was highly motivated to "come from behind."

Near the end of the first week, when her students were having a good day, Mrs. Maestra let them earn one minute more of recess. This gave them a taste of success. For the rest of the days Mrs. Maestra played the Scoreboard Game, she never rewarded or penalized more than two or three minutes of recess. Her students almost never received three extra or three fewer minutes. These had to be saved for extraordinary days, positive or negative, or these marks lost their "specialness." (When Mrs. Maestra worked in a school with a tight recess schedule, she gave her students "in class" recess for the extra minutes they earned.)

When adding or subtracting recess minutes began to lose its motivational power, Mrs. Maestra substituted one page more or less of homework. Mrs. Maestra understood many great truths of Whole Brain Teaching. Here is another:

Students will work extremely hard to avoid a small amount of work.

When Mrs. Maestra added extra homework, she was putting pages "in the bank." Her students weren't aware of it, but they were ahead of where Mrs. Maestra needed them to be... thus, Mrs. Maestra could give them homework reductions and know she was still moving at the pace she wanted.

If her students complained about the game or the penalties, Mrs. Maestra give them a quick Frowny and explained, "Sorry. Complaints about the Scoreboard Game never make the Scorekeeper happy. Class! Tell your neighbors how important it is to keep your dear Scorekeeper happy and never complain about how she keeps score!"

Mrs. Maestra gave no warnings.

She never said, "Now, class if you're not listening to me more carefully, I'm going to give you a Frowny face. I mean it class. You better really listen to me now, because if you don't, you're going to get a great, big Frowny." Mrs. Maestra either gave a Frowny or ignored the bad behavior. Sometimes, when her class was very unruly, Mrs. Maestra didn't give Frownies at all, especially when the Frownies were three marks ahead of the Smilies.

If a few penalties weren't motivating her class, lots of penalties wouldn't improve their behavior. Instead, on days when the class as a whole was seriously misbehaving, Mrs. Maestra would say something like, "You know what? There are several people in here who are doing an outstanding job. In fact, everyone at table three is really working hard. Here's a Smiley for the whole class as a gift from hard working table three! Give them a cheer!"

Students invariably cheered for the classmates who earned them a Smiley... and Mrs. Maestra had her students focused on following her directions. They had cheered when she told them to cheer.

Mrs. Maestra knew some teachers began the Scoreboard game and *gave no reward at all*. Many classes would work fairly hard just to see more Smilies than Frownies. Go figure.

Because the Scoreboard game was fundamental to her year long classroom management system, Mrs. Maestra, as described above, overcame her students' tendency to habituation by varying the rewards and the way the sides of the Scoreboard were labeled. In addition, she could also segment the Scoreboard in a variety of ways. Occasionally, she might draw a horizontal line across the diagram, and label it as follows.

Girls	
Boys	

With the Scoreboard labeled Girls vs. Boys, the game could be played in one of two ways. First, Mrs. Maestra could give separate rewards and penalties to the girls and boys (always observing the Plus/Minus Three rule for each group.) For example, if the reward was extra recess, and the girls won by one point, they could have one minute extra recess. Or, second, Mrs. Maestra could total the girls and boys scores and let them "work together." Thus, if the reward was extra recess, then the total of the boys and girls positive points had to exceed the total of their negative points before the class earned extra recess. An alternative to Boys vs. Girls was to pit the right side of the class against the left, or even better, to name two captains, and let them choose teams (and then seat them on the right and left side of the class).

For even more Scoreboard flexibility, Mrs. Maestra was delighted to find the following article in the Levels menu at WholeBrainTeaching.com.

Because you'll be using the Scoreboard all year, here are a variety of Scoreboard strategies... but don't employ them too often! It's a long time until spring.

Ping-Pong: Named by our WBT kindergarten pro, Andrea Schindler, you either reward for a positive behavior and then quickly follow up with a negative point or vice versa. You ping-pong the Scoreboard, point on one side, point on the other. Say, "That back row is doing great! Give me a Mighty Oh Yeah!" (And make a mark on the positive side.) Continue, "But unfortunately, some of my students are not using vigorous gestures! Oh no! Mighty Groan!" (And make a mark on the negative side.) Obviously, you can go the other way, negative point first and then positive point.

Marker Move: Your marker is in a tray at the bottom of your blackboard. Say, "You kids are doing really well. I'm going to move my marker a little closer to the positive side of the Scoreboard. Give me a 'ooooooh, goody!'" Also, when kids aren't doing quite so well, you move your marker slightly further away from where it would need to be to make a positive mark.

Boombox: You go in with a boombox and place it in the front of the room, far from where it would be hooked up. Each positive mark on the Scoreboard gets a "Mighty Oh Yeah" and you move the boombox closer to where it could be plugged in.

Eventually, you plug the boombox in... but then, oh no! You see some negative behavior and the box must be unplugged! Eventually, the kids get to hear 30 seconds of music (maybe the second day of this routine.) Let them beg to play "boombox" again for several days and get your most popular kids to suggest music (that you preview at home to be sure it is PG.) When the boombox reward is won, you keep the music period short... it's a long year... by the spring they should have worked hard to earn three minutes of music at the end of the day.

Fake: Say, "Wow, you kids are doing really well. Where is my marker..." Then pick up the marker and move it toward the board, ready to make a positive mark. Then, say, "But not quite well enough to get a positive mark!" And put the marker down underneath the Scoreboard... done correctly, your kids will say "awwww" and be eager to get an actual positive mark.

Doubler: For late in the year, say "Today, we're going for double points!" Then, whenever there is negative behavior, make two marks and get a double Mighty Groan. Whenever there is positive points, make two marks and get a double Mighty Oh Yeah. When you have some positive and some negative behavior, make a quick mark positive and a quick mark negative. As you can tell, the score will end up to be about the same as when you are making single marks, but it feels much more exciting.

Pirates: Say, "today we're going to play Pirates. I'm the Captain, you're the Crew." Label the Scoreboard appropriately. Say, "When the Crew scores a point, shout 'Yo, ho! ho!'" When the Captain scores are point, hold your hand out in a hook and say, "Arrrrgggg!" Obviously you can change the labels in other ways, Queen vs. Subjects, Farmer vs Turkey (yum, yum, gobble, gobble!), etc.

Drum roll: Right before you make a positive mark, say, "Drum roll!" The kids pat their hands very fast on their desk, saying "ahhhhh!" louder and louder as you approach the board. You make the mark, point at them and they explode, "OH, YEAH!" Jay Vanderfin, one of Whole Brain Teaching's co-founders, throws in the "In your face!" Kids get to say this to their instructor instead of the Mighty Oh Yeah!

Beat the Clock: Go in with a kitchen timer, pick the rule you want to work on, then say, "Okay, I'm going to set the timer. Let's see how long we can go without... (insert negative behavior, like talking without raising a hand to speak)." When the negative behavior occurs, stop the timer and write down the "class record" on the board. Then say, "Okay, let's try again. If we beat that record, everyone will get a Smilie! Tell your neighbor how desperately you want to win a Smilie!" The goal is for students to go for 20 minutes without the negative behavior. When this goal is achieved, and it's possible even in kindergarten, every time they hit the 20 minute mark, give them all a Smilie.

Vertical Morphin' Scoreboard: After using your Scoreboard for awhile, extend the center line upward and then draw another line crosswise on top of this center line. You now have what looks like one Scoreboard on top of the other; the Scoreboard has morphed into a Higher Power. Label the top Scoreboard with another set of Smilies and Frownies, or whatever you are currently using. Also add a note that this Higher Board is the next grade higher for your students. Thus, if your students are 4th graders, the higher board is a 5th grade standard. Point out that energy that might have scored a Smilie in 4th grade, could earn a Frownie in 5th grade. Use the higher board rather ruthlessly for a few quick Frownies when students are a hair slow or a hair less focused than you wish. As the day, or week proceeds, add categories to the higher board: speed, eye focus (every eye on you when you're talking), full turn (students fully turned in their seats when teaching their neighbors), gestures (emphatic gestures used when teaching their neighbors). In the morning add one category and mark Higher Smilies or Higher Frownies in that category; then add a second category later in the morning and mark both categories and so forth through the day. In the last hour, when student energy is normally the lowest, they have the most higher categories used as motivators.

Obviously, you could morph the Scoreboard to an even higher level, call it College. So then, you'd have a triple Scoreboard, one on top of the other. This higher Scoreboard is a "challenge"..."let's see if you can hang at the college level..." In general, when you get them at this highest level, make sure they win so that they feel wonderful about their maximum energy.

Horizontal Morphin' Scoreboard: Extend the normal Scoreboard horizontally so that you have two Frownie Categories and two Smilie categories. Thus, you have four columns. The leftmost column has two Frownies, the next column has one Frownie, the next column has one Smilie and the next column has two Smilies. Now, when the students are "really slow" make a mark in the Double Frownie column... that counts as two Frownies! Ditto for the Double Smilie column. Obviously, the overall score doesn't need to change from the normal Scoreboard, but kids will really be sizzling when they are zonked with Double Frownies or Smilies. For madcap energy, combine the Horizontal Morphin'

Scoreboard with the Vertical Morphin' Scoreboard... so kids are at the College Level and can add double or even triple! Smiles or Frownies!!! Don't overdo this... at this highest or most extreme level, kids should only be working a few minutes at a time, usually when their energy is the lowest in the last minutes of the day.

Team Scoreboard: Draw a horizontal line across the middle of the Scoreboard. This will give you a higher and lower Frownie and a higher and lower Smilie. You are now ready to play Teams. Two excellent teams, as mentioned above, are boys against the girls, or left half of class against right, or back half against front half... or even nominate two captains on opposite sides of the room and give the kids a count of 15 to divide equally, half sitting with one captain and the other half with the other. If you play one team against the other, then the winning team gets the prize... one extra credit point or lining up before the other team, or whatever. Keep the reward small so that later in the year it can be doubled or tripled. You can also play cooperatively with teams scoring points for the class as a whole. When both teams have, say, a total of three more positives then negatives, give the teams a prize, playing Mind Soccer for two minutes, for example.

Mystery Road: Draw a circle on the upper right of the whiteboard (your students' right). Label this circle with the prize, say Music Time. Then, draw a "road" from the upper left of the whiteboard all the way to the Prize. Now, as the class proceeds, draw a line down the middle of the road, this marks their progress toward the prize. "Oh, you're getting closer... oh, you moved even further, oh, you zoomed ahead!" Of course, they can also go off the road... even go back toward their starting point! The line eventually looks very zig-zaggy, shooting forward, veering off the road, looping back. Students cheer forward motion and groan at backward motion. When they complain, of course that means they are going even further backward, further away from the Prize. For even more fun, put several question marks along the road. These are Mystery Spots. When the line gets to a Mystery Spot, then you stop for some kind of special exercise. For example, students summarize everything from a lesson on a previous day, or make diagrams illustrating everything you've said thus far, or use a pencil as a prop to describe actions in a story etc. Mystery Spots should be relatively short breaks in the overall progress of the day.

Leaderboard: Have the class nominate five or so classroom leaders. Make one column on the whiteboard and label it, Leaders Rule. Now, when the Leaders are working hard, being great leaders, totally focused, highly energetic in teaching their neighbors, etc. make a positive mark in the Leaders Rule column. When the marks reach 10, the class earns the Prize. NOTE: Don't make any negative marks in the Leaders Rule column... you don't want to turn the classroom leaders against you! If you wish, you can, over several days, add columns to the Leaders Rule chart. One column could be speed, another eye focus, another, gestures, another great questions, etc. Add the columns slowly. Then make a mark in the appropriate column when you see one or more leaders demonstrating that leadership virtue. For even more tension and engagement, add the leaders' names to the Leaders Rule column. Now, you can reward individual leaders for individual achievement (using or not using the columns for specific kinds of engagement).

Gridboard: Under the Frownies write "Slow" and under the Smilies write "Fast." Now you are marking for one individual class virtue, speed. As the day, or week, unfolds add other virtues: sleepy/energetic gestures, partial turn/full turn, little focus/max focus.

Virtueboard: Only on the Smiley side, add special Smiley categories like Great Question, or Excellent Leadership or Politeness or Generous Sharing, Unselfishness, Kindness, Honesty or even Excuselessness (when a kid is accountable for his/her actions). Don't make any equivalent Frownie category for these! It would be awful to have a kid ask a question and you say, "Oh, awful question! Here's a Frownie!" Because we want our kids to be virtuous, to develop strong, moral characters, you might have the Virtueboard be entirely separate, on the other side of the whiteboard from the regular Scoreboard. The Virtueboard would be an excellent way of monitoring outside of class behavior (lunch, playground, lines). You might even have Virtue Captains whose job it would be to occasionally make a mark on the Smilie side of the Virtueboard for virtuous actions they observed.

Scoreboard Rewards: As mentioned earlier, you can use slightly more or less recess or homework as Scoreboard rewards. However, the rewards, so long as they are small, are as unlimited as your imagination. Instead of showing a video, let students earn "video minutes" that they save until Friday. Or, give them one point more or less extra credit (my favorite college motivator.) Use learning games as rewards (but use a kitchen timer set to 3-5 minutes to keep the games tantalizingly brief!) Many WBT teachers believe that Mind Soccer (see the Appendix, Mind Sports) is one of the all time best academic review games. I've often noted that students never pay attention more intently than when I get off the subject and tell a story about something that happened to me when I was younger. So, "True Story" time could be a great motivator... but stop the story at an exciting part... your students only get to hear the story's end if they win the Scoreboard by 3 points tomorrow. Now, let me tell you about the time I met Cesar Chavez alone on a moonlit road in the Tehachapi Mountains. He was standing there with his two big dogs, Huelga and Boycott. He looked at me with that wonderful, saintly face and said, quietly, "Hi!" I said... oh, maybe you'll hear tomorrow what I said.

WARNING: Don't keep switching up the games above. Use one occasionally... and see how long you can keep engagement by using it. Then, eventually, go to another. Too much variety in how you're using the Scoreboard will make your class less, not more, focused on the goal of positive, learning behavior.

In upper grades, Mrs. Maestra could introduce some of the basics of Whole Brain Teaching briefly in the first hour of the first day of class. It took her little time to teach her students the Class-Yes, Five Classroom Rules, Teach-Okay, Teaching and Listening Gestures and the Scoreboard Game. She knew other teachers who started much more slowly; in fact, some rookie Whole Brain Teachers simply used the Class-Yes and nothing else for weeks. One of the features Mrs. Maestra loved about Whole Brain Teaching was that it was a highly structured system, with a clearly laid out set of incremental steps, that could also be restructured, mixing, matching and redesigning elements however the individual teacher wished.

Some instructors loved noisy, high energy classes and had great fun with the Mighty Groan, the Mighty Oh Yeah and encouraged students to use intense, flamboyant, teaching and listening gestures. Other instructors wanted their students to be self controlled, diligently serious; they taught their classes the Whisper Groan, the Whisper Oh Yeah, and Teensy Weensy Gestures.

Dr. Patricia Hutinger, Director of the Center for Best Practices in Early Childhood Education at Western Illinois University, describes a learning experience similar to methods employed by Whole Brain Teaching. "Children can learn one set of concepts using a variety of modes. Imagine a first grade class learning rather difficult conceptual words such as 'that', 'them', 'when', 'what', and 'got'. The teacher writes the words on the board (visual) then they chant the words (combining visual and auditory). Then, they sing the words to the tune of 'row, row, row your boat' as she points to the words. Next, they write the words in their 'journal' (motor/kinesthetic) and finish with another round of song. (A child could easily do the pointing). That teacher makes use of visual, auditory, music, and kinesthetic modes with an entire group of 20 highly engaged children."

Hutinger's conclusion would be echoed by Mrs. Maestra and thousands of Whole Brain Teachers around the country, "If you plan learning experiences that incorporate a wide range of modalities you are likely to produce a group of enthusiastic, engaged learners." Mighty Oh Yeah!

Thus far, you have learned five of the Big Seven: Class-Yes, the Five Classroom Rules, Teach-Okay, Switch and the Scoreboard (Level One). In the next chapter, you'll learn the last two, Mirror and Hands and Eyes.

CHAPTER 12

Mirror, Hands and Eyes

Two powerful student engagers

Mirror is one of WBT's simplest and most powerful techniques. You say "mirror" and your students respond "mirror." They then pick up their hands ready to mimic your gestures.

As students imitate the motions you use to teach a lesson, their motor cortex, the brain's most reliable memory area, is automatically engaged. Mrs. Maestra used mirror when telling a story, giving directions, describing the steps in a procedure, demonstrating a process... anytime she wanted her class locked in to what she was saying.

Here is the script Mrs. Maestra mentally followed when introducing Mirror.

SCRIPT: MIRROR

Teacher: Class!

Students: Yes!

Teacher: Here is a simple, new, fun learning technique. When I say "mirror," you say "mirror" and pick up your hands, ready to mirror my gestures. Mirror!

Students: Mirror! (Students hold their hands in the air.)

Teacher: Great job, but let's do it a little faster and maybe you'll get a Smilie. (very quickly) Mirror!

Students: Mirror! (Students quickly hold their hands in the air.)

Teacher: Fantastic! (Walking to the board. Making a mark on the Smile side of the Scoreboard.) Hold it! Hold it! (Rapidly pointing to her class.)

Students: (Clapping their hands loudly.) Oh yeah!

Teacher: Good job. Mirror!

Students: Mirror!

Teacher: Now, mirror my gestures. Today we are going to talk about a great big problem (spreading her arms out wide... students mirror this gesture) but we're going to break it down into little pieces (holding her fingers close together... students mirror this gesture.) Tell you neighbor what I said... using my gestures! Teach!

Students: Okay! (Students use the teacher's gestures to teach their neighbors the teacher's points.)

In general, there are three kinds of gestures you can use while teaching:

- **casual:** these are hand motions that you naturally use while speaking
- **graphic:** match your gestures to exactly what you are saying. For example, if you're talking about walking somewhere, walk your fingers through the air. If you want to explain a hard problem, scratch your head. If you are presenting a big idea, spread your arms far apart.
- **memory:** these gestures are linked to core concepts and/or state standards. Every memory gesture should be unique. For example, a memory gesture for a fraction might be one fist above the other, with the top fist standing for the numerator and the bottom fist standing for the denominator. Or, a memory gesture for a period might be pushing your hand out as if giving a "stop" signal. Other memory gestures might include pretending as if you are writing in the air as the memory gesture for author, making an "X" with your arms for multiplication, dealing imaginary cards for sorting and so forth.

For additional student engagement when using mirror, add elements of silliness and exaggeration to your gestures. As a variation, say "mirror words" and your students respond "mirror words." Then, speak slowly and match your arm movements to what you are saying. Your students repeat your words and mimic your gestures. Five brain activities are now involved: seeing (motor cortex), saying (Broca's area), hearing (Wernicke's area), doing (motor cortex) and feeling (limbic system). Another name for this quintuple learning is Teacher Heaven.

Fairly often, Mrs. Maestra wanted to make a Big Point and she needed intense attention from her class. Maybe she was describing exactly how a form had to be filled out by her students' parents or the heading she wanted on every paper turned in or the rule for reducing improper fractions to whole numbers. For this special, intense attention, Mrs. Maestra used Hands and Eyes.

SCRIPT: HANDS AND EYES

Teacher: Class!

Students: Yes!

Teacher: The next technique is very simple. Whenever I need to make a big point, I'll say "hands and eyes." You say "hands and eyes" and fold your hands and stare at me, as if you can't wait to hear the words I'm going to say. Let's try it: Hands and eyes! (The teacher folds her hands quickly.)

Students: Hands and eyes! (The students quickly fold their hands and stare intently at the teacher.)

Teacher: Great! Let's try it again! Hands and Eyes! (The teacher folds her hands quickly.)

Students: Hands and eyes! (Folding their hands even more quickly.)

Teacher: Fantastic. Now, here is my big point...

Note this: the teacher does not give a Smilie point every time her class follows directions... or a negative point every time they don't follow directions. If this was the case, the game would be controlling the instructor, instead of vice versa. The beauty of the Scoreboard is that, never forget it, you are the Scorekeeper. Points are marked entirely at your discretion. And if a student complains that they should be getting a Smilie, you have the option of marking a quick Frownie... *because pressuring the Scorekeeper never makes her happy!!!*

Here's a review of the Big Seven:

1. The Attention Getter: Class-Yes

When you say "Class!" your students respond, "Yes!" By varying your call, "Class! Class!," "Classity! Classity!," "Oh, Class!," "Class, classity, class, class!" your students will vary their response and thus avoid habituation. For additional variety, change your tone of voice... or even use attention getting gestures. The mirror neurons in many of your students' brains will take over, mimicking you. Think of the Class-Yes as a brain switch that readies your kids' prefrontal cortex to focus on your next instruction.

(As the year progresses, substitute a bit of core knowledge for your "Class!" For example, if you call out "First President!" your students respond, in place of "Yes!" with "George Washington!" or if you say, "Four times Four!: they respond "16!")

There is something quite odd, mysterious about what happens when you say "Class!" a variety of ways and your students respond "Yes!" Amazingly enough, this routine makes the class momentarily merry. I use Class-Yes! a thousand times a semester. Students are still grinning in the final week. Further, I and other Whole Brain Teachers have noted, that if you laugh when saying "Class!" many of your students will laugh as well. This is because one of the primary learning mechanisms in the brain, as I noted earlier, are mirror neurons. We learn by imitating, mirroring. It is not just monkey see, monkey do. It is monkey see, monkey's brain rewires itself.

2. The Organizer: Five Classroom Rules

Note that three of the rules, "Follow directions quickly," "Raise your hand for permission to speak," and "Raise your hand for permission to leave your seat" are behavior specific. They describe exactly what you want your students to do. The last two rules, "Make smart choices" and

"Keep your dear teacher happy!" are general principles which cover a host of situations in and out of the classroom. For variety, always important!, select one of the first three rules as a "special focus" for the day. Tell your students that the majority of the points you mark on the Scoreboard will reflect how well, or poorly, the rule is followed.

By rehearsing the rules several times a day, with gestures, you will engage whole brains in hearing, seeing, saying, doing and feeling the principles that create an orderly classroom.

3. The Whole Brain Activator: Teach-Okay

If you can train yourself to speak briefly, your students will have few problems with becoming teachers of their neighbors. Kids love to talk and be active. Teach-Okay gives them the chance to use their energy to nourish their, and their classmates', learning. You need to make two important points to your students about Teach-Okay. First, each student must be making speaking or listening gestures. Second, students continue teaching each other, even if they are repeating themselves, until you call out "Class!" The last thing you want in a Whole Brain Teaching classroom is for pairs of students to fold their arms and zone out after teaching each other your lesson once.

Occasionally, a few students may complain that making gestures distracts them. Use your instructor's intuition, judge by their tone of voice and past behavior, if their complaint comes from genuine mental difficulties or from a determination to do as little work as possible. If the former is the case, then ask the student to slightly nod her head when listening and to try, occasionally, to make small gestures. If the latter is the case, and the student is particularly stubborn, encourage her to learn in the same way as the rest of your students (and make a mental note that this pupil will be a prime candidate for Level Two of the Scoreboard... when you introduce consequences for individual, not group, behavior.)

If Teach-Okay is difficult for you, then practice dividing a lesson into short chunks at home; write notes in your lesson plan to guide you through Teach-Okay presentations.

4. The Motivator: The Scoreboard

Remember that you begin the Scoreboard at Level One (additional levels will be introduced beginning with chapter 14.) Your initial goal is not to transform the behavior of every student, but to unify as many students as possible behind your leadership. Consistent use of the Scoreboard, early in the year, means that the positive and negative marks, per day, total at least 15. As the year unfolds, you'll find yourself having to make fewer and fewer marks. While you can use the Scoreboard to point out individual positive behavior, *never use it to penalize individual negative behavior.* You will quickly turn the class against you if you punish everyone for the actions of one student. But what do you do about individual misbehavior? Wait until Level Two (chapter 14)!

5. The Involver: Switch

Typically, in a WBT classroom students teach their neighbors the instructor's lesson every minute or so. When we judge that a lesson is particularly difficult, we move into Switch. Giving each student several turns explaining and listening to information provides the repetitions necessary to begin to grow new dendrites. Award winning journalist, Judith Horstman in *The Scientific American Day in the Life of Your Brain*, makes the point clearly, "The more you repeat something—an action or a thought—the more brain space is dedicated to it." Switch, as you have probably already deduced, is especially powerful for English learners. ESL students need hundreds of hours of practice acquiring new language skills, most comfortably in the privacy of conversations with a friend.

6. The Class-Unifier: Mirror

Use Mirror to directly and energetically involve your students' whole brains in your lessons. We have found there are at least three kinds of gestures: casual (hand motions you naturally use when speaking), graphic (gestures that tell a story or describe a process), memory (gestures that are unique for each core concept or state standard).

Andrea Schindler, our veteran WBT kindergarten specialist, enlivens her class with "mirror check." The routine goes like this:

SCRIPT: MIRROR CHECK

Teacher: Class!

Students: Yes!

Teacher: Mirror!

Students: Mirror! (Imitating the teacher's gesture.)

Teacher: Great! Now, let's do mirror check. Mirror my gestures (the instructor then begins waving her arms about in a variety of callisthenic gestures. Her students follow suit.)

Late in the afternoon, when your, and your students are feeling drowsy, a minute or so of mirror-check calisthenics is a great way to get the blood pumping.

7. The Focuser: Hands and Eyes

Whenever you have a big point to make about *anything*, use the Focuser. Don't be afraid to use the technique too often. In college, I employ Hands and Eyes about once every five minutes. Typically, introduce the Focuser with Class-Yes... which will gain the attention of most of your students, and then tighten student engagement by saying "Hands and Eyes" as you make a large gesture, bringing your hands together.

Before we watch Mrs. Maestra solve some of teaching's great, practical problems... like how to hand out papers, open books to the proper page or what to do about that infernal machine, the pencil sharpener... let's think about how the Big Seven addresses problems of teaching challenging students.

Remember in chapter 4, Mrs. Maestra divided her class into four groups, Alphas, Go-Alongs, Fence Sitters and Challenging Students. A *consistent* application of the Big Seven will do wonders to unify the first three groups behind your leadership and reduce the number of students in the last group, the challenging students. We counsel teachers beginning to use our methods to work hard for several months, if necessary, to create a core of group of pupils who understand and support their instructor's leadership. This support is created by consistent, and happy!, use of the Big Seven. As you will see beginning in chapter 15, we will use the peer pressure created at Level One of the Scoreboard as leverage to encourage more and more of a class to become part of the Whole Brain learning community.

A central premise of Whole Brain Teaching is that the more frequently you engage your students' whole brains, the more you will reduce disruptive behavior. Students can't dream up challenging behaviors if they're too busy energetically teaching their neighbors. But you can't have a classroom of whole brain learners unless you are a whole brain instructor. To help your students transfer information from short to long term memory, you must speak briefly, engage their limbic systems with the Scoreboard, activate their motor and visual cortices with vivid gestures that they mirror and teach their neighbors. You have to grow dendrites across your whole brain to grow dendrites across your students' whole brains.

And remember another of WBT's great laws.

If repeating yourself bugs you, don't go into teaching. Teaching is repeating!

If you've read this far and want an even stronger classroom management system because the majority of your students, and not just a few, are immune to penalty. You need a system that is all reward.

Go to WholeBrainTeaching.com. Download, under "Free Downloads" *Industrial Strength Whole Brain Teaching*. This is our suite of techniques designed for the toughest classes. It was successfully piloted by Jackie Pedersen at a middle school in Riverside, California. She had remarkable success with classes of the most resistant kids *in an institution that had a 43% suspension rate! Industrial Strength Whole Brain Teaching* is based on two principles: every class of determined rebels has a few very strong rebel leaders; success with such a class must involve leadership training. The magic of *Industrial Strength Whole Brain Teaching* is that it creates an environment in which rebel leaders can only maintain their positions of leadership, which they desperately want, by gaining their followers the rewards that come from staying on task!

CHAPTER 13

Daily Classroom Procedures

Eliminating challenging behavior during transitions

Mrs. Maestra understood that teaching her students the classroom rules, posting them at the front of the room and rehearsing them several times a day, laid a strong foundation for classroom behavior... but she also knew the real trick was weaving the rules into the fabric of daily instruction. John and Juana, two of Mrs. Maestra's most challenging students, learned the rules quickly, but, without wise guidance, would rarely follow them.

An especially important rule for any classroom is Rule 1: Follow directions quickly. Our goal in a WBT classroom is bell to bell instruction, without a second wasted. Seconds and minutes are lost when classroom procedures are not followed quickly.

A classroom procedure is an activity you want your students to perform many times a day; a rule is a general principle that guides student behavior. In WBT, we distinguish between two kinds of procedures: those that involve the entire class, like lining up, and those that involve individual students, like correcting a wrong answer. The more smoothly your class performs common procedures, the less opportunity there is for challenging behavior.

Here are five of the most common procedures that involve the entire class and that should be performed according to Rule 1: Follow directions quickly!:

- opening books
- lining up
- handing papers in (and out)
- being seated
- lowering the noise level

Before Mrs. Maestra became a Whole Brain Teacher she was frustrated with the amount of class time wasted in transition activities when all she wanted was for her students to open their books to a specific page or to perform similar "simple" tasks. In addition, Mrs. Maestra noted that the more slowly these routines took place, the more likely it was that challenging students, temporarily free of supervision and lost in the chaos of many students performing, or not performing, the same activity, would become disruptive. It was as if her student rebels were suddenly released from captivity… and lining up, or opening their books, become opportunities for mutinies.

Mrs. Maestra was delighted with the following multipurpose script that could be used for many of her most common procedures.

SCRIPT: OPENING BOOKS (AND OTHER COMMON CLASSROOM PROCEDURES)

Teacher: Class!

Students: Yes!

Teacher: I'm now going to show you how I want you to open your books. I will say, page 39! and you say "39! 39! 39!" loudly and then open your books quickly. Hold up both hands when you are at the correct page. Let's practice. 39!

Students: 39! 39! 39! (students open their books, many raise their hands)

Teacher: Classity! Classity! Classity!

Students: Yessity! Yessity! Yessity!

Teacher: You can put your hands down. That wasn't too bad for the first time, but I want you to be a bit quicker. I'm going to count to 10. If everyone has their hands up with their books open to the correct page, I'll give the class a Smilie! Remember to repeat the page number. 142!

Students: 142! 142! 142! (while the teacher counts 1 to 10, students race to open their books to the correct page.)

Mrs. Maestra loved this procedure for many reasons. First, it solved the ongoing hassle of students asking her what page they should open their books to and the teacher having to repeat the page number over and over. Second, the procedure turned opening books into a game, and thus, her students were often engaged in one of Whole Brain Teaching's highest goals, task focused laughter. Third, Mrs. Maestra could use the 10 count to set class "records." She always counted at the same speed, but as the year progressed she would only give a Smilie when the class opened their books before she got to 8, then before she got to 6. This made the book opening game even more entertaining *and wasted even less time*. Fourth, she could use exactly the same script for lining up, being seated, and handing papers in or out and many other frequently repeated procedures. Instead of repeating the page number three times her students said "Lines!" or "Seats!" or "Papers!" three times and held up their hands when the task was accomplished. Mrs. Maestra adjusted the count for each activity.

Mrs. Maestra had 35 students. Here is the count she started the year with for common procedures:

- Opening books: 10 count
- Getting out paper and pencil, with name neatly written in the upper right corner: 25 count
- Handing papers out with the extras passed back to the instructor (and no running in the classroom!): 35 count
- Handing papers in to one student and the student placing the papers in a neat stack on the teacher's desk... without running: 25 count

- Putting away all materials before lining up at the door: 20 count
- Lining up at the door: 20 count
- Being seated, starting from an orderly, silent line outside the classroom: 20 count

For several of her procedures, Mrs. Maestra kept class records on the board, which, because of her students' efficiency, were lowered as the year progressed.

Sharpening pencils was a common activity that Mrs. Maestra *didn't* want all her students to engage in at once. She knew that pencil sharpening could drive a teacher bonkers. Students leave their seats, create disturbances on the way to sharpen their pencils, have problems operating the pencil sharpener, then cause disturbances on the way back to their seat. And this could happen all day long!

Here is a routine I learned from a teacher at one of my seminars... whoever you are, wherever you are, God bless you!

Buy a few hundred pencils and a good electric pencil sharpener. Put a red piece of paper on the front of a coffee can and a green piece of paper on the back. Place a large handful of sharpened pencils in the can and put the can on your desk. Tell your students that when the red paper faces them, no one can trade one of their pencils for a sharpened one. When the green paper faces them, students are permitted to, one by one, trade their pencil for a sharpened one. If students have no pencils, they can get a sharpened pencil when the green paper faces out.

In other words, students never sharpen their pencils in class!

Mrs. Maestra often had to lower the general noise level in her classroom. She could do this either by saying "class," getting everyone's attention and asking her students to work more quietly, or she could use the Magic Invisible Volume-O-Meter.

SCRIPT: SETTING THE CLASSROOM NOISE LEVEL

Teacher: (Using a deep voice) Class!

Students: (Imitating the teacher's deep voice) Yes!

Teacher: When you are too noisy, I'll use my Magic Invisible Volume-O-Meter to set the correct sound level for our current activity. (Raising her hand) When I move my hand move up toward the top of the Volume-O-Meter I want you to say 'yada, yada, yada' louder and louder. When I move my hand down, I want you to say 'yada, yada, yada' more and more quietly. Teach!

Students: Okay! (Students teach their neighbor what the teacher has just said, many of them move their hands up and down imitating the Magic Invisible Volume-O-Meter).

Teacher: Class!

Students: Yes!

Teacher: Okay, now here we go. (She moves her hand up and down and the students, adjusting their volume to her gestures, say "yada, yada" more loudly and then quietly. The teacher then moves her hand down very low, until the students are whispering.) Good! That's the level I want you to speak at.

Mrs. Maestra understood that her class, and especially her challenging students, loved to play games. Her general classroom management strategy exemplified by the Magic Invisible Volume-O-Meter was to set up games that students enjoyed... and that trained them to follow her rules.

Now, let's look at four common procedures that apply to individual students.

- correcting a wrong answer to a teacher's question
- rewarding a correct answer to a teacher's question
- encouraging students to avoid "I can't..."
- raising a hand to ask a question

When Mrs. Maestra was a student, she had seen many of her own teachers tiptoe around correcting pupils when they answered a question incorrectly. The teacher didn't want to hurt anyone's feelings. If a student thought the area of circle was found by using a formula for squares, the teacher might say something like, "That's an interesting answer, Joe. It certainly shows that you know something about math. Now, Juana what do you think of Joe's answer?"

Of course Joe, as soon as the teacher went to Juana, knew he was wrong. His feelings weren't being protected... in fact, his misery was drawn out, especially because many students might chime in with the right answer or, worse, laugh at Joe's mistake.

Mrs. Maestra wanted her students to know that they were in a "no failure" class. She wanted them to understand it was okay to make mistakes... and no one would mock them for their errors.

SCRIPT: CORRECTING STUDENT ERRORS WITH "IT'S COOL"

Teacher: Oh, classss!

Students: Oh, yesss!

Teacher: Hands and Eyes! (Spreading her arms out wide, and then bringing them together and folding her hands.)

Students: (Imitating her gesture.) Hands and Eyes!

Teacher: Great! You did that so well, I'm going to give you a Smiley! (Walks to board, gets a marker.) Hold it! Hold it! (Makes a mark on the Smiley side of the Scoreboard. Then, whirls and points at her class.)

Students: (Clapping their hands!) Oh yeah!

Teacher: Wonderful! Now, here is my big point. If someone makes a mistake when I ask them a question, I don't want anyone to correct them and I certainly don't want anyone to laugh at them for being wrong! Teach!

Students: Okay! (Students teach each other what the teacher has just said.)

Teacher: Class!

Students: Yes!

Teacher: Everyone will make mistakes. It's okay, no big deal. The worst thing that will happen to you if you make a mistake is that everyone will tell you, "it's cool." For example, Jason... what year was the French Revolution?

Jason: 1920?

> **Teacher:** No, it was 1789. Tell Jason "it's cool."
>
> **Students:** It's cool!
>
> **Teacher:** Maurice. What is the capital of Florida?
>
> **Maurice:** I don't know.
>
> **Teacher:** It's Tallahassee. Tell Maurice "it's cool."
>
> **Students:** It's cool!

Mrs. Maestra valued the "it's cool" routine. Students quickly learned that there was no humiliation in missing an answer and Mrs. Maestra found it much easier to immediately correct a student's wrong response than hunting around the classroom to find a student who knew the correct response. In fact, Mrs. Maestra's students became so used to saying "it's cool" that they would use it when she made an error... and Mrs. Maestra had to admit that it felt pleasant to have everyone support her when she was mistaken.

Early on in Whole Brain Teaching, we decided teachers needed an entertaining way to quickly reward students when they answered a question correctly. We certainly didn't want to hand out candy or pass out play money; the first was unhealthy and the second took too long... and students became upset when they misplaced their cash. We wanted a reward that was instantaneous and that would add to what we called "educational tomfoolery." Here is one of our first scripts.

> **SCRIPT: INSTANTLY REWARDING STUDENTS WITH A "WOO!"**
>
> **Teacher:** Class!
>
> **Students:** Yes!
>
> **Teacher:** Whenever someone gives a right answer, or does something else worth a reward, we're going to give them a woo. Watch, I'll demonstrate. Cathy, you did a great job of helping your partner with her spelling. Give her a 10 finger woo! (The teacher extends her arms, points 10 fingers at Cathy, wiggles her fingers and says, with delight...) Woo! Go on, give Cathy a 10 finger woo!
>
> **Students:** (Laughing and pointing wiggly fingers at Cathy) Woo!

Mrs. Maestra and other Whole Brain Teachers quickly created a variety of woos. If a student was half right, she got a five finger woo; if a student was only a little bit right, and had a good sense of humor, he got a pinky finger woo. If Halloween was coming they got a 10 finger "boooo-woooo"; Thanksgiving brought out the 10 finger "gobbledy-woo." And so forth.

When her students did something exceptional, Mrs. Maestra called for a 10 finger rolling woo... and added a rolling motion with her hands to the 10 wiggling fingers. Occasionally, maybe only twice a year, a student deserved an extraordinary woo. Mrs. Maestra invented the "10 finger rolling woo with the grand salami!" She would point 10 wiggling fingers at the wondrous student, roll her hands in the air, then throw her arms up and bring them down as if bowing to the student while she exclaimed, "Grand Salami!" All her students followed suit and everyone laughed.

Thus, far we've looked at two techniques, "it's cool" and "woos" that are a common feature of Whole Brain Teaching classrooms when the instructor is engaged in an interchange with an individual student. Mrs. Maestra knew that many times during the year her challenging students, and many others in her class, would become frustrated because some learning task seemed impossible. A typical complaint would begin with, or contain the phrase, "I can't..." Mrs. Maestra knew that almost always when students said "I can't" their minds closed, making a difficult learning task even harder for them. Anticipating this problem, Mrs. Maestra used the following script.

SCRIPT: REMOVING "I CAN'T" FROM STUDENT VOCABULARY

Teacher: Class!

Students: Yes!

Teacher: There are two words which we never, ever, ever say in our class when we are working on a lesson. Those words are "I can't" Teach!

Students: Okay! (Students teach their neighbor what the teacher just said.)

Teacher: Class, class!

Students: Yes, yes!

Teacher: Whenever you say "I can't..." you are putting yourself down. Putting yourself down is never a smart choice. You're breaking rule 4! Teach!

Students: Okay! (Students teach their neighbor what the teacher just said.)

Teacher: Class, class!

Students: Yes, yes!

Teacher: So, instead of saying "I can't" I want you to say "I can't yet." Just add that one word. And here's the deal, whenever I hear you change an "I can't" to an "I can't yet" I'm *may have the whole class give you a Rolling 10 Finger Woo! You know how hard those are to get!* Teach!

Students: Okay! (Students teach their neighbor what the teacher just said.)

Teacher: Class, class!

Students: Yes, yes!

Teacher: Okay, let's practice. I want you to say "I can't," and then change it to "I can't yet." Here we go. No matter what I ask, say "I can't" and then change it to "I can't yet!" Timmy, can you lift 200 pounds over your head?

Timmy: I can't. I can't yet!

Teacher: Great job. Class, give Timmy a 10 Finger Rolling Woo!

Students: Woo!

Teacher: Bethany can you solve college algebra problems?

Bethany: I can't. No, I mean I can't yet!

Teacher: Wonderful! Give her a 10 Finger Rolling Woo!

Students: Woo!

Mrs. Maestra knew that many times during the semester her students would say "I can't," but she also knew that if she practiced the routine above, they would, little by little, learn to correct themselves.

Mrs. Maestra's classroom rules instructed her students to raise their hands for permission to speak and for permission to leave their seats. These were wonderful rules, but they caused two problems: first, when

Mrs. Maestra's students raised their hands, their minds, many times, went blank and they stopped listening to what she was saying; second, Mrs. Maestra might be making an important point, and couldn't stop to call on a student with a raised hand. To solve both these problems, she used the following short script.

SCRIPT: THE GRABBER

Teacher: Class!

Students: Yes!

Teacher: We're going to practice raising hands in a moment. I want a few of you to raise your hands and then I'll reach out like this (making a gesture as if she was reaching out and closing her hand around the raised hand). That means I've got your question. Then, when you see me make the reaching out gesture, put your hand down in a fist on your desk. When I've finished talking, I'll take questions from students whose hands are down in a fist. (The teacher then had a few students raise their hands; she "grabbed" their question; the students put their hands down in a fist on their table.)

In the next chapter, you'll get an overview of the six levels of the Scoreboard.

CHAPTER 14

Scoreboard Levels

*A year long classroom
management system*

There are two major components to Whole Brain Teaching's instructional system. First, the Big Seven (Class-Yes, Five Classroom Rules, Scoreboard, Teach-Okay, Switch, Hands and Eyes, Mirror) provide a set of techniques that engage your student's whole brains in instruction. Think of the Big Seven as your daily teaching tools. A second component is a multileveled game that evolves from the Scoreboard as an ongoing system of rewards and penalties. The Scoreboard provides year long motivation for the Big Seven's daily learning routines.

Here are the seven Scoreboard levels, with a brief description of each.

Level One: The Scoreboard (described in chapter 9) rewards and penalizes the behavior of your class as a whole. Though individuals may be rewarded for positive behavior with a Smiley, they are never punished for negative behavior because the class will soon rebel for being punished for the behavior of one student. The Scoreboard is used on the front board for the entire year; each succeeding level does not reduce, but only enhances its powers.

Level Two: Super Improvers Team - Using a color coded scale, students advance from the lowest to the highest level for improvements in academic or social behavior. Instead of competing against each other, kids strive to set and break personal records in everything from reading speed to lunch room behavior. The Super Improvers Team can be adapted to help challenging kids focus on easy to improve negative habits.

Level Three: Practice Cards provide a powerful tool to address individual behavior problems... and successes. When students receive a white card, they briefly rehearse at recess the rule they broke and take a note home to their parents describing their negative behavior; when students receive a purple card, they take a note home to their parents describing their positive behavior; when students receive a green card, they practice in class following the rule they have broken.

Level Four: The Guff Counter is added to the Scoreboard to remedy the problem of students who speak, or act, disrespectfully to their teacher or classmates. One of the many beauties of the Guff Counter is that the guffing student finds herself isolated; the instant she speaks or acts disrespectfully the entire class exclaims, "Please, stop!"

Level Five: The Independents is added to the Scoreboard. This new feature of the game miraculously turns rebellious cliques of students against each other.

Level Six: The Bullseye game, and the next level The Agreement Bridge, is reserved for your most challenging students, those who are immune to penalty and punishment. In general, you'll only be able to identify your most stubborn rebels after they have resisted Levels One through Four. When students play the Bullseye game, they are involved in a brief, daily, one on one exercise that rewards them for seeing their behavior from the instructor's point of view.

Level Seven: The Agreement Bridge, frankly, is seldom needed by WBT educators. This game establishes a context for long term counseling with students who engage in structured, no punishment, dialogue with a teacher, mentor or administrator. The goal of the dialogue is to negotiate a contract which both counselor and student sign and frequently reevaluate.

Before we investigate the Super Improvers Team, note the strategy of the seven levels of the Scoreboard. Your plan is to begin with the easiest to solve behavior problems and proceed to the most difficult. Why? Because by having larger and larger groups of students enter your learning community, you free up the time you will need for work with your most disruptive kids. In addition, the more students who support you, the smaller the support system is for your rebels.

The classroom is too often a power struggle, and yes, it is often us against one or more challenging kids... that is the blunt and unhappy truth. But anyone can teach compliant kids. Mrs. Maestra's glory, which will soon be yours, was that she had the skill and techniques to bring even her loudest squawkers under the warm shelter of her wings.

CHAPTER 15

The Super Improvers Team

Rewarding student improvement

Level Two of our yearlong classroom management system, The Super Improvers Team, addresses a universal student need; our kids crave recognition. But what form should it take... and what activities should they be rewarded for? In WBT, we believe students should be rewarded for academic and behavioral improvement. We don't want to reward students for where they are now, but for how far they've come since last month.

A system that rewards for intellectual and social growth is perfectly democratic and superbly differentiated. From Special Ed to gifted, students' goals should be the same... to surpass their previous best effort. In every classroom across the land, we should be giving our classes the same, invigorating message, "Go out there and break your personal records!"

Imagine a system that graded students solely on foot speed. The teacher calls you and I out to the track and says we're going to race. We both run hard and you beat me. I get an "F," you get an "A." Tomorrow we have the same race. Same result. After about a week, you don't run hard, just enough to win. And I, because I know I can't beat you, slack off. Before long, you loaf and I quit. Isn't that what happens in traditional education? Our best students do just enough to get by and our weakest students, because they know the can't win, bail out.

But what would happen if we changed the race? The teacher calls us out to the track. New rules. The racer who beats their previous best time, *by the greatest amount*, gets the top grade! Oh no! You have to run like crazy. And so do I. Every day! Every race! Beating me is not the point. You've got to keep beating yourself. And you know what ... if you keep running hard, you will beat your previous best time. And so will I. The race is more rewarding and motivating when we stop racing each other and race against ourselves.

If we focus on student improvement in academic activities and social growth, then scores on state tests *will take care of themselves*. Nothing will produce higher test results than a class of students who are continuously striving to break their own personal records.

In WBT, we want to set up a system in which every kid has an equal chance for success. Putting this another way, we want to create a classroom atmosphere that is brain friendly. Every brain is unique, but all brains grow dendrites, nerve fibers that expand knowledge. In 12 years of experimenting in classrooms across the country, we have found nothing that motivates students more intensely than setting and breaking their own records. Brains seem to be nourished by their own growth. Exhilarated by its sprouting dendrites, the brain sprouts more dendrites. Kids' brains love to feel like they are getting bigger. Brain growth fuels the appetite for brain growth. WBT learning is like a magic meal. The more you eat, the hungrier you become!

So, let's focus on student improvement as our educational target not on academic excellence. Every child, in every way, can grow.

A WBT classroom with its many rules, routines, procedures, and games is a garden of student growth. You can observe individual growth in following the five rules, teaching neighbors, responding to the Scoreboard, lining up, handing papers out, neat writing, improved scores in SuperSpeed games, outstanding homework (see appendix), growth in Oral Writing (see appendix), using good manners, etc.

To reward student improvement, create a Super Improvers Team with every student's name written on a individual piece of white paper (half a sheet of typing paper will work... if you have 30 students, then you will have 30 half sheets of typing paper on your wall.) In addition, create a color scale with smaller pieces of paper about the size of 3 x 5 cards. From bottom to top, each color should be different. For example, white, blue, red, green, orange, purple, yellow, metallic bronze, metallic silver, metallic gold (we suggest these last three for the three highest levels). Now, you're ready to chart and reward improvements (see diagram below).

Super Improvers Team

	Student	Student	Student	Student
Gold				
Silver	Student	Student	Student	Student
Bronze	Student	Student	Student	Student
Yellow	Student	Student	Student	Student
Purple	Student	Student	Student	Student
Orange	Student	Student	Student	Student
Green	Student	Student	Student	Student
Red	Student	Student	Student	Student
Blue	Student	Student	Student	Student
White	Student	Student	Student	Student

When you observe students improving in any school activity, give them verbal praise, "you're really doing better lining up... wow, what a great improvement in your SuperSpeed 100 score... what a remarkable increase you've demonstrated in keeping your hands to yourself on the playground... you are using gestures to teach your neighbor much better now than this morning." After you've made several verbal comments, add a star to the child's name on the Super Improvers Team. When a child has earned 10 stars, change the color of the paper their name is on. In the color system described above, every child starts at the white level, then advances to the blue level, then to the red, etc. Every ten stars, they climb higher in color code. With 10 colors, this means your Super Improvers Team has room to note 100 improvements for every child in your class!

If your room is arranged so that it might be difficult to add stars to the names on the wall, give each child a card that they keep on their desk. When you are ready to award a star, mark a star on the child's card. Then, at recess, lunch or after school, transfer the stars from the cards to the Super Improvers Team. If your students go to other classrooms for a period or two, and if the other teacher is willing, give the teacher a hand stamp. When the teacher sees improvement, the wonderful child gets his hand stamped... and then has the opportunity when he returns to your classroom to show you how wonderful he has been!

Children love to be recognized, love to feel like they are making progress. "Last week I was just a blue, but now a few more stars and I'll be a red!... Gosh, someday maybe I'll be a metallic gold!!!!"

If you wish, the 10 color levels can have names. For example, using a fish theme, the 10 color levels could be

Metallic Gold: blue whale
Metallic Silver: tiger shark
Metallic Bronze: dolphin
Yellow: sword fish
Purple: giant sea bass
Orange: king salmon
Green: doitsu koi
Red: guppy
Blue: minnow
White: tadpole

I'm especially fond of a sports theme... and if you have rowdy boys, the scale below is almost irresistible.

Metallic Gold: Living Legend
Metallic Silver: Hall of Fame

Metallic Bronze: SuperStar

Yellow: MVP

Purple: All Star

Orange: Team Captain

Green: Team Leader

Red: Starter

Blue: Rookie

White: Fan

Here is the sports themed Super Improvers Team with stars and a few students who have advanced beyond Fan.

Super Improvers Team

Living Legend				
Hall of Fame	Student ★★★ ★★ ☆	Student ☆	Student ☆☆	Student
Super Star	Student	Student	Student	Student
MVP	Student ☆	Student ☆☆☆	Student ☆☆	Student
Star	Student	Student	Student ☆	Student
Captain	Student ☆☆☆	Student	Student	Student ☆☆☆
Leader	Student	Student ☆☆	Student	Student
Starter	Student ☆	Student	Student	Student
Rookie	Student	Student ★★★	Student	Student
Fan	Student	Student	Student	Student

After several months, you can add even more motivation to the Super Improvers Team.

Bring in your camera and when a student at any level over red earns a new color, take the student's picture with any friends he or she chooses. *Encourage the kids to make funny faces.* Children love to see pictures of themselves making funny faces.

Develop the picture and bring it to class. Do not show the child the photo but replace their name on the Super Improvers Team with the picture, *image side to the wall* (but maintain the color coding.) For example, Maria advances from green to orange. Take her picture as she poses with her friends. Bring the picture in, put it on an orange sheet of paper, with the image side to the wall. At this point, Maria wants more than anything in the world, to have the photo turned around and see her funny face picture with her friends.

As you note continued improvement, put a star on the back of the photo. When the photo has ten stars, make a big production of turning it around. Viola! Announce that your Super Improver has become a Student Leader! We almost guarantee that at least once a day, the student and her friends will go up and look at the picture.

What should Student Leaders do?

For one day, assign leaders to perform, at your request, any of the following call outs: class!, hands and eyes, mirror, papers, seats, lines, switch, teach, Mighty Groan, Mighty Oh Yeah. Change leader tasks daily... not everyone who has a photo turned face outward, will be a leader every day. By making your most improved kids part of your daily routine, you are creating mini-Whole Brain Teachers. If you attend a WBT conference, you can purchase leadership buttons for these students.

Student leadership, in this system, is hard earned, based on self improvement. We especially stress the importance of recognizing students who make dramatic gains in the SuperSpeed games as part of their homework (see appendix, Universal Homework Model). When your students ache for the recognition that comes from setting and breaking personal records... ache so much that they work hard at home on reading and math... you're in Teacher Heaven. All your racers are racing against themselves.

Recently, Deb Weigel, a member of our Executive Board, sent me a description of how to significantly simplify the construction of the Super Improvers Team. Instead of using colored sheets of paper on the scale on the left that ascends from lowest to highest, Deb suggested simply writing the levels in different colors of marker. It's far simpler to find and buy a set of 10 colored markers than packs of colored paper. Next, instead of changing the color of the sheets of paper that a student's name is on, simply write their names in the appropriate marker color. Thus, let's say Maria was moving from the green to the blue level. You would take down the white sheet of paper with her name in green and replace it with a white sheet of paper with her name in blue. A lovely next step would be to give Maria the lower level sheet, name in green with the 10 stars, to take home and show her parents.

In the diagram below, imagine that the different shades of gray on the ladder on the left correspond to 10 different colors. The color of the students names would correspond to the colors on the left ladder. Thus, the whole wall is made from white paper; color coding is handled by markers.

Super Improvers Team

Living Legend				
Hall of Fame	★★★★ Student ★★★★	☆ Student	★★★ Student	Student
Super Star	Student	Student	Student	Student
MVP	☆ Student	★★★★ Student	★★★ Student	Student
Star	Student	Student	☆ Student	Student
Captain	★★★★ Student	Student	Student	★★★ Student
Leader	Student	★★ Student	Student	Student
Starter	Student ☆	Student	Student	Student
Rookie	Student	★★★ Student	Student	Student
Fan	Student	Student	Student	Student

But what happens if some marvelously improving students reach the top level, Living Legend in the sports theme above? When a student gets ten more stars, she becomes Living Legend 1.0; 20 stars and she advances to Living Legend 2.0. The Super Improvers Team has no top rung; the climb, as it should be, is infinite.

A further, and powerful refinement of the Team, was suggested by Kate Bowski, a WBT intern for 2012-2013. Kate's students are encouraged to nominate classmates for Super Improver stars. Isn't that wonderful?! Her room is filled with children looking for other kids to reward for improvement. Kate's view, and it certainly makes sense, is that we should do as much as possible to empower students, to give them ownership of learning systems we create for them. If your students are eagerly recognizing classmates' improvement, then everyone is not only improving academically and in terms of behavior but also in open hearted generosity.

The Super Improvers Team, as you may have guessed, provides powerful incentives to improve the behavior of your most challenging kids. Follow these steps:

1. Early in the year, focus on creating systems and procedures that your most amenable students will follow. Unite as many of your kids as possible behind your leadership. Praise frequently and, as the first weeks unfold, begin to award stars.

2. Understand that every truly challenging kid has a host of disruptive behaviors... that's what makes them so challenging. Your challenging kids will see that students are getting rewarded for improvement, not academic ability or social maturity. Take your special student aside, indicate some activities that might be improved and then *pick the easiest behavior to fix*. "John, if I could see you keeping your feet off your desk before first recess, that would be an improvement that could gain you a star."

3. After a few weeks, to continue to move forward, give your special student a list of behaviors. Let him or her pick the one they want to work on. Now, your challenging kid is making decisions about how to develop a pattern of success. (Remain calm if you don't see as much improvement as you wish... there are many more strategies in the chapters ahead! Our system is like a video game; each level is more powerful than the last.)

Now, please listen to me. I made a terrible mistake in my 40 years in the classroom. I had marvelous students but I never created a system for remembering them. Use the Super Improvers Team to make a permanent record of your best, most improving kids. Tell your students something like the following, "If you make it to the top level, Living Legend, I'll take your picture and put it at the top of the wall. As long as I teach, no matter where I go, your picture will be there, looking down on my future students. Every child who comes through my classroom will look up to you... and so will I. In my world, you will always, always be a Living Legend."

As you'll see in the next chapter, an especially powerful way to use the Super Improvers Team is to employ its star system to reward students for excellent test preparation practice for the dreaded state tests.

CHAPTER 16

Improving State Test Scores with The Super Improvers Team

Climbing a ladder of stars

There are many reasons why students score poorly on state tests, but let's focus on two: they don't receive enough practice taking tests and they have little motivation to employ sound test taking procedures.

Assume I'm going to teach you how to play tennis. I spend a lot of time encouraging you to try your hardest. I show you many ways to improve your game. I tell you that it is very important for you to play tennis excellently. I do everything I can to focus your attention on The Big Game that will occur at the end of the year. Occasionally, I let you actually play a few sets of tennis. At year's end, we're both upset when you do poorly in The Big Game. Nonetheless, when you're my tennis student the next year, I follow the same procedure. Large quantities of talk, direction and urging by me... little actual tennis playing by you.

If you'd need lots of daily reps practicing your strokes to improve your tennis, then our students need lots of daily reps practicing test taking procedures. Just as we would advance from simpler to more complex tennis skills, so we should advance from simpler to more complex test taking procedures. We suggest that students spend 20 minutes of class time, *daily*, practicing test taking and test procedures (10 minutes on math, 10 minutes on language arts).

High test scores benefit teachers and, in some states, can save principals' jobs, but don't do much for our kids. It takes so long for tests to be graded, students don't learn the results until months later... *if at all*. So, how can we motivate students to work as hard as possible on a arduous task, if an excellent score means little or nothing to them?

Stop here a second. Think back to the Super Improvers Team. *What if we rewarded kids for outstanding improvement while they were practicing test taking procedures?* Do you see the power of that? Students would suddenly have motivation for ramping up their testing skills. Every day they would have a new opportunity to climb up the Super Improver Ladder. "If I get better at solving math problems, I could advance from a Rookie to a Starter!" Oh goodness!

Here is a sample of a year long sequence of test taking strategies.

Week 2-6: Prove It! + Show Work (math)

Project sample test questions on the board or hand out samples. Students turn to their neighbor and prove one answer is correct and the other three answers are incorrect. They use the following sentence frames, "_____ is correct because _____." Or, "_____ is incorrect because _____." When they say the word "because" they clap their hands; this is the Because Clapper and emphasizes "because" as a key word in reasoning. Listen to students' responses. Point out that a "weak because" would be something like "Answer B is wrong because it is not right." A "strong because" would be something like "Answer B is wrong because to find the area of a rectangle you have to multiply two sides, not add all the sides on the perimeter."

As an alternative to talking to their neighbors, students can use a class set of whiteboards. They write down the correct answer with the reason why it is correct and the incorrect answers with the reasons whey they are incorrect. At your signal, your kids hold up their whiteboards and you check their responses. Note: don't wait until the slowest student is finished!; also, tell the fastest students that when their work is complete, they should use gestures and teach their shoe (!) the correct and incorrect answers. (Prove It! was inspired by a program developed by Linda Mikels of Sixth Street Prep in Victorville, California. Linda's techniques produced some of the highest test scores in our state.)

Stress that on all math questions, students must show their work. Use a computer projector to illustrate strong examples of "showing your work" and weak examples. Occasionally, ask students to create several examples of the wrong (messy, sketchy) way to show work and the right (clear, detailed) way to show work.

Award Super Improver stars as students improve in neatness, accuracy, speed, strength of "becauses" or "shoe teaching," and showing their work.

Week 7-12: Prove It! + Show Work (math) + Doofus/Trickster/Smarty

Teach students that there are three kinds of answers to every state test question. The Doofus answer is totally wrong... not even close. The Trickster answer is designed to fool kids... it looks correct but it is absolutely wrong. The Smarty answer is, of course, right. Tell students to label answers Doofus, Trickster, Smarty and then use the Prove It! and the Because Clapper to explain their reasoning. The power of this approach is that it turns a dry reasoning technique, process of elimination, into a lively game. Award Super Improver Stars for improvements in accuracy, lively gestures while teaching neighbors and "strong becauses."

A very powerful test taking strategy would be for you and your grade level team to create special banks of test questions. Early in the year, give your kids the Doofus Bank in which every answer but one is a Doofus, obviously wrong. This will make the questions as easy as possible, build student confidence and also increase the strength of their "becauses." Next, about a month before Christmas, give students the Doofus-Trickster bank in which there are two Doofus answers, one Trickster and one Smarty. After Christmas, use test release questions which typically have a mixture of Doofus and Trickster answers. About a month before test taking, give students, if they are ready, some Triple Tricksters in which three of the answers are as tricky as possible and only one is a perfect Smarty.

Weeks: 13-18: Prove It! + Show Work (math) Doofus/Trickster/Smarty + Double Underlining

Students read through a math problem or language arts section and underline key words and phrases. Then, they *reread* the section and double underline the most important words and phrases. The power of Double Underlining is that students must read a section twice… and you can visually monitor their progress. Show students examples of poor underlining (too much or too little underlined) and excellent underlining (single underlining identifies key ideas; double underlining highlights the most important information in the passage.) In math, emphasize that the second underling should always highlight numbers and language that indicates the math operation that should be employed. Award students Super Improver stars for improvements in neatness and an appropriate amount of single and double underlining.

In California, second grade students are not allowed to write in their test booklets. Therefore, we teach "light underlining" that can be erased when the test is completed.

Weeks: 19-36: Prove It! + Show Work (math) Doofus/Trickster/Smarty+ Double Underlining + Headings

Teach students that before they solve any math problem, they should complete the following heading:

- Key Words: (fill in key words)
- Key Numbers: (fill in key numbers)
- +, -, x, /: (fill in whether the problem involves addition, subtraction, multiplication, or division)
- Procedure: describe what you have to do to solve the problem
- Show Work: Show your work very neatly

Award Super Improver stars for improvement in any of the above categories.

For language arts, students should complete the following headings:

- Key Words/Phrases: (list double underlines here)
- One Third Summaries: Students divide the reading section into three parts and briefly summarize each unit before answering questions.

By using Headings, students take the complex task of answering test questions and break it down into a clear, detailed, set of steps.

An excellent way to set up your Super Improver Team would be to put up a list of signs that indicated what activities you were emphasizing. Thus, you might have Prove It, Double Underlining, Heading, Doofus/Trickster/Smarty, etc. as separate signs and put sticky notes on the activities that you were rewarding with stars.

We believe state test practice using the above techniques should begin the second week of the year. We call our method DVR. Practice testing should be daily (D), involve visible (V) techniques and be Rewarded (R) with Super Improver stars.

If we don't give students daily practice in rehearsing test taking skills, we can expect what we typically get ... poor scores on state tests.

We must teach students test taking techniques that are visible. This is crucial. Instead of telling students to "read carefully," "use the process of elimination," and "think critically" we tell them to double underline, label every answer a Doofus, Trickster or Smarty and consistently use Prove It. Each WBT technique is visible... students have something concrete and specific to do as opposed to engage in mystifying mental activities. We can track, evaluate and reward student activities like the detailed Headings we described above. Too often in traditional practice test taking, teachers can't tell if students are employing the strategies they have been taught.

Who will work hard, long and hard, for no reward? Education, and the test taking procedures we described above, can be a long, unpleasant grind. But not with the Super Improvers Team! Begin by handing out stars sparingly when students daily practice their test taking skills. Lots of praise, lots of encouragement, a few stars. And be sure you are rewarding for improvement not academic achievement. Children are competing against themselves, not each other. As the year unfolds, award more stars. After Christmas, have special "double star" days when clear improvement can earn two stars... wow! Then, during tests, tell your kids that outstanding effort, working long and hard, can earn five stars! Oh, my goodness! Cover the clock. Don't let children hand in their tests. Keep pushing them to go back to write out their Prove Its.

Chris Rekstad, a co-founder of Whole Brain Teaching, used the above strategies wonderfully and found his fourth graders, who had previously averaged an hour and 15 minutes to finish the math portion of their state tests took two hours and 45 minutes. Chris drank deeply of the sweet spring in Teacher Heaven.

Finally, here is a list of suggestions that can be used anywhere you think appropriate in the process of preparing students for state tests.

1. **Whiteboard Game:** students put their answers labeled Doofus, Trickster or Smarty with the reasons for their choices on a small whiteboard. If everyone correctly identifies a Doofus, everyone gets a star on the Super Improver Team. Weeks later, if everyone identifies the Trickster and the Doofus correctly, everyone gets a star (and so on).

2. **Answer Nows:** language arts questions (not the reading passages) are flashed at students. They decide if the question is an Answer Now and use the because clapper to explain why to a neighbor. An Answer Now is a question that does not require returning to the reading passage. For example, students might be asked which pair of words are synonyms or to identify a definition of a vocabulary word.

   After a few weeks, students might explain why a question is an Answer Now or a Flipper (a question requiring re-reading of a passage).

   Finally, they explain why a question is an Answer Now, a Flipper or a Returner (a question so challenging that they should mark it R and come back later).

3. **Multiplication grids:** beginning with 0 and 1, students race to complete as many multiplication grids as possible in three minutes. As the year unfolds, they add other numbers and a longer time for completion. In California, students are allowed to make detailed notes during test taking. Many teachers have found that math scores increase when students make a complete 0-10 multiplication grid to guide them in answering questions that involve multiplication.

4. **Add, subtract, multiply, divide:** shown a math problem, students tell their neighbor, using the because clapper, if the answer will involve adding, subtracting, multiplying or dividing.

5. **Key words:** shown a question, students tell their neighbors what the key words are in the question using the because clapper.

6. **First Step:** shown a question, students tell their neighbors what the first step would be in answering the question using the because clapper. Later, they explain the first two steps, and so on.

In the next chapter, we'll explore Practice Cards, Level Three of our classroom management system (the Scoreboard and the Super Improvers Team were the Level One and Level Two, respectively).

CHAPTER 17

Practice Cards

Targeting individual behavior problems

There are many excellent classroom management systems but one of the most popular uses color cards to underscore a students' positive or negative actions. Here is a sample of how the cards are coordinated with student behavior:

green card student had a great day

gray card student receives a warning

purple card student receives a time out

red card student is given a note to take home

black card student is sent to the principal's office

Not all color card systems are the same but they generally follow a similar pattern. Colors are used to identify an ascending set of consequences for inappropriate activity. There are three problems with this system. First, the colors don't identify the specific problem that students need to work on. Second, the cards give students no practice in changing their behavior. Third, all the cards but one indicate negative actions.

To solve these problems, Jay Vanderfin, a co-founder of Whole Brain Teaching, came up with Practice Cards. He created one card for each of Whole Brain Teaching's five classroom rules. (A full description of Practice Cards is available at WholeBrainTeaching.com.)

Here are the rules we covered in chapter 6:

Rule 1: Follow directions quickly.

Rule 2: Raise your hand for permission to speak.

Rule 3: Raise your hand for permission to leave your seat.

Rule 4: Make smart choices.

Rule 5: Keep your dear teacher happy!

Each Practice Card is printed with one of the classroom rules. Thus, there is a set of Practice Cards labeled, Rule 1: Follow directions quickly. Another set of Practice Cards is labeled Rule 2: Raise your hand for permission to speak... and so forth. When students break a classroom rule, the teacher places a white Practice Card for that rule in their pocket on a pocket chart at the front of the room.

Let's see how Practice Cards work for our wonderful, Whole Brain Teacher, Mrs. Maestra.

After several months of playing Level One of the Scoreboard game and Level Two of the Super Improvers Team, Mrs. Maestra's students came in one morning and were intrigued to note Level Three written at the bottom of the Smiley-Frowny Scoreboard. They listened with great interest as Mrs. Maestra explained the new, higher level.

Here is how the game worked out for Juana, one of Mrs. Maestra's most challenging students.

Juana had a common problem; she often spoke without raising her hand. Frequently during the day, Juana broke Rule 2: Raise your hand for permission to speak.

Whenever Mrs. Maestra believed Juana needed to practice following Rule 2, she placed a white Rule 2 Card in Juana's slot on the pocket chart. The advantage to Mrs. Maestra is obvious. She didn't have to stop teaching to address Juana's problem. Mrs. Maestra simply continued with her lesson, while she picked up a white Rule 2 card and placed it in Juana's envelope on the chart. If Mrs. Maestra had several disruptive students who were breaking a variety of rules, she never had to wonder at recess who needed to practice following which rule... she simply looked at the cards she had placed in the pocket chart.

The Practice Card was also an advantage to Juana. She was not "bad," she simply needed additional practice in following a classroom rule. Juana was not scolded by Mrs. Maestra; neither of them liked a scolding session. Juana merely received additional time to focus on a problem she was having with a specific behavior.

And so, what does Juana do at each recess and lunch? She sits at a desk with a kitchen timer in front of her; for two minutes she raises her hand over and over, while she whispers, "Rule 2: Raise your hand for permission to speak." Try this yourself for two minutes to see what a powerful effect it has. Two minutes of hand raising and whispering feels like forever. If one arm gets tired, raise the other!

While Juana is practicing Rule 2, Mrs. Maestra is free to engage in whatever work she wishes. If Mrs. Maestra has yard duty, then Juana sits on a bench outdoors and practices following the rule she broke. If Juana refuses to practice the rule, then Mrs. Maestra does not quarrel with her. She says, "You can do it for two minutes my way... by practicing. Or sit for four minutes your way, by not practicing." Juana soon learns it's easier to do things Mrs. Maestra's way.

Mrs. Maestra believes, along with contemporary brain researchers, that it is not the size of the penalty, but its frequency that changes behavior. It is more effective for students to have five short practice sessions, than one long one. Thus, it is Mrs. Maestra's principle that even on Juana's worst day, *she never receives more than two white Practice Cards*. If four minutes of hand raising and whispering doesn't motivate Juana, then eight or 10 minutes will be no better. Mrs. Maestra knows it is a long year; in September she gives her students two minutes of practice, understanding that late in the spring, when the classroom management levels increase, she will need to double, or, at Level 6, even triple the rehearsal period.

When Juana receives a white Practice Card, this also means she will receive a note that goes home to her parents. This note informs parents about the rule that the student needs to work on, and encourages them to have the child practice at home. In most cases, the white Practice Card stays in the student's pocket chart for the next day, *unless the note comes back signed from home*. Thus, Juana is highly motivated to bring Mrs.

Maestra evidence that her parents have read the note. (Copies of note sent home to parents can be found in the Appendix.)

Luckily for Juana and other challenging kids, Mrs. Maestra is a realist. She knows some parents will follow through by signing the note and some parents won't. Juana's parents are very involved in their child's education; they can be depended on to do anything the school asks of them, including promptly signing notes. And so with Juana, Mrs. Maestra is quite strict about keeping the white Practice Card in Juana's card pocket for the next day (which means practice at every recess and also at lunch), unless she receives the signed note from the girl's parents. However, Jack is a different story.

Jack's parents are space cases. Mrs. Maestra knows, realistically, there is no chance in the world that Jack can get his folks to do anything to support his education. Mrs. Maestra cuts Jack a special deal. She finds an adult on campus, usually another teacher, to be Jack's substitute parent. When Jack has received a white note, he goes to his parent sub and the two of them have a conversation about Jack's problem. Thus, every student in Mrs. Maestra's class is assured of being under an adult's watchful eye.

To sum up, students receive white Practice Cards, never more than two, whenever the teacher decides they should spend time at recess and lunch practicing a rule they have broken. The practice involves two minutes, initially, of repeatedly whispering the rule and making the corresponding rule gesture. The cards are not viewed as punishment, only as an opportunity for additional rehearsal. If students refuse to practice, they are not scolded but the time lost at recess is doubled. The white Practice Card stays in the student's card pocket for the next day unless a signed note is brought home from the parent. Students whose parents are unreliable are assigned a substitute parent.

Mrs. Maestra understood that her students' brains were always learning. Negative inclinations were not innate, but learned. Negative behaviors, as well as positive behaviors, grew dendrites. Pulitzer Prize winner, Ronald Kotulak points out in *Inside the Brain*, "The problem is that the brain can organize itself in good ways, like learning to play a violin or mastering calculus, or in bad ways. When the brain wires itself in negative ways the result is learning disabilities, obsessive-compulsiveness, or other behavior problems." Mrs. Maestra's use of white practice cards went a long way toward stunting the growth of her students' negative dendrites.

CHAPTER 18

More Ways To Use Practice Cards

Rewards and in-class practice

After Jay Vanderfin, my Whole Brain Teaching colleague, had been using Practice Cards for several months, we realized that they could be used in two additional ways: as rewards for good behavior and as prompts for in-class practice of individual rules.

Jay made three sets of Practice Cards; each card, remember, had one of the five classroom rules. White cards were used as described above, to signal that a student needed time to rehearse a rule. Purple cards (also called Wisdom cards) became rewards for good behavior. Green cards were placed on a student's desk and guided in-class rule practice.

Here's how the whole system worked for Mrs. Maestra.

When Juana was having problems with a rule, she received one, or at most, two white cards. She stayed in two minutes at recess for each card to practice the rule she had broken. After this had been going on for several months, Mrs. Maestra dramatically reinvigorated her system by introducing purple cards. When Mrs. Maestra noted that Juana was doing a good job of following a rule, she put a purple card in Juana's pocket chart. A purple card canceled the effect of a white card; Juana was always highly motivated to get back on track and earn a purple card when she knew she had practice time ahead. If Juana managed to end the day with one or more purple cards (and no white cards) then Mrs. Maestra sent a congratulatory note home to Juana's parents. (Copies of notes sent home to parents can be found in the Appendix.)

As the year unfolded, Mrs. Maestra saw that Juana's number of white cards decreased and her purple cards increased... but the energetic girl still needed additional guidance. It was not enough that Juana knew the rule, had practiced it over and over, and was taking positive and negative notes home. Juana needed help in class... *she needed practice actually following the rule when surrounded by the lively atmosphere of a classroom.* To address this issue, Mrs. Maestra put a green Practice Card on Juana's desk. The card was labeled with the rule Juana needed to focus on; in her case it was almost always Rule 2, raise your hand for permission to speak.

Mrs. Maestra explained the green cards to Juana as follows, "You're doing a great job with the Rule 2 and I really appreciate the effort you have put into practicing. I love to give you purple cards because I want you and your parents to know when you are excelling in classroom behavior. So, here is a green Rule 2 card. Each time during class you actually raise your hand for permission to speak, I want you to make a tally mark on the green card. At the end of the day, I'll look at how many tally marks you have accumulated on the green card, showing that you have been following the rule. If I think you have been doing a good job raising your hand for permission to speak, then you'll have a good chance of earning a purple card."

Thus, green cards guide student practice *in class.* Juana now has a chance to apply what she has learned about controlling her impulse to speak. Her goal is identical to Mrs. Maestra's, to see how many times during the day she can follow Rule 2. The green cards are a simple way of tracking and nourishing her positive behavior.

It turns out that Juana eventually went overboard with raising her hand for permission to speak. She so enjoyed making tally marks on the green card that could earn her a purple card, that she shot her hand up at every opportunity. Mrs. Maestra, ever the resourceful Whole Brain Teacher, was prepared for this.

She took Juana aside and said, "You are doing fantastic following

Rule 2. You are always raising your hand for permission to speak. But I need you to let other students follow this rule as well. If you always have your hand up and focus too much attention on yourself, then that isn't fair to others. In fact, I may think you are breaking Rule 4: Make smart choices. Or even worse, I might feel you were breaking Rule 5: Keep your dear teacher happy. We certainly don't want to start getting white Practice Cards for those rules! You've lost enough recess time already with Rule 2."

Several additional points should be noted. When using the green card, Mrs. Maestra *did not say how many tally marks Juana needed to record*. Nor did she guarantee that a heavily tally marked green card would earn Juana a purple card. Mrs. Maestra deeply believed in one of Whole Brain Teaching's favorite sayings, "We use the system. The system doesn't use us." Mrs. Maestra valued the freedom of making decisions based upon her best intuition as a teacher. She did not want to be confined by an arbitrary rule like, "If you make 10 tally marks on the green card, then I'll give you a purple card." Mrs. Maestra had no wish to be involved in this kind of bookkeeping for 35 kids. In addition, she wanted the flexibility of being able to give, or withhold, purple cards whenever she judged it was the best for her students.

Occasionally, Mrs. Maestra had a student who couldn't be relied upon to make tally marks on the green card. Joanie nibbled on her card; Janey couldn't resist tearing the corners off. In cases like these, Mrs. Maestra gave the green card to a dependable student, someone who could do excellent work and make a tally mark whenever the challenging student followed the card rule.

Finally, Mrs. Maestra knew that one of the most difficult aspects of classroom management was to keep the system from becoming stale. Techniques that worked in September, often had little effect in December. Thus, she saw the Practice Card system as having three phases, white cards, white cards plus purple cards, white cards plus purple cards plus green cards. By stretching out each phase as long as possible, Mrs. Maestra kept her students engaged for many months.

Now, here's a summary of the points we've made about the Level Three Practice Cards.

1. Kids receive a maximum of two white Practice Cards to practice the rule(s) broken in class. Initially, the practice is for two minutes per card at each recess and lunch.

2. A note is sent home to parents describing the rule broken. If the note isn't signed and returned, kids continue to practice for the following day (unless the teacher assigns the student an on-campus parent sub.)

3. Later in the year, purple Practice Cards are awarded for positive actions. A note is sent home informing parents about their child's excellent behavior.

4. A purple Practice Card cancels a white Practice Card.

5. Still later in the year, at the teacher's option, green Practice Cards are placed on a student's desk during class. Students make a tally mark on the card each time they follow the card's rule. At the end of the day, the teacher may decide that the student's work with the green Practice Cards merits a purple Practice Card.

6. If the student cannot be relied upon to put tally marks on the green card, another student may be given this task.

7. Practice Cards are introduced at Level Two of Whole Brain Teaching's classroom management system. For each level the class moves up, an additional minute of practice time is assigned to the Practice Cards. This underscores the importance of using a short practice time when the Practice Cards are first introduced. As the instructor moves up levels, the system becomes increasingly rigorous, and the Practice Cards become more and more powerful motivators.

Let's stop here for a moment.

Giving seminars to thousands of teachers over the last 12 years, I learned the not surprising truth that the number one classroom management problem in America, and perhaps the world, is students speaking without raising their hands. Thus, we designed a multistage solution to this substantial problem. Here are the stages (all of which we have already covered):

- Students learn Rule 2: Raise your hand for permission to speak and practice rehearsing it several times a day.
- After the concept is mastered, and a student fails to follow the rule, the teacher has the option of raising two fingers in the air and saying, "Rule 2!" The class choruses, "Raise your hand for permission to speak!"
- At Level Two with the Super Improvers Team, students can earn stars for showing improvement in raising their hands for permission to speak.
- At Level Three, white Practice Cards, accompanied by notes home, give students penalties for not following Rule 2.
- Purple cards are then added to reward students, at the instructor's option, for following Rule 2. (Of course, a student doesn't get a purple card every time she raises her hand!)
- Green cards are eventually added, if necessary, to give students in-class practice following Rule 2.

So, if early in the year, you have many students who speak without raising their hands... don't despair. Your colleagues at Whole Brain Teaching created the system above just for you.

CHAPTER 19

The Guff Counter

What to do when students talk back

The goal at the Scoreboard's Level Four, the Guff Counter, is to introduce techniques that directly target disrespectful behavior, talking back, eye rolling, groaning. What we want to do is change the classroom dynamic, introduce structures that will divide rebel students from peer support.

One of the major causes of challenging behavior is the perception by mutinous pupils that they have the strong backing of their friends and the silent support of the majority of their classmates. To see that this is true, perform this thought experiment.

Imagine that a bold, disruptive student, like John in Mrs. Maestra's class, is thrust into a new school where he knows no one. He is transformed, becomes New Quiet John and draws into his shell; he doesn't disrupt class but instead works hard at establishing a network of friends and allies. Once he has backing, New Quiet John becomes Old Rowdy John. Without friends and allies, his challenging behavior was temporarily stifled. With support for his antics, John blossoms into his full blown rebellious nature. Virtually all disruptive students are nourished by the understanding that key allies in their class endorse their conduct.

Our goal at Level Four of the Scoreboard is to target challenging students and turn the majority of the class, *including their friends,* against their disruptive behavior. We will demonstrate to the rebel that the dynamic is not students vs. teacher but one rebel student vs. all the students backed up by their teacher.

But how, and on what kinds of occasions, is this to be accomplished? If you haven't already, please go get a large hanky we mentioned early on our journey. The next paragraphs will have you weeping joyfully.

It is astonishing how often teachers have to endure disrespectful remarks. Students are very skilled in making comments, sometimes only partly heard, that almost, but don't quite, cross the line into completely rude behavior. Taken individually, these remarks aren't terribly hurtful, but they add up... until you're ready to scream. Right?

After months of training her class in Whole Brain Teaching, coaching them in how to respond to her directions, Mrs. Maestra was ready for Level Four.

One day she made the following changes to the Scoreboard.

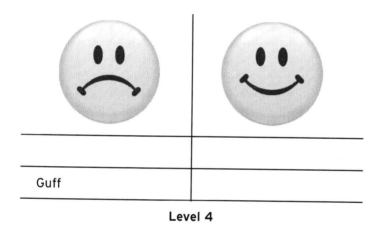

Guff

Level 4

Using her voice of command, Mrs. Maestra said, "Guff is any remark that makes a teacher unhappy. For example, if I say to Melanie, 'please work harder' and she says, using an irritated tone of voice, 'I am working harder'... that's guff. I'm asking her to do something that will help her be a better student, and she's refusing. Amazing guff! Students in most classes make these kinds of statements all day long! BUT NOT IN MRS. MAESTRA'S CLASS. If a student gives me guff, and the class doesn't say anything, *then that means everyone silently supports that remark! I'll add 1 mark in the Guff Counter for every word of guff!* The marks in the Guff Counter mean that everyone loses one minute of recess for each mark!!! However, if someone says something that is guff, and everyone firmly says 'Please, stop!' that means the class doesn't silently support the guff... and recess time isn't decreased. In fact, I may even make a mark on the positive side, which will increase the recess by a minute. Teach your neighbors what I said!"

After students reviewed her points, Mrs. Maestra continued.

SCRIPT: THE GUFF COUNTER

Mrs. Maestra: (Pointing at Darla, an amiable, non-guffing student) Okay Darla, we're going to practice guffing. I'm going to pretend like I'm talking. I'll say 'yada, yada, yada' and then I'll say to you, 'please pay attention' and you give me some guff, like 'I am paying attention.' Okay?

Darla: Okay.

Mrs. Maestra: Yada, yada, yada. Darla, please pay attention.

Darla: (after a moment's hesitation) I am paying attention!

Mrs. Maestra: Oh goodness, that was excellent guff! She said four guffing words... now I'm going to count them with four marks in the Guff Counter. (After months of putting only one mark at a time on the Scoreboard, making four marks on the Frownie side stuns Mrs. Maestra's class.) Those are just pretend... Class, tell each other how you'd hate to see four, real Frownie marks! Teach!

Students: (Relieved laughter) Okay!

Mrs. Maestra: Let's have more practice in guff. I won't make any more practice marks... you get the idea. One Frownie for every word of guff. Yada, yada, yada, Mark, look at me.

Mark: (a bright, resourceful boy who is always quick to catch on) I am paying attention to you, jeez! (Students laugh)

Mrs. Maestra: Great guff! That 'jeez' was pure guff! All in all, that was seven words of wonderful guff! Give Mark a 10 finger woo! (Mrs. Maestra calls on a few more students, giving them permission to back talk, and includes John, a notorious guffer, near the end.)

Good job. Now, let's go over this again. The reason any student gives a teacher guff is that they believe they have everyone's silent support. In the future, if I hear one word or see one act of guff, even a sigh, even rolling your eyes, I'll instantly decrease everyone's recess... unless everyone points their hand at the guffer and instantly, forcefully says, 'Please, stop!' Then maybe they'll get a positive mark. Now, let's practice that. As soon as Darla says the smallest guffing word, jump in immediately, point your hand at her and say loudly and firmly, 'Please, stop!' Okay, ready Darla?

Darla: I think so.

Mrs. Maestra: Yada, yada, yada. Darla pay attention to what I'm saying.

Darla: I am paying attention.

Several students: (Slowly and weakly) Please stop!

Mrs. Maestra: Oh, that was not fast enough. Everyone would get Frownies for sure! Let's try it again! The instant you hear anything that sounds like guff, you've got to very, very quickly cut that guffer off with 'Please stop!' or you'll all get a handful of Frownies. Teach!

Students: Okay! (Students teach their neighbor that they have to be very quick in order to get avoid a handful of Frownies.)

Mrs. Maestra: Class!

Students: Yes!

Mrs. Maestra: Here we go Darla. Yada, yada, yada. Darla pay attention.

Darla: I am...

Students: (Very quickly pointing their hands) Please stop! (Everyone laughs)

Mrs. Maestra: Excellent. (Mrs. Maestra practices with several more individuals, rehearsing just as she had with Darla. By the end, the class is saying "Please stop!" so quickly that guffing students can hardly open their mouths.)

(After about a week, Mrs. Maestra introduced the concept that students should not guff each other... with a routine similar to the above. Her class learned that the Guff Counter could be marked for disrespectful talk addressed by students to their teacher or their classmates.)

Note Mrs. Maestra's strategy. Instead of scolding her students about guffing, she turned it into a game. She rehearsed correct and *incorrect* behavior.

Mrs. Maestra ended her first presentation of the Guff Counter by saying, "Sometimes you may not hear or see the guffing behavior. When I do, I'll say, 'that sounded like guff! Where is my marker?' As soon as you hear that, say 'Please, stop!' and no one will suffer a penalty. And here is the truth. If you are very quick with your 'Please, stop!' you may never get a mark in the Guff Counter all year.'"

Please, pay close attention. *The Guff Counter is the only technique we threaten with... but never carry through.* If you made a mark for every word of Guff, you would quickly break the Plus/Minus Three Rule; the difference between rewards and penalties should never exceed three. The real purpose of the Guff Counter is achieved as soon as your students silence the guffer. All Mrs. Maestra had to do to achieve this purpose was say, "that sounds like guff! Where is my marker?"

Here is the amazing phenomenon that Whole Brain Teachers notice when they use the Guff Counter. A rebel student's friends are among the quickest and the loudest to say "Please stop!" Isn't that amazing?

Challenging students' strongest allies are the first to turn on them.

I believe the readiness of friends, especially boys, to chastise each other, given the safe opportunity (and having the teacher's encouragement, and the support of the entire class, is a safe opportunity) tells us something important about student cliques. Listen carefully to how rebellious students talk to each other... there is a continuous struggle for hierarchy, authority and power inside their group. They support each other out of fear of not being supported and of being ostracized, but their ongoing battles build up enormous reserves of bitter energy. Given the opportunity, and the "Please stop!" is the perfect opportunity, *most challenging students will turn on each other in a flash.*

Now, here is a last point. Many times your students so energetically support the Guff Counter that they are exclaiming, at the slightest indication of disrespectful behavior, "Please stop!" When this happens, proceed as Mrs. Maestra did above; teach your class that they should only say "Please stop!" when you say, "That sounds like Guff... where is my marker?"

But what do you do if, even after the application of the Guff Counter, you still have challenging cliques of rebels? You go on to the Scoreboard's Level Five.

CHAPTER 20

The Independents

*Watch in amazement as rebel allies
turn against each other*

Mrs. Maestra started class one morning by drawing the next version of the Scoreboard on the whiteboard.

Guff	
Independents	

Level 5

Mrs. Maestra said, "Notice that now we are at Level Five! We're going to play a more advanced version of the Scoreboard Game. We'll have two groups, the class as a whole, and a smaller group, the Independents. These are students who just won't go along with everyone else. Some of you may already have an idea of who these pupils are. Many times over the last months their behavior has caused the entire class to get Frownies. But that's over now! GIVE ME A MIGHTY OH YEAH!"

Mrs. Maestra's students responded with a delirious "Oh, Yeah!!" even the rebels, because they didn't know what was coming.

Mrs. Maestra continued, "Here is what we're going to do. If I come to you outside of class and tell you that you're in the Independent group, then you'll have your own score separate from the rest of the class. There's only one catch. If someone else in the Independent group is misbehaving, you get the Frownie along with them! In this case, the Frownie will be an automatic White Practice Card. However, you only have to stay in the Independent group one day. All you have to do to get out, is come to me and say, 'I don't want to be in that Independent group anymore!'"

Mrs. Maestra loved this modification of the Scoreboard Game. Her "independent" students, especially Joan, John and Jason, all close friends, often tried to support each other's challenging behavior... as much as possible, given the system of Practice Cards and the Guff Counter. By grouping the rebel friends together in the Independent group Mrs. Maestra established a powerful new principle. When one acted up, they all got a Frownie, a white Practice Card. Negative behavior by Joan, earned recess practice for Joan, John and Jason.

Do you see the wonder of this?

Rebellious behavior by one student has an immediate unpleasant effect upon the other students in the Independent group. Instead of disrupting the class, rebellious behavior now turns the clique members against each other! Joan and Jason might be, briefly, behaving themselves, but then John acts up... and all three pay the price!! The behavior that they had intended as teacher-aggravating is now buddy-infuriating. Remember our earlier point. Rebel students, even close friends, are always ready to harass each other, because harassing each other is their way of life, the way they maintain rank in their group.

Think of a clique of challenging students this way: you've got Leaders, Followers and Bottom Dwellers. There is usually one Leader, call him El Supremo (or La Suprema, if you wish) and many Followers and Bottom Dwellers. El Supremo maintains his position by harassing Followers and

Bottom Dwellers. Followers maintain their position by harassing other Followers and Bottom Dwellers. Bottom Dwellers maintain their position by harassing each other, and, when it is safe, joining in the harassment of Followers who are being harassed by other Followers and/or El Supremo.

So, these cliques are small societies that run on humiliation, intimidation and reprisal. They are only truly united when they face Outsiders, especially Outsiders who are in Authority. Someone exactly like you. Teachers provide a necessary ingredient in rebel cliques; they are the agreed upon target for group bonding rebellion.

The normal, galvanizing polarity of the rebel clique is Us against Outsiders. However, by putting a few rebel students into the Independent group together, the polarity becomes Us against Us. If you only put a few challenging students together at a time in the Independent group, not only will they harass each other, but the challenging students who aren't Independents will mock them!

Oh, sob for joy my dear colleague!

Mrs. Maestra was more than ready for the parents who might complain about their child being put in a "special group."

She told the parents, "On the first day I introduced this concept, I told my class that they only had to stay in the Independent group one day. All they had to do to get out, was tell me they wanted out. I need my students to learn the very important life lesson that if they choose the wrong group, actions by even one member of the group can have a negative effect on everyone in the group." Mrs. Maestra never had a parent who wanted their child to be in the wrong group. In fact, many of the parents of challenging kids believed deeply and ardently that their child was *already* in the wrong group... and, once the principle of the Independents was explained to them, fully supported Mrs. Maestra.

Now, I hope you can see the importance of the incremental, step by step approach we have been suggesting since the opening chapters. You can most powerfully play the Independent game, after you have gotten as many students as possible unified behind your leadership and accustomed to following rules and procedures that eliminate classroom chaos. The Scoreboard game, Super Improvers Team, Practice Cards and the Guff Counter, set up the Independent group later in the year. When you divide your pupils into the Class and the Independents, this has an enormously unifying effect upon all your respectful, hardworking kids. After you announce that the whole class is no longer going to pay the price for the actions of the rebels, *the faces of your faithful students will shine with joy.* Not only does using the Independent group have, ultimately, a positive effect upon your rebels, it also further unifies the students who have been following you since the first week.

The instant Mrs. Maestra made the surprising modification to the Scoreboard, every faithful student beamed at their beloved teacher. Their faces glowed with silent, joyful passion, "Oh, Mrs. Maestra we are behind you! Yes! Yes! Sock it to those rebels!" When students deliberately chose to leave the Independent group, Mrs. Maestra knew she had helped them make an important moral decision. They had decided to separate from a group that got them into trouble. Some students went in and out of the Independent group, asking over and over to be let out. This was fine with Mrs. Maestra. These were precisely the pupils who needed long practice in seeing how unpleasant life could be when chained up with a group of outlaws.

CHAPTER 21

The Bull's Eye Game

One on one with challenging students

Late in the school year, Mrs. Maestra turned to one of Whole Brain Teaching's most effective strategies for reforming the behavior of challenging students. The Bull's Eye game involves no punishment, and yet has produced remarkable results with hardened rebels. After going through five levels of the Scoreboard, Mrs. Maestra learned that John, one of the most challenging students in her career, was immune to every form of penalty. Mrs. Maestra was not distraught. The Bulls Eye game was 100% reward.

Mrs. Maestra used the following game materials:

- A large, 5 circle, bull's eye that she drew and posted prominently in class.
- A "Sticker Bank" of 25+ stickers ranging from simple to elaborate designs.
- Sheets of paper divided into 5 boxes. These would be John's "weekly Bull's Eye calendar" for pasting stickers and recording behavior scores.

On the day Mrs. Maestra posted the five circle bullseye on the front board, she also wrote "Level 6" under the Scoreboard. The students were eager to know what was next on Mrs. Maestra's entertaining agenda. She said, "Level 6 and the bullseye is a game that I'm going to play with one of my friends in class."

When Mrs. Maestra knew she would have a few minutes to work one on one with John, she took him aside and explained the Bullseye Game.

SELECTING A BEHAVIOR GOAL

Mrs. Maestra showed John the bull's eye diagram with five circles. The circles, from inside to outside, were numbered 5, 4, 3, 2, 1. Mrs. Maestra explained that when John scored a "bull's eye day" he had perfectly achieved the behavior goal that he chose (and Mrs. Maestra agreed to). Examples of Mrs. Maestra's behavior goals were:

- raising your hand for permission to speak
- raising your hand for permission to leave your seat
- not speaking during "silent work" periods
- following the teacher's directions
- looking at the teacher when she speaks
- standing in line with your hands folded
- not touching others

Note that Mrs. Maestra's goals were very specific. Challenging students need easy to understand standards. Goals like "playing safely," "speaking respectfully," "being good" are, for many challenging students, nebulous.

Mrs. Maestra found that encouraging John to choose his behavior goal significantly deepened his involvement in the game.

REHEARSING THE BEHAVIOR GOAL

In their one on one meeting, John and Mrs. Maestra took turns rehearsing the behavior goal, "following the teacher's directions" that John chose. To rehearse "following the teacher's directions" Mrs. Maestra gave normal classroom directions and John followed them. Then, to make the rehearsal entertaining, John gave normal classroom directions and Mrs. Maestra followed them.

Mrs. Maestra then asked John to model inappropriate behavior. Mrs. Maestra gave directions and John stared around the classroom, or laughed, groaned, banged on his desk.

Next John and Mrs. Maestra changed roles; she became the challenging student who did not follow directions. Much to John's delight, Mrs. Maestra modeled John's typical avoidance behavior. Role switching rehearsal of appropriate and inappropriate behavior continued until John clearly understood the behavior goal.

Mrs. Maestra understood that the rehearsal stage was very important. Not only did it begin to imprint John with the difference between appropriate and inappropriate behavior, but also, and more importantly, rehearsal created an entertaining bond between them.

EXPLAINING THE BULL'S EYE GAME

Mrs. Maestra told that John that his task was to try to score Bull's Eye days by perfectly hitting the behavior goal. She and John would meet several times a day (for example, at the start of each recess, at lunch and after school) to evaluate John's performance. Initially, she had many meetings with John; later she only had to meet him at the end of the day.

Mrs. Maestra said, "When we meet, I will write down what I think your score is... 5 is a perfect bull's eye... but I won't show you what I've written. You then tell me what me think your score is and explain your reasoning. Next, I'll show you my score. If you are only 1 point away from my score, you'll receive one point. If your score matches mine, you'll receive 2 points. If you are more than 2 points from my score, you don't score anything. Now, here is very good news... if you finish the day with what we both agree is a Bull's Eye day, you'll receive 5 points. You can use your points to buy stickers from my special Sticker Bank."

(Mrs. Maestra's one point stickers were small and single color. Two point stickers were larger and had two colors... and so on up to Mrs. Maestra's gaudy, wonderful 10 point stickers. Mrs. Maestra knew that one of John's special passions was Batman... so, all her stickers portrayed the Caped Crusader, his friends or enemies.)

PLAYING THE GAME

Mrs. Maestra met John several times a day to compare scores, and add up points. *It was very important that Mrs. Maestra honestly evaluated*

John's behavior. For example, John would learn nothing if Mrs. Maestra was "nice" and gave a 3, when John only earned a 1. Mrs. Maestra believed that honest evaluation was an excellent way for challenging students to learn a teacher's standards.

When John, from Mrs. Maestra's point of view, scored a 1 or 2 on the Bull's Eye, she and John rehearsed the behavior goal several times, often switching roles, with Mrs. Maestra taking John's part.

Mrs. Maestra kept a daily record on the calendar of her and John's scores and what behavior goals were targeted. Stickers that John had purchased from the Sticker Bank were put on the calendar. Each Friday, Mrs. Maestra made a copy of John's weekly calendar page and gave the original to John.

When John had difficulty meeting a behavior goal, Mrs. Maestra encouraged him to choose a new goal. As he became more successful in meeting his behavior goals, other goals were added.

After a week or two, Mrs. Maestra offered to help John, saying "If you want, you and I will have a secret sign. When you see me point at my head, that mean's that you have to think more carefully; you're missing the bull's eye. When you see me pointing at my eye, that means you're really hitting the bull's eye. Then you should nod, so that I know you've gotten my secret message."

ADVANTAGES OF PLAYING BULL'S EYE

Mrs. Maestra realized that the Bulls Eye game had many potent advantages.

- By allowing students to choose their behavior goals, student involvement in the classroom management system is greatly increased.
- By focusing on only one behavior goal at a time, the Bull's Eye game vastly simplifies classroom management... for both the challenging student and the teacher.
- During brief counseling sessions, teachers can refocus the student on the behavior goal.

- During rehearsals, which are powerful alternatives to scolding, the student is imprinted with the difference between appropriate and inappropriate behavior and, because of role switching, an entertaining, positive bond develops between teacher and student.
- The weekly calendar provides a simple way to evaluate a student's progress; this is especially important when behavior changes are slowly achieved.
- Challenging students are trained in the high level intellectual skill of objective, self-critical evaluation of their own behavior.
- *A challenging student can be successful even on the worst days, simply by matching the teacher's low score.*

We have had more success with the Bulls Eye game in reforming the behavior of extremely challenging students than with any other strategy. However, the game will fail if you have not been able to establish a conversational bond with your rebel. You may have students who are so defiant that they refuse to sit down with you, or when they do, you're met with an icy glare. If this is the case, then you may have to precede the game with weeks of short, casual conversations, giving appropriate praise, offering academic help or counseling. You have to build a bridge to your most rebellious student before you can walk across it.

Occasionally, Mrs. Maestra didn't have the amount of time she needed, as described above, to play the Bullseye game with her most challenging kids. In those unfortunate cases, she simply taught the game to her rebel, which took no more than five minutes, and then evaluated progress at the end of each day, rewarding with stickers as appropriate. This "shorty" Bullseye game never took more than 5 minutes per day and often had remarkable results.

CHAPTER 22

The Agreement Bridge

Collaborative problem solving with your toughest kids

The Agreement Bridge is a unique tool in Whole Brain Teaching's workshop. At the highest level of the Scoreboard, Level 7, the Agreement Bridge is a game that unites challenging kids with their teachers in collaborative problem solving. The problems addressed can include, but are not limited to: conflicts with other students or the instructor, gang activity, lagging social skills, anger management, patterns of weak academic performance, poor attendance, disruptive classroom behavior. If you have a kid who cusses you out, or who brings drugs to school or who merely never does homework, the Agreement Bridge provides a flexible, entertaining environment for discovering solutions that satisfy not only the teacher, but also the rebel student.

That point should be stressed. Any solution to a school problem which is not endorsed by the student involved is likely to quickly fail. Solutions that are imposed on challenging kids are quickly shrugged off. The point is not to punish troubled students but to give them life skills that will help them succeed; two important, but rarely taught, life skills are negotiation and compromise. The goal of the Agreement Bridge, which can sometimes be achieved fairly quickly, is to generate a solution to a problem that suits the student as well as the instructor.

Our game can be successfully played in a five to 10 minute session or, to address more difficult problems, it can be adapted to longer exchanges over several days or even weeks. (A complete description of the Agreement Bridge is available as a free download at WholeBrainTeaching.com.)

The Agreement Bridge is inspired by Ross W. Greene's *Lost at School,* a remarkable description of collaborative problem solving techniques that have proven effective in schools across the United States. I strongly recommend Greene's book as a useful resource, a second line of defense, if a student's problems, after successive sessions playing the Agreement Bridge, prove intractable.

Though the Agreement Bridge is designed to be played between a teacher and a student, the teacher's role can be taken by an administrator, counselor or any responsible person who is interested in helping the challenging student. One of the most intriguing partnerships in the Agreement Bridge is between a student and a peer mentor. The remarkable flexibility of the game even allows it to be adapted to dealing with groups of students.

In the next section, the players are Mrs. Maestra and her student, Juana.

MATERIALS NEEDED

A ruler, two markers, two coins, two copies of the Agreement Bridge game board (Appendix), an Agreement Contract (Appendix).

PROCEDURE

Mrs. Maestra and Juana sit on opposite sides of a table with a ruler between them. One end of the ruler points at Mrs. Maestra; the other end points at Juana. The ruler represents the "distance" between them.

One marker representing Juana, stands at her end of the ruler; the other marker representing Mrs. Maestra, stands at her end of the ruler. (If markers are unavailable, any other small objects may be used, chalk, paperclips, etc.). The goal of the game is for the two players to participate in a structured discussion that eventually arrives at a mutually satisfactory agreement resolving the problem that separates them.

Mrs. Maestra and Juana have a copy of The Agreement Bridge game board (Appendix) and talk about the subjects it presents. After each subject is discussed, one or both players have the option of moving their markers closer to the center of the ruler if they feel the distance between them has decreased. The game is completed when the markers of both Mrs. Maestra and Juana arrive at the middle of the ruler; this symbolizes that the distance between them has been removed and they are ready to fill out an Agreement Contract (Appendix).

Before going further, look at a copy of the Agreement Bridge game board. Note the six squares: Hello, Problem, Swap, Smart Choices, Foolish Choices and Change. Each square introduces a new subject for discussion between the players.

Mrs. Maestra explains that each topic on the Agreement Bridge game board introduces a new subject for conversation.

The subjects, described in detail below, are: Hello, Problem, Swap, Smart Choices, Foolish Choices and Change. The players decide who should go first. With shyer students, Mrs. Maestra automatically took the lead. The first player puts a coin on one square on the board, introducing the subject he or she wants to talk about. When the first player is finished talking, the second player puts a coin on the same square and discusses the same subject. When the conversation is completed, the second player moves her coin to another square and talks about the new topic.

Essentially, the players engage in follow the leader. First one player chooses a subject and talks about it; then the other player talks about the same subject and, when finished, picks the next subject. The topics may be selected as many times as the players wish. After each topic is discussed, one or both players, if they believe the distance between them has decreased, moves their marker closer to the middle of the ruler.

Mrs. Maestra explained each topic to Juana as follows:

Hello: The players ask each other anything they want about the other player's life... except the problem that has brought them together.

Problem: Each player describes the problem from his or her point of view.

Swap: The players swap markers. Each player describes the problem from the other player's point of view.

Smart Choices: Each player describes, in regard to the problem's solutions, as many smart choices as possible.

Foolish Choices: Each player describes, in regard to the problem's solutions, as many foolish choices as possible.

Change: Each player describes what he or she is willing to change to solve the problem.

Mrs. Maestra believed that the Agreement Bridge had several, powerful advantages over typical confrontations between teacher and challenging student.

- By setting the problem in a game context, a potentially explosive encounter becomes less volatile.
- The subjects on the game board provide a clear, but flexible pattern for discussion.
- The teacher has no advantage over the student, because the behavior of each player is prescribed by the topics.
- Moving markers closer along the ruler clarifies the progress and the goal of the discussion.
- Because the subjects may be chosen in any order, as many times as the players wish, the game adapts to a range of problems and personalities.
- The challenging student's typical defensive and/or belligerent attitude is defused because he or she is not being scolded but is a partner in problem solving.

THE TEACHER'S STRATEGY

Each topic holds unique advantages for collaborative problem solving. The more often Mrs. Maestra played the Agreement Bridge, the more skilled she became in knowing what subject to choose and how to exploit the game's conversation structure. Here are some suggestions she found useful:

Hello: Use this subject to get to know your student and also, reveal as much personal information as you are comfortable with. This is your chance to take off your teacher's hat and to investigate, without drama, aspects of your student's life that you are not familiar with. Select this topic as often as you need to during the game, especially when it seems useful to lower your student's, or your own (!), emotional heat.

Problem: You need to hear what your student has to say about the problem that divides you. Listen and ask non-threatening questions.

Seek clarity about your student's perspective, needs, goals. Then, take your time in explaining, in a calm tone, your own perception of the problem.

Swap: Selecting this topic will provide an excellent opportunity to develop objectivity, both for you and your student. Model, as well as possible, what it means to see the world from someone else's perspective. The more skillful you are in understanding the problem from your student's point of view, the more he or she will be encouraged to adopt your perspective.

Smart choices: You may need to choose this subject several times as you and your student share perspectives describing the best possible solution to the problem. Encourage your student to explain his or her reasoning in selecting a choice that seems like an intelligent response to the current difficulty.

Foolish Choices: If it seems appropriate, you can have fun with this topic. Talk about all the absurd, irrelevant choices you could take in response to the problem. This may help lighten your student's mood. You can also discuss choices that are available to you that you believe are genuine options but that would make the problem worse. If you know several failed approaches that have been tried with the student, and that you believe were ineffective solutions, you can present these as some of the choices you believe are foolish.

Change: This subject is quite powerful and can have, if played wisely, a positive effect upon your troubled kid. Your student's education is your responsibility. If he or she is having problems, you need to make changes. Too often we want kids to adapt to a system, that refuses to adapt to them. Your offer of change can be no more complex, but nonetheless powerful, than saying something like, "The change I suggest is that we need to talk to each other a little more. I'll rearrange my schedule and be happy to chat with you a few minutes tomorrow morning... and at other times we set up." Or, "I can certainly change my tone of voice in the future when I talk to you about this problem." Or, "I'll be happy to set up a record keeping system, so that you and I can chart your progress."

Now, let's see how the game played out between Juana and Mrs. Maestra.

THE HOMEWORK PROBLEM

Juana, a withdrawn fourth grader, and her teacher Mrs. Maestra meet to discuss the problem that divides them: Juana never does her homework. Mrs. Maestra sets up the ruler, diagrams and markers, and explains the game, indicating that Juana can make the first choice. Juana shyly puts her coin on the Hello square. Under Mrs. Maestra's coaxing, she shares information about her life at home with her mother and three brothers. Mrs. Maestra doesn't ask about Juana's absent father. Mrs. Maestra also learns that Juana lives near Carla, Juana's best friend and also one of Mrs. Maestra's most reliable students. Mrs. Maestra takes her turn with the Hello topic. Understanding that anything she says is likely to become common knowledge among her students, she talks about her own relationship with her siblings. She is quite close to her brother but has had difficulty forming a bond with her sister.

Mrs. Maestra can tell by Juana's attention that the game has already had a positive effect on her shy student. Perhaps the girl didn't know that teachers had brothers and sisters, much less had relationship problems! When Mrs. Maestra is finished with the Hello subject, she says, "Juana, I think we have moved a little bit closer together. It's good to get to know you and I'm always happy to share parts of my life with my students. I think I'll move my marker a bit closer to the middle." Juana, unable to resist her teacher's initiative, also moves her marker closer to the middle.

Mrs. Maestra then moves her coin to the Problem square and describes her view of the difficulty separating them. She says that she wishes Juana would take more advantage of the study tips she has offered and the opportunity for before and after school help.

Mrs. Maestra says that there is a real possibility that if Juana doesn't improve her math and language arts scores, she won't go on to the fifth grade with Carla and her other friends. Juana moves her coin and then says her problem is "not doing homework" but doesn't offer much more. However, under Mrs. Maestra's questioning, Juana reveals that her favorite activity at home is looking at Facebook on the internet and texting on her cell phone... for about five hours a day. Mrs. Maestra stores this information away for future reference, perhaps another round of The Agreement Bridge.

Mrs. Maestra asks if Juana thinks they have gotten any closer together and Juana replies, "I don't know." Mrs. Maestra smiles and tells her student to pick the next topic. Juana is uncertain which subject to choose; Mrs. Maestra reviews the topics and then, after more hesitation on Juana's part, suggests she select Foolish Choices.

Under Mrs. Maestra's guidance, Juana comes up with two Foolish Choices she could make in regard to the homework problem. The choices are: ask her older brother to do the homework, forget homework and find a job that paid her to text on her cell phone.

Mrs. Maestra describes her own Foolish Choices in regard to Juana's homework problem. She could ignore Juana and let her fail, call Juana's mother and blame her for her daughter's problem, make Juana stay in for recess until she had completed all her past homework, double the amount of homework Juana receives. Mrs. Maestra grins and says, "I think we can both agree that your Foolish Choices and my Foolish Choices were wacky. Right?" Juana laughs and nods.

Mrs. Maestra moves her marker closer to the middle and so does Juana. The game continues with Juana opening up a bit more and taking more initiative in choosing the subjects she wants to talk about. Eventually, Mrs. Maestra and Juana arrive at the following two agreements that they record on the Agreement Contract:

1. We agree that Mrs. Maestra should give Carla and Juana one point extra credit for every day that Carla helps Juana finish her homework.
2. We agree that we should play the Agreement Bridge next Monday to see how we are doing on the homework problem that has separated us.

The best agreements are the most specific, and thus are the most easily evaluated for success. In almost all cases in the Agreement Bridge, the contract should include deadlines. The student and teacher agree to do something by some date, usually in the near future. At that time, they meet, evaluate, and often renegotiate the agreement. You can't expect troubled kids to make permanent changes based on one discussion! The fewer agreements entered in to, the better, not only for your student but also for you. Life is chaotic; the fewer promises made, the easier they are to keep. In general, two agreements are plenty. So, here are characteristics of a good agreement: be specific, set a date, be open to renegotiate, make no more than two agreements.

Special emphasis should be placed on establishing clear-cut, easy to evaluate contracts. The best agreements always specify some behavior that will, or won't, be engaged in. On the following page is a sample, blank Agreement Contract.

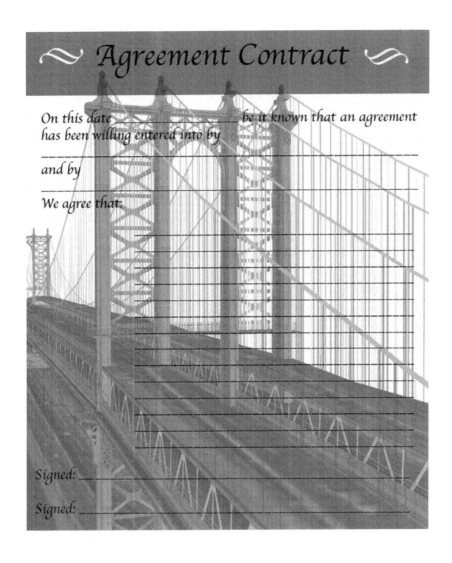

Agreement Contract

On this date _____ be it known that an agreement
has been willing entered into by

_____

and by

_____

We agree that:

_____

_____

_____

_____

_____

_____

_____

_____

_____

_____

Signed: _____

Signed: _____

Here is a game of the Agreement Bridge Mrs. Maestra played when she taught sixth grade at an inner city school.

THE FIGHTER

Joelle, a large, aggressive sixth grader, meets with Mrs. Maestra, the only teacher she respects. Mrs. Maestra explains the Agreement Bridge and the game begins.

Joelle puts her coin in the Problem square and says she has a problem with kids hassling her all the time. She says if it continues she is going to "smash someone's face in."

Under Mrs. Maestra's questioning, Joelle reveals that she hates to hear comments about her weight. Mrs. Maestra, moving her coin the to Problem square, talks about her view of the situation. She says she completely understands Joelle's sensitivity. Mrs. Maestra talks about verbal abuse and agrees Joelle has been a victim... words can make deep wounds.

Mrs. Maestra wisely resists adding anything like, "But Joelle, hitting people will just make your problem worse. That isn't the mature way to handle problems." Mrs. Maestra knows Joelle has heard this kind of comment many times before and it hasn't changed her behavior. When Mrs. Maestra is finished, she sees from Joelle's expression that she doesn't feel the distance between them has decreased, so she makes no offer of moving her marker.

Mrs. Maestra moves her coin to the Hello square. She asks questions about Joelle's life and is happy to see that Joelle is eager to know about her teacher's interests outside of school. Mrs. Maestra understands that she will need many sessions with Joelle and so she lets the conversation go on for as long as the girl wishes.

At the end, Mrs. Maestra says, "Well, it is great getting to know you better. I had no idea you had such an interest in basketball! I'd love to come see your travel team play some day." Mrs. Maestra knows that in order to help Joelle, she must find a point of positive contact with her. Discovering an interest in basketball she can share with her student may go a long way in decreasing the distance that divides them.

Mrs. Maestra says happily, "Just thinking about watching you play, makes me want to move my marker closer to the middle, how about you?" Joelle agrees and moves her own marker forward.

Under Mrs. Maestra's encouragement, Joelle chooses Swap as the next subject. Mrs. Maestra volunteers to go first. She gives a lively, accurate description of what it feels like to be Joelle and to hear mean comments from other students.

Mrs. Maestra dramatizes Joelle's rising anger, "Oh, man. When I hear someone mouthin' off at me, I just feel myself gettin' madder and madder... right?"

"Right!," exclaims Joelle.

"And then all of a sudden, before I even know it, I'm ballin' up my fists and I just hope they say one more thing because I'm going to blast them. Right?"

"Right!"

And so Mrs. Maestra continues her reenactment of Joelle's anger. She can tell that her student is delighted to see someone else knows what it feels like to be her... perhaps, Mrs. Maestra guesses, this is the first time she's ever had anyone empathize with her.

When Mrs. Maestra is finished, she offers to trade chairs with Joelle. Her student happily agrees.

Joelle talks to Mrs. Maestra about the problem, as she thinks Mrs. Maestra sees it... and the girl is quite accurate. Joelle discusses the difficulties that she sees ahead and how disappointed she is, as a teacher, in Joelle's conduct. Both players enjoy the role reversal, and have several laughs as each tries to mimic the other.

At the end of the discussion, Mrs. Maestra and Joelle move their markers closer. Mrs. Maestra, believing that she has made significant progress, decides to see if an initial Agreement can be reached. She knows that Joelle is going to be a long term project and does not want to push forward too quickly.

Their Agreement Contract reads:

1. We agree to talk for at least five minutes at the end of every lunch for a week, with, or without, the Agreement Bridge, as we wish.

Mrs. Maestra knows they are a long way from crossing the distance between them, but she and her student have made a good start.

Here are sample effective agreements (in the following the students' names are Jack and Joanie; the mentor is Paulina.)

1. We will meet tomorrow at 3:15 to play another round of the Agreement Bridge.
2. Jack will draft a letter to his mother explaining why he has been angry.
3. Paulina will ask Joanie's teacher for additional time to complete Joanie's research paper.
4. Jack will complete one diary entry of at least one full page about his problems with his former girl friend before Wednesday's meeting at 2 PM.
5. Mrs. Maestra will send Jack two text messages to see how he is doing before their next meeting on Tuesday.
6. Joanie will not call or text her boyfriend before the next meeting on Thursday at 9 AM.
7. Jack will get a list of math assignments from Mr. Warren before the next meeting on Friday at 3 PM.
8. Joanie will complete three, one hour guitar lessons, before the next meeting on Monday morning at 8 AM.
9. Jack will not use drugs or alcohol for 24 hours, and will report on his progress at the next meeting at 3 PM.

Now, here is a list of ineffective agreements (with suggestions for improvements in parenthesis):

1. Jack will stay away from his old friends. (How does he do that? They are students at the same school. And what does "stay away" mean? Never speak another word to? Better would be, "Instead of going to Robbie's house tomorrow after school, Jack will go to the weight room.")
2. Joanie will not have anything to do with Tamara. (Better would be, "Between now and Tuesday morning, Joanie will keep a diary entry

of each conversation with Tamara. The fewer the entries, and the shorter the conversations, the better.")

3. Jack will work harder on his math assignments. (Much better would be, "Jack will meet tomorrow with Robby, his math tutor, from 3 to 3:30 PM in room 214.")

4. Joanie will not let her brother aggravate her. ("Agreement One: Joanie will ask Paulina to role play her brother being aggravating at least two times before Friday at noon. Joanie will practice controlling her tone of voice and/or walking away when she feels upset. Agreement Two: Joanie will keep a record of how many times she responds angrily to her brother before the next meeting with Mrs. Maestra on Friday at noon at the lunch tables.")

5. Jack will stop using drugs. ("Jack will keep his appointment with his drug abuse counselor tomorrow at 4 PM.")

6. Joanie will find a new group of friends who have positive attitudes toward life. (This is a huge undertaking that may be necessary, but will take months. Better would be, "Joanie will have lunch tomorrow with Andrea." Andrea has been identified as a friend who has no involvement with drugs.)

A substantially expanded version of The Agreement Bridge is available at WholeBrainTeaching.com.

In the next two chapters, as a bonus, I've included descriptions of how Whole Brain Teaching can be adapted to one of education's highest goals, helping students develop critical thinking skills.

CHAPTER 23

Whole Brain Teaching and Critical Thinking

Open ended questions lead to Higher Order Thinking Skills (HOTS!)

Many of the techniques in this book are designed to keep students on task and to help them master core knowledge. Over the last 10 years, we have focused on these two areas because most educators we talked to identified them as their core teaching problems. Now that we have some solutions to these issues, we have developed a set of critical thinking techniques that are remarkably easy to adapt to a WBT classroom.

To begin, I'll define what I mean by critical thinking... and then propose a more useful term. In philosophy, a subject I've taught for 40 wonderful years, critical thinking involves creating strong evidence for clear-cut conclusions. It is useful to think of evidence as "because" statements and conclusions as "therefore" statements. For example:

Because I want my students to master core knowledge, *therefore* I have them rehearse it frequently with their neighbors.

Because I love a lively classroom, *therefore* I encourage my students to make large, flamboyant gestures when teaching course material to their neighbors.

Because/therefore thinking is at the root of the kind of logical analysis important to instructors at every level of our system. However, we want students to do more than reason carefully, we want them to engage in original, outside the box thinking. We want our pupils to come up with ideas, approaches, strategies that we, their teachers, never imagined. I've found it easier when talking to students and teachers to abandon the phrase critical thinking... which often doesn't mean much to my audience... and use the simpler, clearer term, *creative thinking.*

Creative thinking is easy to define. Its primary characteristic is that it is new thinking, ideas you haven't heard before. Thus, creative thinking could include new combinations of because/therefore structures, or new insights into a story, or new ways to express an idea in an essay.

Creative thinking is, surprisingly, easy to initiate in a WBT classroom. When students have been taught to teach their neighbors what the instructor has presented, creative thinking is initiated *by simply having students answer a question posed by the instructor.*

When students are talking to each other about the instructor's question, without being given the answer in advance, they are automatically inventing material that is new, creative... the answer is coming from them and their neighbor, not their teacher.

Additional levels of Whole Brain creative thinking are developed by adding gestures specific to a variety of complex thinking tasks.

For example, if you want students to practice using because/therefore thinking, teach them corresponding gestures. (I describe 12 of these gestures, Brain Toys, in the next chapter.) Clap one hand on the other for "because." Making a closed fist represents the "therefore" that concludes one or more "becauses."

Because (hand slap) I want my students to master core knowledge and *because* (hand slap) I love a lively classroom, *therefore* (closed fist) I have them rehearse lessons frequently with their neighbors.

Give your students a question that requires using because/therefore reasoning and then ask them to practice using the gestures above as they develop creative thinking answers.

Sample questions might be:

- How could you prove that basketball is, or isn't, more fun than baseball?
- What evidence could you use to argue that Batman is, or isn't, a better crime fighter than Superman?
- Try to convince me that you should get extra recess today.

Another common creative thinking activity involves comparing and contrasting. A gesture for comparing could be lacing your fingers together (showing two things are joined together, similar); a gesture for contrasting could be bumping your fists together (showing two things don't fit together, are different). Present compare/contrast tasks to your class and ask them to use these gestures as they generate answers with their neighbors.

Sample tasks might be:

- Compare and contrast baseball and basketball.
- Compare and contrast whole numbers and fractions.
- Compare and contrast California with Mexico.

We often want students to illustrate their written points with examples. A simple gesture for an example would be pretending to pull the example out of the top of your head. The example gesture could be combined with either because/therefore or compare/contrast tasks to create fairly complex sequences of creative thinking.

Sample tasks that students could explore with their neighbors might be:

- Try to prove to someone, using because/therefore gestures, that it is a good idea to go to college. Include examples, with gestures, that support your reasoning.
- Compare and contrast, using gestures, the pigs and the wolf in the "Three Little Pigs." Use example gestures to illustrate parts of the story.

- Compare and contrast, using gestures, a poem and a novel. Then, try to prove that one is more fun to read than the other. Use gestures for because/therefore, compare/contrast and examples.

You can probably tell that creative thinking, as described above, would be an excellent precursor to writing essays. We agree and call these activities, oral writing. To learn more about our approach to writing, download "The Writing Game" at WholeBrainTeaching.com.

CHAPTER 24

More Critical Thinking: The Illustrious Brain Toys

What's more fun than a dozen mind games?

Let's continue our investigation of making abstract thinking, visual. There are three levels of understanding: memorization, paraphrasing and critical thinking. Brain Toys are gestures used to engage the prefrontal, visual, motor and auditory cortex in original thinking, learning's highest level.

1. **Props:** books, pencils, papers, keys, even a whole classroom can become problems, ideas, characters, abstractions, etc. For example, your class has just finished reading "James and the Giant Peach." You say, "Okay. I want you all to pick up your pencil, turn to your neighbor and use your prop, in as many ways as possible, to retell the story." You then clap twice and instead of saying "Teach," say "Props!" Your students respond, "Okay!" and boom! They're using props to vigorously animate "James and the Giant Peach."

2. **Air Whiteboard:** You clap your hands twice and say, "Whiteboard!", your students clap twice and chorus, "Okay!" They lift their hands, mark the outlines of an imaginary whiteboard in the air, use a palm to clean the dirty left corner (for some reason, kids love dong this) and

then they make invisible diagrams illustrating the relationship between ideas, creating outlines, anything that can be drawn.

3. **Story Gestures:** Students talk to their neighbors and use their hands to act out a story. "First, (hold up one finger) the man drove his car to town (pantomime driving a car)... Second, (hold up two fingers) he ate a pizza (eat an imaginary pizza), then..." etc.

4. **Sockless Hand Puppets:** Lift your hands as if there is a sock puppet on each hand. Use one sockless hand puppet to talk to the other. This is a great technique for conversations between characters or to represent opposing points of view. Sockless hand puppets can be used to compare (left hand) and contrast (right hand) or in any dialogue situation. Or, let's say one of your kids needs a partner... let her talk to herself creating a sockless hand puppet conversation. A very entertaining addition to sockless hand puppets is to ask kids to use a different funny voice for each hand.

5. **Infinity Sack:** Use the Infinity Sack when you need something that can't be illustrated by a single prop. Make a half circle with your arm, resting your fist on your hip. The opening your arm makes is the mouth of the Infinity Sack. Pull anything you want out of your magic bag: mountains, cities, people, an ocean, a mouse, a planet of daffodils to use in any explanation... the prop of all props!

6. **Example Popper:** We frequently want students to illustrate their points with examples. As they speak to each other, or to the class, they should pull examples out of the top of their heads. Demonstrate by bringing your fingers and thumb to a point, put the point on the top of your head, and then pull upward and viola... you're example popping! Whenever students use the Example Popper, they should say, "For example,..." and then speak in a complete sentence.

7. **Because Clappers:** "Because" is probably the single most important word in creative thinking, because it introduces evidence for your

conclusions. Teach your students to clap one hand on the other when they use "because" to show they are "building" evidence.

8. **Vocabulary Candy:** Pop an imaginary candy in your mouth and automatically use a vocabulary word in your next sentence! Here is a note I posted on our website, WholeBrainTeaching.com, describing advanced ways to use Vocab Candy.

No More Stale Candy!

At the highest level, you would call on a kid who would say "Class!" Everyone would respond "Yes!" The kid would say "Mirror!" Everyone would say "Mirror!" Then she would toss an imaginary piece of candy into her mouth and say "Yum!" Everyone would toss a piece of imaginary candy into their mouth and say "Yum!" The girl would use a vocabulary word in a sentence WITH the word "because" and use a because clapper. Then she would add an air punctuation mark at the end of the sentence. Then your student would add an "adder" which would be another sentence that added information to the "vocab candy because sentence" and conclude with air punctuation. Then the energetic girl would clap twice and say "teach!" and everyone would follow suit.

Why so many steps? Because this is ULTIMATE VOCAB CANDY! You would move up to this level throughout the year, to keep adding new challenges... and to keep the Vocab Candy fresh. Who wants stale candy?

You could even say, "Who's ready for EVEN SWEETER VOCAB CANDY?" as you moved up in levels.

8. **Two Finger, All Terrain, Action Figures with Anti-Gravity Boots:** Use these wonderful action figures to recreate any sequence of events in a story or a process. Using two fingers, walk your Action Figures on your desk, in the air, up your arm, anywhere. They're All Terrain! And, jumping into the air, they hop free of gravity! My college students especially love using their Action Figures in ArmWorld. Beginning on the back of one hand, they walk their fingers up to their shoulder, jump over their head, switch hands and walk their fingers

down to the other hand. Why? They are repeating all the steps in a philosophical argument... or, step by step, reviewing a historical sequence or important events in a story.

10. **Compare/Contrast:** Bump your fists together when contrasting; lace your fingers together when comparing. Compare/Contrast is probably the most powerful, most deeply explanatory of all Brain Toys... use it frequently!

11. **Adders:** We frequently want students to "say more" or "give more details." To encourage this, point your index fingers at each other and roll them in small circles as if saying "more." Adders, adding details to explanations, are crucial in language development.

12. **Combos:** Use any combination of the above.

HOW TO USE BRAIN TOYS

1. **Levels:** Brain Toys provide a year long critical thinking curriculum if you introduce about one a month.

2. **Reading comprehension:** divide a reading selection into short units, about half a page. Have pairs of students read a unit, use a Brain Toy to explain it to each other and then go on to the next unit.

3. **Teach-Okay:** Explain complex concepts and then select a Brain Toy that students will use to explain the ideas to each other.

4. **Mirror:** Explain a concept using a Brain Toy as students mirror you. Students then use the same Brain Toy to teach each other or, for a challenge, use a different Brain Toy to teach each other.

5. **Switch:** When you call Switch, point at a new Brain Toy on the board for students to use as they teach each other.

6. **Hands and Eyes:** Students watch you using one or more Brain Toys and then imitate you as they teach their neighbor.

7. **360 degree Learning:** When we fully understand a topic, we can explain it in multiple ways. Pick any challenging subject, ask students to use four Brain Toys to explain key points. Then, have them stand in small groups and practice using the Brain Toy to teach each other. Finally, select individuals to present the Brain Toy explanation to the class. This is a good occasion for students to practice being WBT teachers beginning with "Class" and ending with "Teach!"

8. **Math word problems:** Give students a list of word problems. Ask them to use one or more Brain Toys to explain the problems to each other, *without even trying to find a solution*. Next, ask them to use Brain Toys to explain the steps in the solution. If the word problem has multiple choice answers (like the state standards tests), ask students to use Brain Toys to prove their answer is correct and that the other answers are incorrect. It is better for students to spend 10 minutes on one problem than racing through 10 problems in 10 minutes.

9. **Prove it:** Put a multiple choice test problem on the board, or project one from a computer. Ask students to use Brain Toys to prove which answer is correct and which answers are incorrect. This is an especially powerful technique to prepare students for state testing. The "prove it" technique with Brain Toys is adapted from Linda Mikels' 10-a-day, 5-a-day strategies used to make 6th Street Prep one of the top ranking elementary schools in California.

CHAPTER 25

Smart Cards

Low tech device for student assessment

Many underperforming students have one, superb skill. They are outstanding at hiding their ignorance from their instructors. When the teacher asks, "does everyone understand?," the cunning underperformer grins broadly and nods her head. When the teacher poses a question to the class, the underperformer hesitates a moment and then responds as she hears the majority responding.

Faced with a direct question, "Do you understand how to multiply fractions?" the underperformer, unwilling to be embarrassed by her ignorance, gives whatever response she believes will move the teacher on to another student. Then, to further hide her inabilities, she does her best to copy her smartest neighbor's work.

Underperformers spend their lives masking their inabilities. They live in the secret land of I Can't. Teacher and student work at cross purposes. The teacher wants to cure ignorance; the underperformer denies her illness.

We would have few education problems in the U.S., if students eagerly came to us for help. We know how to teach reading, writing and math. Millions have been spent to develop wonderful textbooks and potent instructional technologies. We have bags full of cures but our students, daily, hide their disease.

Teachers need an instant assessment tool to measure student comprehension; smart boards with student clickers have provided a powerful, but expensive answer. The teacher flashes a question on the board; students click their answers. The teacher sees an instant readout of how many students are on the right track.

Wonderful!

But few schools can afford the $3,500 per classroom that smart boards cost. That's about $100 per kid!

As you'll soon see, Smart Cards are far cheaper and a remarkably flexible method of evaluating student comprehension.

WHAT IS A SMART CARD?

A Smart Card is simply a 3x5 index card with Yes on one side and No on the other. A Slightly More Sophisticated Smart Card is a red and a green 3x5 card stapled together. The green side is labeled Yes; the red side is labeled No.

When a question is posed in class, students hold up the Yes side, if they believe the answer is affirmative, the No side when they believe the answer is negative. Thus, every student responds, every student instantly reveals their understanding. Because the cards are held up silently, no student is embarrassed by verbalizing an incorrect answer.

If students have no idea of the correct answer, they *should not be encouraged to guess.* Kids should signal unsure answers by holding their card with the edge pointing toward the instructor. We would much rather have students knowing they are uncertain rather than believing, incorrectly, they are right.

USES OF YES/NO SMART CARDS

Whenever you want to determine how many of your students understood part, or all, of your lesson, simply ask them several questions that can be answered Yes or No. Having color coded Smart Cards (green for Yes, red for No) makes it even easier to quickly evaluate your students' comprehension.

Mrs. Maestra, our veteran Whole Brain Teacher, used the following script to incorporate Smart Cards into the Teach-Okay pattern.

SCRIPT: SMART CARDS

Teacher: Class!

Students: Yes!

Teacher: You all have your Smart Cards. I'm going to ask you a question and then say "Vote!" If your answer is Yes, say "Okay!" and hold up the Yes side of the Smart Card. If your Answer is No, say "Okay!" and hold up the No side of the Smart Card. Teach!

Students: Okay! (Students teach their neighbor what the teacher has just said.)

Teacher: Class!

Students: Yes!

Teacher: Now, I'm going to ask the question. *But don't hold up your Smart Cards, until I say Vote!* Would you like an hour recess today?... Vote!

Students: (Laughing) Okay! (Students hold up their Yes Smart Cards.)

Teacher: Class!

Students: Yes!

Teacher: Great job! Now, let's take this one step further. I'll ask a question and say Vote! You say Okay and hold up a Smart Card. I'll look at the Smart Cards and say, "Unvote!" and you say Okay and lower your card to your desk. Teach!

Students: Okay! (Students teach their neighbor what the teacher has just said.)

Teacher: Class!

Students: Yes!

Teacher: Excellent! Okay, let's try Vote and UnVote. Here's the question, "Is Sacramento the capital of California... Vote!"

Students: Okay! (Students hold up their Smart Cards.)

Teacher: Good! (looks at the response by her students) UnVote!

Students: Okay! (Students lower their Smart Cards.)

There are only two problems that may develop with Smart Cards. First, students may speak their answer in place of silently holding up their card. We want a silent response because we need to measure students' understanding, not their reaction to classmates. To solve the problem of oral responses, use one of WBT's standard strategies; practice the incorrect behavior while identifying it as incorrect. Ask students to respond orally several times and, at each response, point out this is the wrong way of using Smart Cards.

The second problem that may develop with Smart Cards is that students, out of the corner of their eye, may "read" other students' movements for clues about how they should answer. For example, let's say you ask an easy question and everyone holds up a Yes card. Next, you ask a hard question with No as the correct answer. If many of your students lower their Yes card and then hold up their No card, your underperformers may read this visual change of cards and simply follow suit, though they have no idea of the correct answer. To avoid this, simply require after each vote that the card be lowered to the desk. This is the point of the "Vote!" and "UnVote!" procedure in the script above. Students begin with both cards on their desk; they listen to a question and raise a card when you say "Vote"; you inspect their answers and say "UnVote!" They lower their cards and wait for the next question.

Here are some sample uses of Smart Cards:

Language Arts

1. **Parts of speech:** If students are all using the same book, read one of the sentences aloud. For example, "John went to the big store to buy tamales." Ask, "Is John a noun?... Is big a noun... Is store a noun?" Pause after each question to let your students vote with their Smart Cards. When 80% of your kids can identify nouns, then go on to adjectives. Then add, nouns and adjectives. Next, focus on verbs. Finally, quiz on nouns, adjectives and verbs. Using the sentence above, you would ask, "Is John a noun?... Is big a verb?... Is store an adjective?"

2. **Capitalization:** While your students are engaged in other activities, write several sentences on the board. Include correct and

incorrect capitalization. Then, get your kids' attention and point at various words. Ask students to vote whether or not a capitalization mistake has been made. As the year unfolds, include other kinds of errors in your board sentences.

3. **Spelling:** Spell commonly misspelled words aloud, sometimes correctly, sometimes incorrectly. When the word is spelled correctly, students hold up the Yes card; when the word is spelled incorrectly, they hold up the No card.

4. **Subject/verb agreement:** Speak aloud short subject/verb pairs. For example, "We is... They are... I was... They is... I were... John was" When the subject/verb agreement is correct, students hold up the Yes card; when it is incorrect, they hold up the No card.

5. **Sentences and fragments:** Read aloud a collection of sentence and sentence fragments. When students hear a sentence, they hold up a Yes card; when they hear a fragment, they hold up a No card.

6. **Vocabulary:** Read aloud words and their definitions, occasionally inserting incorrect definitions. Students vote after every definition. They hold up the Yes card when the definition is correct and the No card when the definition is incorrect.

Math

1. **Math procedures:** As you work a problem on the board, ask students if you have just made the correct step (make occasional errors.) Students hold up Yes if you are right; No if you have made a mistake.

2. **Fill in the blanks:** While students are engaged in other tasks, put multiple step math problems on the board, for example, long division problems. Leave several blanks in each problem. Point at the blanks, offer a sample answer. Students hold up the Yes card if you are right; the No card if you are wrong.

3. **Math facts:** Slowly speak a group of math facts (addition, subtraction, multiplication, division). Make occasional mistakes. Students hold up the Yes card when you are right; the No card when you are wrong.

4. **Word problems:** Including several mistakes, suggest various ways to solve a word problem. Students hold up the Yes card when you are right; the No card when you are wrong.

5. **Board diagrams:** Label and mislabel diagrams on the board. Then point at parts of the diagrams. Students hold up the Yes card when you point at correctly labeled parts; the No card when you are pointing at incorrectly labeled parts.

General

1. **Smart Card SuperSpeed:** Follow any of the procedures above but tell students they are in a one minute race against the clock. Every time they get an answer correct, they should make a tally mark on a sheet of paper. Their goal, each time they play Smart Card SuperSpeed, is to beat their previous best record.

2. **Assignments/Instructions:** Give your students an assignment or a set of instructions. When you are finished, check their comprehension by making statements about what you said. Students hold up the Yes card when you are right; the No card when you are wrong.

3. **Worksheets:** Before students begin filling in a worksheet, review some of the tasks. Occasionally make mistakes. When your students' votes demonstrate an understanding of the material, allow them to begin filling the worksheet on their own.

4. **Core concepts:** Assign gestures to core concepts: period, preposition, multiplication, more than/less than, etc. Speak the concept and make a gesture. When the two correctly match, students hold up the Yes card and the No card otherwise.

5. **Preview/Review:** Use Smart Card voting at the start of a unit to determine how much your students know, or at the end of a unit to determine how much they remember.

6. **Critical Thinking:** After any vote, say "Prove it!" Students then turn to their neighbors and give reasons justifying the answer on their Smart Card. This is an extremely powerful exercise that should be used often to develop higher order thinking skills.

What we need is a fast, simple method for determining, lesson after lesson, how many students understand what we are teaching. There is no sense in going on to lesson B, if lesson A lost half our class. If you can't afford smart board technology, spend a few pennies on a class set of Smart Cards.

CHAPTER 26

Leadership Training and the Self Managing Class

*The Gold Treasure at rainbow's end...
is closer than you think*

Mrs. Maestra didn't just want her students to follow the five rules, learn energetically, and develop their critical thinking skills, she also wanted her kids to become better human beings. She tried many avenues for moral development, but she eventually saw that leadership training dovetailed with many WBT techniques. Becoming better leaders increased her students' self confidence, taught boisterous kids consideration of others and brought quiet students out of their shells. Mrs. Maestra often noted a positive link between growing leadership skills and improved academic performance.

About the second month of class, Mrs. Maestra used a simple technique for leadership training. She began to turn over her oral cues to individual students. At the start of each class, she selected students who would lead the rules rehearsals, be in charge of the Class-Yes, Teach-Okay, Mirror, Hands and Eyes and Switch. Whenever she tapped Juan on the shoulder, he would vigorously exclaim, "Class!" and the students would respond "Yes!" Janie, a high energy student became responsible for the "Teach-Okay." When Mrs. Maestra pointed at her, the lively girl would clap 1 to 4 times (or use some other innovative Tickler) and exclaim "Teach!" The students would chorus, "Okay!" and teach their neighbors Mrs. Maestra's previous point. Mrs. Maestra followed a similar procedure for her other, frequent verbal cues. She found students who liked to say "Mirror," "Hands and Eyes," "Switch," "Papers, papers, papers" etc. For some of these techniques Mrs. Maestra found it easiest to use a light shoulder tap to spark her leader into action; for other cues, all Mrs. Maestra had to do was look at the leader, smile and slightly nod her head.

Mrs. Maestra didn't use her leaders every time she needed a verbal cue, that might have slowed down her class, but she found that allowing leaders to give cues not only increased their self confidence, but also provided needed pedagogical variety.

Another leadership technique Mrs. Maestra found effective was to count her class off into 1s, 2s, 3s, and 4s. She could then say, "Ones, I want you to stand up be energetic teachers of your three neighbors. Teach!" As the day progressed, she gave the other group members the opportunity to be the standing leaders. On other occasions, she said, "Twos, show everyone how we energetically say Yes!, when I say Teach!" Or, she might say, "Threes let me hear a big Mighty Oh Yeah!"

Mrs. Maestra's most advanced technique for leadership training was to take small groups of students aside and introduce them to new material. She would explain concepts, get their feedback in creating learning gestures, assign a teaching point to each one. Then, she would use these leaders as part of her new unit. Every year, Mrs. Maestra was delighted to find students who were able to lead entire lessons. She, and her class, loved watching these marvelous leaders get everyone's attention with "Class!," and creatively employ Mirror, Hands and Eyes, Switch and Teach-Okay. She noted with joy that her students were becoming Whole Brain Teachers.

As each year progressed and Mrs. Maestra's students mastered the five rules, the various classroom procedures, the WBT teaching techniques and especially as her leaders developed, Mrs. Maestra caught glimpses of her highest goal, the self managing class.

Mrs. Maestra had become a teacher because she wanted to communicate her intellectual passions to students. She loved the intricacies of math, the unending universes of literature, the mesmerizing variety of social studies and history. As a new teacher, she had not realized that in order to communicate her passions, she would first have to teach her students to pay attention, get their books out quickly, line up in an orderly fashion, not interrupt when classmates were speaking. Before long Mrs. Maestra learned that in order to Teach, she would have to master Crowd Control. Developing leaders went a long way in turning the routines of classroom management over to the students themselves. As the months passed, the class, under the direction of its leaders, began to run itself, monitor itself, correct and guide itself. With a nod, a smile, a shoulder tap from Mrs. Maestra, students shaped their own positive behavior. Year after year in the company of her self managing class, Mrs. Maestra explored the golden corridors of Teaching Heaven.

CHAPTER 27

Whole Brain Teaching Review

All about Everything (and more!)

A nd so there you have it, the Whole Brain Teaching system. You use the Big Seven daily instructional techniques within a year long, six level classroom management system (adding creative thinking as you wish). Here's a review, with several new points thrown in:

THE BIG SEVEN

1. **The Attention Getter: Class-Yes** – To gain students' attention, the teacher says "Class!" or "Class! Class!" or "Classity Class!" with various tones of voice and students respond "Yes!" or "Yes! Yes!" or "Yesity Yes!"

2. **The Organizer: Classroom Rules** – Rehearse class rules at least once a day with gestures. The teacher says the rule number and students repeat the rule number and rule. For example, the teacher says, "Rule 1" and the class says "Rule 1: Follow directions quickly!" and makes the Rule 1 gesture.

    Rule 1: Follow directions quickly!
    (Gesture: raise one finger, then swim your hand rapidly through the air.) To use this rule in class, count aloud beginning at one, to "time"

various activities like opening books, lining up, being seated. Keep track of class times; when the class does well, give them a Smiley mark (see below).

Rule 2: Raise your hand for permission to speak.
(Gesture: raise two fingers, then make a talking motion with your hand.) To use this rule in class, when a student speaks without raising a hand, say "Rule 2!" Your class responds, "Rule 2: Raise your hand for permission to speak."

Rule 3: Raise your hand for permission to leave your seat.
(Gesture: raise three fingers, then walk two fingers through the air.) To use this rule in class, follow the same procedure as for Rule 2.

Rule 4: Make smart choices.
(Gesture: raise four fingers, then tap your temple three times with one finger.) To use this rule in class, follow the same procedure as for Rule 2.

Rule 5: Keep your dear teacher happy!
(Gesture: raise five fingers, then use both hands framing your mouth and make a smiley face.) To use this rule in class, follow the same procedure as for Rule 2.

3. **The Whole Brain Activator: Teach/Okay** – Speak briefly, using gestures, usually no more than 30 seconds to 1 minute. Then (this can be seen in the videos at WholeBrainTeaching.com) clap your hands one to five times and say, "Teach!" Your students repeat your hand clap, and say "Okay!" They make a full body turn to their neighbor and, using gestures, teach their neighbor what you have just taught the class. While students are teaching each other, move around the class; check for comprehension. *All students should be gesturing!* For students who are listening, but don't know what gestures to use, ask them to mirror the gestures of students speaking. Praise students who are energetically on task; briefly encourage students who are off task to become more involved (usually this means, asking them to make gestures as they speak or listen.)

4. **The Motivator: The Scoreboard –** To keep your students intensely involved, make a Smiley/Frowny diagram on the front board. (For variety, use other symbols or terms besides Smiley/Frowny.) When students are on task, mark a Smiley point. Then point at them; they clap their hands and exclaim, "Oh, yeah!" When students are off task, mark a Frowny point. Then point at them and students lift their shoulders and groan, "Awww!" *Never let the difference between Smiley and Frowny points be greater than 3.* If you reward too much, students lose energy (the game is too easy). If you punish too much, students become unhappy (the game is too hard). At the end of the period, if there are more Smiley points than Frowny points, students receive a small reward of extra recess, free time, or a learning game equal in minutes to the number of Smiley points they earned. For example, if they have 2 Smiley points, they have earned two minutes of game time. See the Appendix for three of our favorite learning games: Mind Soccer, Mind Basketball and Mind Volleyball.

5. **The Class Unifier: Mirror –** When you want your class deeply involved in your lesson, hold up your hands, ready to make gestures, and say "Mirror!" Your class says, "Mirror!," picks up their hands and mirror your gestures as you teach. When you want your class to mirror your gestures and repeat your words, say "Mirror words!"

6. **The Involver: Switch!** Count your class off in 1s and 2s. When students are teaching their neighbors, after Teach-Okay, the 1s teach with gestures and the 2s mirror the gestures. When you shout, "Switch!" all students shout "Switch" and the 2s teach and the 1s mirror their gestures. Even more fun, students can shout "Uh, oh! Switch!" and then they reach up and pull down a large, imaginary switch ... and then teach their neighbors.

7. **The Focuser: Hands and Eyes –** When you have an important point to make, say "Hands and Eyes!" Your students say "Hands and Eyes!" and fold their hands and stare at you intensely.

SCOREBOARD LEVELS

Add each Level's rules to previous levels.

Level 1 – Scoreboard: Students earn small rewards or penalties, as determined by their positive or negative behavior. (Note: we have met some instructors who strongly object to using additional homework as a penalty. However, all the veteran WBT instructors I know, believe homework is one of their strongest motivators. Shortening or lengthening recess, or free time, has, thus far, not met with any objections. Best of all, might be the opportunity to play a learning game; our favorites are in the Appendix. No matter what reward/penalty you choose, you'll have to change it occasionally to avoid students' habituation as described in Chapter 4.)

Level 2 – Super Improvers Team: Using a color coded scale, students advance from the lowest to the highest level for improvements in academic or social behavior. Instead of competing against each other, kids strive to set and break personal records in everything from reading speed to lunch room behavior. The Super Improvers Team can be adapted to help challenging kids focus on easy to improve negative habits.

Level 3 – Practice Cards: Use a card pocket chart with each pocket labeled with students' names or numbers. Create sets of Rule 1 cards, Rule 2 cards, Rule 3 cards, Rule 4 cards and Rule 5 cards. You will need three sets of each. One set is white; one set is purple; one set is green. *Stay at each card level as long as possible, before introducing a new color of cards.*

- **White Cards:** Penalties: No more than 2 cards per day. Each card stands for 2 minutes of recess rule practice (increases one minute as each new level is added). A note goes home asking parents to help with rule practice. The card stays in the pocket for one day, except in special cases, until the note comes back signed from home.
- **Purple Cards:** Rewards: purple cards are awarded when a student has done an outstanding job of following one of the five

rules. A purple card and a white card cancel each other. If a student has one or more purple cards at the end of the day, a praise note goes home.

- **Green Cards:** In-class practice: A student records a tally mark on his/her green card, every time a rule is successfully followed in class. At the end of the day, the teacher has the option of sending, or not sending, a white card or purple card note home.

Level 4 – Guff Counter: the teacher announces that a Frownie mark will be recorded for each word or act of guff between student and teacher or student and student. Students respond to guff by exclaiming, "Please, stop!" The threat of the Guff Counter, and active student support, eliminates the need for making marks in the Guff Counter.

Level 5 – The Independents: rebel cliques of students receive their own place on the Scoreboard. Students only have to stay in the Independent group one day. When one misbehaves, they all get a Frownie, a White Practice Card. The misbehaving student receives a note home; all students in the Independent group practice at recess and lunch, the rule they broke.

Level 6 – The Bullseye Game: for students who have proven to be immune to penalty. Students are rewarded for evaluating their behavior from the instructor's point of view.

Level 7 – The Agreement Bridge: Collaborative problem solving for students who have demonstrated long term behavior problems.

As the year progresses, turn more of your routine tasks over to selected students. You can keep these leaders for a week, or swap them daily. Give one student the task of saying "Class!" when you point at her; give another student the pleasure of exclaiming "Papers! Papers! Papers!" when it's time to hand out papers; let another student be in charge of Teach-Okay. As you distribute your most frequent cues to individual kids, you'll be developing leadership and providing needed variety to your daily routines. Your goal is the same as Mrs. Maestra's, to train leaders who will nurture a self managing class. Take some time to communicate your experiences to other instructors at WholeBrainTeaching.com...the electronic portal to Teaching Heaven.

A few last words. If you have a question or comment about any of the above, please post your remarks on our forum at WholeBrainTeaching.com. You'll receive responses from WBT teachers across the country (and around the world). At our website, you'll also find thousands of pages of free downloads. As a follow-up to this book I especially suggest, "The Agreement Bridge" a considerably amplified presentation of our strategy for your most challenging kids. At WholeBrainTeaching.com you'll also find classroom tested games for increasing student reading speed and comprehension, math accuracy, and mastery of state standards.

I'd love to hear from you. Email me, Chris Biffle, at ChrisBiffle@WholeBrainTeaching.com.

Power to the Teachers!

CHAPTER 28

Whole Brain Teaching and Learning Research

The following article written by Angela Macias and Brian Macias, Whole Brain Teaching board members, documents the substantial body of research supporting WBT methodology. Especially valuable is their description of the relationship between Whole Brain Teaching and several of the most widely used and successful instructional techniques, including Direct Instruction and Collaborative Learning.

ABSTRACT

Whole Brain Teaching combines attributes of Direct Instruction and Cooperative Learning into one system of strategies designed to be centered around student learning. A theoretical background is provided from a constructivist point of view as a rationale for using Whole Brain Teaching in relation to Vygotsky's Social Learning Theory and Wenger's (2006) framework Community of Practice. The article concludes with specific benefits for teachers and students in a Whole Brain Teaching classroom.

WHAT IS WHOLE BRAIN TEACHING?

Whole Brain Teaching is a set of strategies that combines the best attributes of Direct Instruction and Cooperative Learning to create an engaging classroom environment for students and an enjoyable workday for teachers. WBT combines both classroom management as well as sound teaching pedagogy in one system.

Direct Instruction (DI) can be defined as "academically focused, teacher-directed classroom instruction using sequenced and structured materials" (Kousar, 2010, p.99). Kousar goes on to explain that key elements of DI are clear goals, structured time, and immediate academic feedback to students. Whole Brain Teaching utilizes all of these teaching tools. For example, a WBT lesson is carefully structured around a few major concepts, which are chunked into short micro-lectures. Each concept is taught one at a time. Students practice and review the concept until the teacher is satisfied with the level of comprehension. Feedback is given immediately as the teacher listens to student discussions and calls on students to explain concepts. When students need more review, it is given immediately without consequence or punishment.

Cooperative Learning (CL) is another successful teaching model which Whole Brain Teaching utilizes. CL involves student interaction as the basis for learning. Students problem solve together, discuss ideas together, and complete practice together. Thousand, Villa, and Nevin (1994) describe five key elements to cooperative learning:

1. Clearly perceived positive interdependence
2. Considerable promotive (face-to-face) interaction
3. Clearly perceived individual accountability and personal responsibility to achieve the group's goals
4. Frequent use of the relevant interpersonal and small-group skills
5. Frequent and regular group processing of current functioning to improve the group's future effectiveness

Whole Brain Teaching effectively uses all five elements of Cooperative Learning while still keeping a strict Direct Instruction model of teacher facilitated lecture-based lessons. Teachers facilitate a well-structured lecture, but switch back and forth between this lecture and pair-share discussions. Students learn in three dimensions: as a class team, as a small group or pair, and as an individual. There are also multiple opportunities for learning social skills as student roles and procedures are rehearsed. Students know what is expected of them at all times.

RATIONALE BEHIND WHOLE BRAIN TEACHING

Vygotsky's Social Learning Theory (SLT) is a fundamental aspect of constructivism. Vygotsky believed that social interaction is vital to learning and development. There are two basic elements to SLT: the More Knowledgeable Other (MKO) and the Zone of Proximal Development (ZPD) (Learning-Theories.com). The MKO is normally a teacher or instructor; one who yields higher education than the student. The traditional More Knowledgeable Other is responsible for facilitating learning through social interaction. In Vygotsky's theory, the teacher must be aware of the Zone of Proximal Development, which is the gap between a student's ability to solve a problem with guidance and his or her ability to solve a problem independently. The More Knowledgeable Other using the WBT methods creates peer based learning in which the Zone of Proximal Development gap can be closed.

One Whole Brain Teaching method that stems from Vygotsky's theory is the Teach / Okay. This involves the teacher training students to become MKOs. The process begins with the teacher creating micro-lectures involving memory retention strategies. After a short amount of information is taught, the teacher says "Teach" and the students respond with "Okay" followed by students re-teaching the micro-lecture to their peers. Eventually students take the concepts and paraphrase, give examples, and create new ideas with the concepts given by the teacher. Students become increasingly responsible for their learning because they teach concepts to one another. This micro-lecture structure with Teach/Okay holds the academic rigor of Direct Instruction while still reaping the benefits of Cooperative Learning at the same time.

Vygotksy's theory is a fundamental starting point of Wenger's Community of Practice (CoP) theory. Wenger's theory resulted from studying groups of people working to better themselves in certain practices. "Communities of practice are groups of people who share a concern or a passion for something they do and learn how to do it better as they interact regularly" (Wenger, 2006). Wenger explained that these CoPs can be incidental resulting from people joining together and unintentionally learning from one another, or they can be intentionally created, such as a classroom situation.

A Community of Practice has three major attributes: a domain, a community, and a practice (Wenger, 2006). A domain refers to a shared interest that joins people to share in a group identity. A community results from relationships being built through discussions and activities. The final piece is the practice. Wenger is careful to point out that a practice is not simply the shared interest. Instead it is what results from the actions of the community involved. He explains, "They develop a shared repertoire of resources: experiences, stories, tools, ways of addressing recurring problems–in short a shared practice." (Wenger, 2006)

A Whole Brain Teaching classroom exemplifies Wenger's CoP theory in several ways. First, students work as a team and in small groups towards one clearly defined learning goal. Second, the methods used are systematic, practiced, and reinforced by all members of the classroom community creating one unifying experience. Third, WBT includes valuable tools such as memory gestures to cover each new concept. All members of the classroom community are expected to not only utilize the methods and tools, but are encouraged to improve upon them for the benefit of everyone. Finally, a WBT classroom addresses recurring problems by rehearsing rules and procedures instead of punishment; the teacher is not pitted against the students, instead students practice together in order to set good examples.

BENEFITS OF WHOLE BRAIN TEACHING

Benefits for Teachers

There are three major benefits for teachers using WBT methods: (1) positive behavior reinforcement, (2) memory retention, and (3) student engagement. These benefits work to reinforce one another as well; as students are surrounded by positive behavior, they can learn better and students will inevitably behave better when they feel more confident in their learning.

1. Positive Behavior Reinforcement

Karaduz (2010) studied verbal stimuli teachers used in the classroom and categorized them as the following: stimuli for getting attention, stimuli for punishment, stimuli for rewards, and stimuli for feedback and correction. Among these types of verbal stimuli, punishment tends to create a lower quality of lesson and feedback and correction have the most potential to affect the students' attitudes toward a lesson (Karaduz, 2010). WBT methods leave no room for punishment verbal stimuli. Feedback and correction in a WBT classroom is always positive and planned. Specific questions are asked of individuals or groups of students. When students have correct answers, the class celebrates. When students do not have a correct answer, everyone responds with "It's cool!" creating a positive atmosphere where students are not afraid to have a wrong answer. Instead, participating is valued and rewarded. Karaduz (2010) pointed out that often students interviewed felt that they could not share their own ideas or opinions, and instead tried to construct responses that they thought would please the teacher (p.703). WBT prevents this because the teacher encourages students to make efforts no matter what the outcome. This occurs through the positive support system created by responses such as "It's cool!" and class cheers for positive ideas and points on the Scoreboard.

The WBT method of positive behavior reinforcement involves teamwork and rehearsing expectations. The central part of classroom management in a WBT classroom is the Scoreboard. This is used to reward positive behavior and correct negative behavior. The reason this works as positive behavior reinforcement is that it creates a team atmosphere as students are all rewarded for following rules, good ideas, pair sharing, participation, politeness, and many other positive behaviors. In other words, if one student follows directions, all can be rewarded.

Negative behaviors can be corrected with the Scoreboard as well. The difference is that negative behaviors are never pointed out in order to focus on an individual student. Instead, all students practice the rules and procedures as a group. In addition, students eventually become the ones who reinforce the rules and procedures to their peers instead of the teacher, creating more ownership.

WBT does have higher leveled tiers of behavior correction for individual students, but these still do not point out any student in front of peers; instead they are conducted in a one-on-one manner between teacher and student. Both the Scoreboard and WBT specific behavior correction such as Independent Group and the Bulls-eye Game maintain a positive atmosphere where no student will be embarrassed. In addition, the Scoreboard is a game. Therefore the mindset of the classroom is lighthearted while still rewarding and correcting within the constructs of the game.

WBT classroom management methods create a classroom community in which students participate as a team to reinforce the rules and procedures and students celebrate positive behavior. Doyle (2009) describes such positive classroom management as "person-centered management" that is built upon contexts within classroom activities and procedures. Doyle wrote "Contexts are, in important ways, jointly constructed by participants and depend upon the willingness of participants to cooperate in creating order together." WBT promotes this by having students rehearse rules frequently with gestures and discussion.

2. Memory Retention

The second major benefit for teachers using WBT methods is memory retention. Many teachers find themselves repeating lessons and wondering why students act as though they never learned content that they have already covered. Self-efficacy of students can be in danger at this point if the verbal stimuli by the teacher is negative as Karaduz (2010) observed many students fear. Martinez (2010) explained that the process of recalling old information and learning new information is best done in chunks. Short-term memory can hold more complex information this way. In addition, Martinez (2010) explained that memory can be stored in images, experiences, and language. WBT micro-lectures utilize visual learning by creating gestures and images for key concepts. An experience is created through cooperative learning pair share discussion and class games. Language is used each day through Teach/Okay. Micro-lectures chunk information in the way that Martinez (2010) describes by repeating short amounts of information, adding complexity each time.

Finally, Martinez (2010) also said that students can utilize this learning more when they work with peers. Martinez said, "When human minds work together productively, the result can be mutually catalyzing, and the combined reach can extend far beyond what the individual mind, acting alone, can achieve." (p.65)

3. Student Engagement

The final benefit for teachers using WBT is student engagement. Common teacher sayings such as students who "fly under the radar" and students who "fall between the cracks" represent those who have learned how to fit into what Pang (2010) calls a "passive learning environment" in which they sit quietly and blend into the crowd. Pang (2010) argued that activity based learning is foreign to many students because they have been trained to be passive learners. Pang explained that metacognitive learning with application happens when students complete activity-based learning. In a WBT classroom participation is expected. Often students are afraid to participate in traditional ways such as raising their hand to ask or answer a question because they fear being different than their peers. However, in a WBT classroom, all students discuss questions with partners and small groups to work out problems and share ideas regularly. Therefore, students who participate do not have to fear being different or singled out.

Snowman and Biehler (2003) explained that some major factors of self-efficacy in children are observation of model behavior and identifying with success. A WBT classroom is structured to foster these two things. Students model the teacher, and each other and are then rewarded with success via the Scoreboard and other WBT games. Creating a learning environment in which students are rewarded for positive behavior and do not have to fear participation allows for better self-efficacy. Snowman and Biehler (2003) went on to say that students with higher self-efficacy tend to use higher-level thought processes and solve complex problems. Therefore, the benefits for teachers lie in the positive behavior reinforcement, memory retention, and student engagement; all can result in better self-efficacy for students as they feel academic success.

Benefits for Students

There are many benefits for students in a WBT classroom. Students can have an overall more empowering experience as they take on the role of a teacher (MKO) instead of traditional classroom models of taking in and regurgitating information. There are three main reasons students can benefit from WBT: (1) motivation, (2) student-centered learning, and (3) application of learning.

1. Motivation

One way that WBT increases motivation is through academic games. Students at all grade levels appreciate games. The most exciting factor in WBT games is that performance is based on intrinsic rewards. Super Speed, for example, is a set of games that help students practice reading high-frequency words and solving common arithmetic problems. The purpose is to break personal time records. By creating an activity in which all students compete against their own score instead of others, everyone can be proud of their improvement. Often, lower skills students improve more than higher skills students in these games.

Another academic game that WBT offers is Crazy Professor. This reading game involves a text and two students working together to read with feeling, create gestures representing events, ask and answer questions, and other comprehension building skills. This game does not involve winning or losing at all, instead it simply allows for fun interaction between students and text.

Mind Soccer is another WBT game that allows for review of any kind of academic content. This game divides the class into two competing teams. Teams answer review questions in order to score points. This game is high energy and can contain any content that the teacher chooses to include. Although in this game students compete against other students, each group has a unified goal to answer questions correctly and there is no extrinsic reward aside from winning points. The teacher is in full control of how each of these games is played and can facilitate multiple opportunities for students to learn and show what they learned. Due to the team structure, students can rely on each other to answer questions as well.

Snowman and Biehler (2003) illustrate the factors of student motivation and list a major one as self-efficacy. As explained earlier, students who can identify with success are more likely to have higher self-efficacy. A WBT lesson provides multiple opportunities for success. Participating in discussion is success. Utilizing learning gestures is success. Following classroom rules is success. Sharing new ideas is success. Helping peers learn a concept is success. Breaking personal records is success. Participating in academic games such as Super Speed, Mind Soccer, or Crazy Professor is success. All students have multiple opportunities to achieve success in a WBT classroom and therefore motivation is a huge benefit for students.

2. Student-Centered Learning

Student-centered lessons are another quality of WBT strategies. Each WBT lesson moves at the pace of students' needs. Marzano, Pickering, and Pollock (2001) discussed how students need to practice new skills up to 24 times before mastery can be achieved. This practice should be concisely planned with chunks of information repeated the first few times and faster repetition later. WBT micro-lectures begin with the teacher giving a few chunks of information that are repeated by students. The teacher adds speed and complexity as the students show comprehension. Review is given as much or little as needed. This is a huge benefit for students because it creates a learning environment where practice is the main focus, not performance or assessment. Students are not assessed on knowledge in a formal manner until they have already had multiple opportunities to practice in cooperative groups and as individuals.

3. Application of Learning

Another product of WBT that provides gains for students is application of higher-level thinking. Marzano, Pickering, and Pollock (2001) list nine strategies for effective classroom instruction. Several of these are non-linguistic representations, summarizing, compare and contrast, and creating and testing hypothesis. WBT lessons follow a specific cyclical structure that includes beginning with memory gestures (non-linguistic representations) and follows with students summarizing each concept using the gesture with a partner or small group. Once students have a basic understanding of concepts, teachers can utilize higher level thinking tools. WBT has two gestures that are consistently used across grade levels and subject areas to represent the words Compare and Contrast. This becomes a powerful tool as it is used repeatedly throughout the school year in various ways. Next, there are also WBT Brain Toys—a set of strategies that challenges students to use their creativity to use the concepts and memory gestures they have learned in a new way. Some involve telling stories, making up new gestures, and creating explanations for questions.

Taking notes in a WBT classroom involves application of higher level thinking as well. Traditionally, note taking involves students recording information delivered in the lesson to be studied later and reproduced on a quiz or test. WBT utilizes notes, but the structure of chunking information and increasing complexity in small amounts is maintained. Therefore, students take notes on one concept at a time and add their own examples to the notes as well. Application of knowledge is extended beyond studying for a test. WBT students use their notes to re-teach or discuss information in groups. This way notes not only have valuable information, but also a purposeful use in classroom activities as well. Compare and Contrast gestures, Brain Toys and WBT note taking strategies provide a cooperative learning structure for higher level thinking with an immediate application for concepts taught by the teacher.

CONCLUSION

Aristotle, one of the original theorists on learning, believed that knowledge can be theoretical and practice based. Saugstad (2002) argued that modern educational theory and practice do not align well because current understanding of knowledge has been narrowed.

In contrast to the contemporary perception of learning, which often involves a mere cognitive-based understanding of learning (as often seen in psychological and educational textbooks), Aristotle expresses a broader and more situated view on learning with room for multiple types of learning, such as practice, exercise, training, imitation and experience-based learning. (Saugstad, 2002, p.378)

WBT exemplifies the philosophy that teachers educate the whole child, not simply teach one subject area at a time. Therefore, classroom discipline and management is equally important to quality lessons, not simply for teachers to have control of the classroom environment, but also for students to build self-efficacy in the process of learning. Schunk (1999) described how social development is directly related to student achievement. There are stages in which a student moves from observing and emulating academic behaviors to finally self-regulated behaviors. Regardless of where a student falls on this scale, WBT has behavioral and academic procedures in place to help the student develop further.

Whole Brain Teaching addresses all of Marzano, Pickering, and Pollock's (2001) strategies for effective classroom instruction in a structure that utilizes the academic rigor of Direct Instruction and the effectiveness of Cooperative Learning. These qualities are what convert WBT classrooms into a Community of Practice (Wenger, 2006) in which all students work towards improved learning together.

References

Doyle, W. (2009). Situated practice: a reflection on person-centered classroom management. Theory Into Practice, 48, 156-159.

Johnson, R.T., & Johnson, D.W. (1994). An Overview of cooperative learning. J. Thousand, A. Villa and A. Nevin, (Eds.). Baltimore: Brookes Press.

Karaduz, A. (2010). Linguistic acts teachers use in the classroom: verbal stimuli. Education, 130(4), 696-704.

Kousar, R. (2010). The Effect of direct instruction model on intermediate class achievement and attitudes toward English grammar. Journal of College Teaching & Learning, 7(2), 99-103.

Learning Theories Knowledge base (2010, July). Social Development Theory (Vygotsky) at Learning-Theories.com. Retrieved July 1st, 2010 from http://www.learning-theories.com/vygotskys-social-learning-theory.html

Martinez, M. (2010). Human memory: the basics. Phi Delta Kappan, 91(8), 62-65.

Marzano, R., Pickering, D., & Pollock, J. (2001). Classroom instruction that works: research based strategies for increasing student achievement. Alexandria, VA: Association for Supervision and Curriculum Development.

Pang, K. (2010). Creating stimulating learning and thinking using new models of activity-based learning and metacognitive-based activities. Journal of College Teaching & Learning, 7(4), 29-38.

Saugstad, T. (2002). Educational theory and practice in an Aristotelian perspective. Scandinavian Journal of Educational Research, 46(4), 373-390.

Schunk, D.H. (1999). Social-self interaction and achievement behavior. Educational Psychologist, 34(4), 219-227.

Snowman, J., & Biehler, R. (2003). Psychology applied to teaching. Boston: Houghton Mifflin.

Wenger, E. (2006, June). Communities of practice: a brief introduction. Retrieved from http://www.ewenger.com/theory/

CHAPTER 29

Additional Research

All of WBT's instructional strategies have been rigorously classroom tested, many for over 10 years. Based on feedback that we receive at conferences, on our website and via emails from hundreds of teachers across the country, we are constantly refining our techniques. Our initial, and primary, research goal was to create a system that instructors would willingly adopt. We believe there is a direct correlation between the effectiveness of a classroom management system and an instructor's enthusiastic implementation of the system. Over the last five years, we have asked instructors at the end of our seminars to answer one question:

Compared to other teaching systems that you are familiar with, Whole Brain Teaching is:

    a. much better
    b. better
    c. about the same
    d. worse
    e. much worse

In one of the largest surveys of its kind, we have polled over 2,000 K–12 educators in California, Arizona, Texas, Montana, Louisiana, Minnesota, Missouri, Florida, Pennsylvania, Arkansas, Tennessee and Alabama. The results have been astounding. Seventy percent of instructors rated our system "much better" and 28% rated it "better." The results are close to unanimous; 98% of educators believe WBT is superior to every other teaching system. *We believe no other instructional strategy can match these numbers.*

Our research continues. In poverty level schools in San Jacinto, California in a district that is 98% free and reduced lunch and 80% Hispanic, students' reading scores in WBT classrooms showed a 12% increase, in three months, over students in non-WBT settings. At San Jacinto Elementary, a team of fourth grade teachers achieved significant results using Whole Brain Teaching with over 120 students. As compared with the previous year, math scores on state tests advanced a remarkable 28%.

Individual WBT instructors across the country report their state test scores exceed those of traditional teachers by 20-30%. Three schools in Hemet, California who have adopted WBT have seen decreases in office referrals and suspensions by as much as 50% in a two year period.

In an intriguing new study from Detroit, Michigan, "Integrating Whole Brain Teaching Strategies to Create a More Engaged Learning Environment," Jesame Torres Palasigue evaluated 9 types of student negative behaviors. The behaviors included head on hand or desk, complaining, staring into space, engaging in off task activities, being out of the proper seat. Palasigue measured the frequency of these behaviors with fifth graders before and after the students were introduced to Whole Brain Teaching. Palasigue reports, "Overall, there was a 50% decrease in student negative behaviors from the pre-observation to the post-observation. The frequency of the nine listed behaviors during the pre-observation markedly decreased in the post-observation." Palasigue's study is published online in Education Resources Information Center, the world's largest digital library of education literature.

Linda Mikels, a strong supporter of WBT and principal of 6th Street Prep in Victorville, one of the top ranked elementary schools in California, reports a remarkable increase in API (Academic Performance Index) ratings. Scores soared from 632 in 2002 to 938 in 2009. Mikels attributes a substantial portion of her school's success to her staff's implementation of Whole Brain Teaching. James Dent, principal at Eliot Elementary in Gilroy, California has seen similar progress. 76% of Eliot's students are English Language Learners and 98% qualify for free or reduced lunch. In 2009-2010, Eliot's test scores leaped over 60 points on

California's API scale. Eliot, in one of the poorest neighborhoods of Gilroy is within a few points of closing the achievement gap with some of the wealthiest schools in the area. Dent believes much of his school's recent success is the result of his teachers' use of Whole Brain Teaching.

WHOLE BRAIN TEACHING BY THE NUMBERS

- **80,000** teachers registered at WholeBrainTeaching.com
- **98%** of 2,000+ teachers surveyed ranked WBT superior to any teaching system they had used.
- **3,000,000** views of free WBT videos on YouTube and TeacherTube
- **10,000,000** pages of free materials downloaded from WholeBrainTeaching.com
- **2010:** WholeBrainTeaching.com becomes one of the largest, free, privately financed, education websites in the world.

WHOLE BRAIN TEACHING AND VICTOR ELEMENTARY SCHOOL DISTRICT

As of November 2010, Victor Elementary School District, Victorville, California had 11,704 students, 61.3% Free/Reduced lunch, 20.8% English Language Learners, 74.4% Hispanic/African American students. Below are the API scores of top 9 of 18 schools in VESD: district average of 810 API, one of highest in the state.

938 Sixth Street Prep School

912 Galileo Academy

901 Endeavour Elementary

871 Discovery School of the Arts

866 The Academy of Performing Arts and Foreign Language

831 West Palms Conservatory

824 Lomitas Elementary

801 Brentwood Elementary

801 Del Rey Elementary

"Once in a great while you come across a solid approach that ensures authentic student engagement for mastery learning. Whole Brain Teaching is such an approach. Victor Elementary School District has for well over a decade seen a continued increase in student learning results. Chris Biffle's approach to WBT comes at a time when teachers need fresh skills that quickly engage students for 'bell to bell' instruction. Though teaching always requires a great deal of energy from any teacher, those who have made WBT routine in their classrooms are finding their energy is well spent on mastery learning for all students. Perhaps the most surprising discovery for our team was how impactful WBT is for our English Language Learners. We are finding since WBT engages students in continuous conversations related to their learning (think-pair-share), language development occurs very naturally, and at an amazing rate. Recently, ELL students at one of our highest poverty schools scored over 94% in ELA and Mathematics. And they said it can't be done!"

Dale Marsden, Ed.D. Superintendent,
Victor Elementary School District

CHAPTER 30

BONUS CHAPTER:
Designing Your WBT
Model Classroom

Okay, you're dreamin' of Teacher Heaven and want to set up a WBT Model Classroom... what should you do?

1. Hanky in hand, read this chapter carefully. When you're done, you'll be weeping tears of joy.
2. Read free WBT eBooks at WholeBrainTeaching.com that are appropriate to your grade level, with special emphasis on Power Pix, SuperSpeed games and *The Writing Game*.
3. Begin designing your lesson plans, using the Five Step Lesson Template described in the next chapter.
4. Make weekly posts about your students' progress in the WBT Schools folder on the forum at WholeBrainTeaching.com.
5. Depending on your grade level, send monthly updates to, and ask for advice from, the co-directors of the WBT Model Classroom Project:

   - K-3: Farrah Shipley at FarrahShipley@wholebrainteaching.com
   - 4-12: Deb Weigel at debweigel@wholebrainteaching.com

HOW CAN YOUR CLASSROOM BE CERTIFIED AS A WBT MODEL CLASSROOM?

After following the guidelines below for a year, submit the following to the project directors, Deb Weigel and Farrah Shipley:

1. An essay describing your yearlong use of WBT methods and materials.
2. A 7-10 minute video of your presentation of a WBT lesson (see below) that also presents edited clips of your students energetically engaged in WBT activities.
3. A copy of your state test scores demonstrating, as compared to your previous year's results, significant improvement in your students' achievement.

If our staff believes your classroom successfully represents the best features of Whole Brain Teaching, you will receive a WBT Model Classroom certificate. Your achievement will be advertized in a nationwide announcement to our 50,000 members and prominently featured at WholeBrainTeaching.com. Finally, WBT staff will energetically guide visitors to your remarkable classroom.

WHAT DOES A WBT MODEL CLASSROOM LOOK LIKE?

Each WBT Model Classroom will have the following:

A. Five Classroom Rules: the set of rules custom designed by Saskia Biffle (a whopping 99 cents each in the store at wholebrainteaching.com) are displayed prominently in the front of the room.

B. Scoreboard: a Scoreboard is drawn on your whiteboard. Signs, magnets, or other items may be added to the display to increase visual interest. In the first weeks of the school year, average at least 20 total marks on the Scoreboard per day, never allowing the difference between positive and negative points to be more than three.

C. Power Pix Wall: a wall divided into two sections, math and language arts, contains your growing display of Power Pix. We suggest you teach a minimum of three new Pix per week. For visual emphasis, your walls should have a color coded border or background, for example, blue for language arts, red for math. In addition, the Power Pix should be arranged in numbered rows and lettered columns. Thus, when you have 50 Power Pix posted, you could say to your kids, "Please review all the gestures in rows 1 and 3 of the math Power Pix." Or, "Please review the questions and answers for language arts Power Pix in columns D and E." Power Pix, available as free downloads at WholeBrainTeaching.com, currently exist for over 200 K-3 state standards. Pix for additional concepts, or for higher grades, are simple to create.

- Change a core concept into a question, for example, "What is an essay?"
- Create a kid friendly answer for the question with an accompanying gesture. For example, "An essay is three or more paragraphs on one big subject." Gesture: Hold up three fingers then one finger.
- Put the concept in large type on a sheet of typing paper; after you have taught the concept, place the paper on your Power Pix wall.

D. Seating: Seat your kids in any configuration you wish, horseshoe, rows, etc. but be sure they are assigned partners for Teach-Okay.

E. Super Improvers Team: See Chapter 15 for a complete description of this powerful, motivational strategy.

F. Genius Ladder: Because we believe students' greatest academic weakness is in writing, excellent writing is the core focus of every WBT classroom. The WBT writing program includes four, interrelated components: *The Writing Game* (a free download at WholeBrainTeaching.com), the *Genius Ladder, Wacky Star Fun Button, 10 Minute Writing* (these last three are described in this document).

The Writing Game provides a complete course in writing from sentence construction to essay design.

The *Genius Ladder* gives students daily practice in constructing paragraphs with complex topic sentences.

The *Wacky Star Fun Button* (see section G below] is an oral writing game that provides students with ongoing practice in writing fluency; learning to speak a paragraph vastly simplifies academic writing assignments.

10 Minute Writing (see section H below) is an end of the day writing exercise; we suggest using either a state standard writing prompt or summative writing.

In general, students begin their day with the *Genius Ladder*, use components of *The Writing Game* during the day and employ the oral writing involved in *Wacky Star Fun Button* in all their responses to their teacher and in many of their interchanges with each other. *10 Minute Writing* is every day's "finisher upper."

The *Genius Ladder* is posted on the front board and changes daily. Students work from the bottom of the ladder, simpler sentences, to the top of the ladder, a paragraph. The rungs of the Ladder are:

Genius Paragraph
Extender Sentence
Spicy Sentence
Blah Sentence

Here is a filled in sample. (Note that when used in class, students work from bottom to top, from Blah sentence to Genius Paragraph.)

- *Genius Paragraph:* The crazy boy runs down the street. He looks like he is being chased by a ghost. No one knows what is wrong with him.
- *Extender Sentence:* The crazy boy runs down the street.
- *Spicy Sentence:* The crazy boy runs.
- *Blah Sentence:* The boy runs.

Now let's look at each rung on the ladder.

The Blah sentence, as you can tell, is composed of an article, "the," a noun subject, "boy" and a verb, "runs." Obviously, an infinite number of sentences can be composed using these three simple components. Here are a few more Blah sentences.

The author writes.
A cat crawls.
An Italian smiles.
The car crashes.

(By having students begin with a Blah sentence, teachers can employ a very useful rule for student writing, "No Blah sentences!")

The Spicy sentence adds an adjective, one of the simplest grammatical devices for increasing the flavor of student writing.. Here are some Spicy sentences.

The famous author writes.
A fat cat crawls.
An old Italian smiles.
The red car crashes.

The Extender extends the Spicy sentence and makes it more complex. This category is extremely rich in possibilities. A Spicy sentence could be extended with "because."

The famous author writes because she wants even more fame.

Or, a Spicy sentence could be extended with a prepositional phrase.

The fat cat crawls in the kitchen.

A Spicy sentence could also be extended with a conjunction. "And" and "but" are two of the most useful.

An old Italian smiles but no one sees him.
The red car crashes and turns over.

An adverb could also be used to extend a Spicy sentence.

A fat cat crawls quickly over the kitchen floor.
An old Italian smiles slowly, but no one notices him.

A Spicy sentence could be extended with dependent clauses (note that a sentence can be "extended" by adding information at the beginning, middle or end.)

> *Standing on the corner, an old Italian smiles but no one sees him.*
> *The red car, a 1965 Ford Mustang, crashes and turns over.*
> *The famous author writes novels, though she would rather be fishing.*

At the top rung of the *Genius Ladder*, the Genius Paragraph, several sentences, called Adders, are added to the Extender.

> *The famous author writes novels, though she would rather be fishing.*
> *Adder: Writing novels is hard work but fishing is nothing but fun.*
> *Adder: The main reason the author writes is to make money to buy a big, fast, fishing boat.*
> *Adder: At the end of every day, she spends hours on the Internet exploring great places to fish.*

Adders are defined as any sentence that adds information to a previous sentence. Thus, Adders make up the bulk of student writing. As you can see, as the student moves up the *Genius Ladder*, the sentences advance, quite naturally, from simple to complex. Fairly sophisticated topic sentences can easily be created.

Now, how should the *Genius Ladder* be used in class?

Each day, create a new Ladder. Use any subject you wish, review material, core concepts, vocabulary words, fiction, anything. Begin with a Blah sentence pattern that contains a few words that can be easily amplified.

As you discuss each rung, erase key words and label them with the appropriate part of speech. Thus, a Blah sentence, "The author writes," could become either:

> *The author [verb] _____.*
> *The [noun] _____ writes.*

Students work in pairs, orally filling in the blanks as quickly as possible. These rapid repetitions develop linguistic creativity, giving your students experience in exploring the rich possibilities of even the simplest sentences.

Next move up to the Spicy sentence. Create a new blank and label it "adjective." Let's say your sample Spicy sentence is, "The famous author writes." After discussion about the adjective "famous" insert a blank.

The [adjective] _____ author writes.

Just as with the Blah sentence, students should work in pairs, orally filling in the blank as many times as possible.

Next, move up to the Extender rung, and create another blank.

The famous author writes _____.
The famous author writes because _____.
The famous author writes [prepositional phrase] _____.

Make the Extender quite simple, as in the first sentence above, or specify the type of grammatical structure you want students to create, as in the last sentence. Additional possibilities for the Extender could be dependent clauses inserted at various points in the sentence.

Because _____, the famous author writes novels.
The fat cat, while _____, crawls across the kitchen floor.
In the _____, the old Italian smiles.

Finally, take one of the sentences students have created and write it in the space for the Genius Paragraph. Ask your class to write as many Adders, supporting sentences, following the Extender topic sentence as possible.

The *Genius Ladder* can be made more complex by adding additional rungs. After the Spicy level, you may want to add a rung for conjunctions, compound sentences or appositives. As the year unfolds, redesign your Ladder in whatever way you think best. To explore core concepts, you could even start the bottom rung with one word, for example "author", and simply require students to add three or more words at each rung as they climb upward toward the Genius Paragraph topic sentence.

There are many, powerful advantages to using the *Genius Ladder*. First, because the Ladder begins with the simplest of sentences, it could be started in kindergarten. Using the Ladder's upper rungs, high school and college students could create sophisticated paragraphs. Because every rung of the Ladder, involves filling in blanks, language tasks are perfectly differentiated. Students create sentences at their own level of ability.

Using the Ladder daily for about 5-10 minutes, students learn sentence construction, the difference between a topic sentence and supporting sentences, parts of speech (noun, verb, preposition, conjunction, etc.), a simple technique for constructing complex sentences and well organized paragraphs. In addition, because much of the activity is oral (only the top Genius Paragraph needs to be written) students, over the course of the year, get hundreds, even thousands, of repetitions in language development. Finally, the *Genius Ladder* can be a simple, powerful core to the development of critical thinking, simply by using "because" or "since" as the key word in the Extender students support their assertions with evidence.

G. Oral Writing And The Wacky Star Fun Button

Before describing the potent force of the *Wacky Star Fun Button*, here is a description of Oral Writing:

Oral Writing is an ongoing exercise, across all subjects and classroom activities, that teaches students how to speak well organized paragraphs as an aid to academic writing.

Oral Writing begins with any question you ask a student.

How was your summer?
What is an end mark?
What do you know about the Amazon?
How should we line up at recess?

Students respond with a complete sentence that includes words in the answer from the question.

This summer I went surfing.
An end mark goes at the end of a sentence.
The Amazon is a big river.
We should line up quietly.

When you ask a question, any question, and students don't respond with a complete sentence, prompt them to try again by smiling and cupping your hand to your ear ("I didn't hear your complete sentence.")

When students have mastered this step, and whenever you want them to add a detail sentence, point your forefingers at each other and spin them in circles ("Give me more.") You are prompting your kids to supply an Adder to their topic sentence.

> *This summer I went surfing. It was lots of fun.*
> *An end mark goes at the end of a sentence. A period is an end mark.*
> *The Amazon is a big river. The Amazon is in South America.*
> *We should line up quietly. If we line up quietly, we will get more time to play.*

As the year unfolds, prompt students to continue to supply Adders by spinning your forefingers, indicating you want more detail sentences. You will probably note that as students become more verbally fluent, they will speak run-ons. To correct this, ask that they end each sentence with an Air Period; jutting their hand forward as if giving a stop signal, they say "errrrt!"... a sound like putting on the brakes. When you note that a student is starting to speak a run on... give the Air Period prompt yourself.

If your students need reminders to start sentences with a capital letter, teach them a capital letter prompt. We prefer putting one hand on top of the other and then lifting the top hand rapidly, to show that a capital is a "large letter."

When students are able to speak short paragraphs with several Adders, teach them the Concluder. A Concluder always begins with either, "In conclusion, " or "To sum up," (and is followed by an air comma... swipe your finger in the air as if making a comma and say, "zoop!").

> *This summer I went surfing. It was lots of fun. I learned how to ride big waves and how to body surf. We spent most of our time at Huntington Beach. In conclusion, I had a blast this summer.*

The prompt for the Concluder is waving one hand above the other, as if signaling "safe... the play is over!"

Note that Oral Writing follows a pattern similar to the *Genius Ladder*, except that Oral Writing starts "at the top" with a topic sentence that is supplemented with Adders, detail sentences.

Initially, as a guide to Oral Writing, put the following on the board:

Question ➜ *Answer*

When this pattern is mastered, add the next step:

Question ➜ *Answer* ➜ *Adders*

Finally, complete the diagram.

Question ➜ *Answer* ➜ *Adders* ➜ *Concluder*

When students have mastered this pattern, and even kindergarteners can learn to speak short paragraphs, you're ready to gain maximum benefit from oral writing. When you wish, pose a question to the class. Students repeat the question to a partner; the partner, using gestures for Adders and Concluders speaks a paragraph as answer. Then, the students switch roles. The Answerer becomes the Questioner and the Questioner becomes the Answerer. In effect, the Answerer is self prompting with Oral Writing gestures.

For example, you have completed a lesson on nouns. Then you ask, "What is a noun?" Students who are Questioners repeat the question; students who are Answerers use Oral Writing gestures to guide themselves through an answer.

For additional complexity, use the following specialized Adders (suggested gestures are in parentheses).

Adjective Adder (kiss you finger tips, and then expand your fingers, as if you were a French chef... adjectives are deliciously spicy.) An Adjective Adder contains, logically enough, an adjective.

Conjunction Adder (link two fingers on one hand with two fingers on the other hand). Teach students that they can use one of three conjunctions as an Adder: and, or, but.

Also Adder (point your forefingers at each other, just as for the Adder gesture, but spin them super fast ... to show that "also" is a Super Adder).

"Also" is an excellent transition to use in mid-paragraph. Teach students to begin a sentence with "also" and then add an air comma... "Also, "

Prepositional Phrase Adder (bring your two hands up, as if you were a squirrel)... prepositions are "squirrel words"... they describe anything an squirrel can do in relation to a log ... over, under, beside, through, on, etc. If a sentence begins with a prepositional phrase, then the phrase should be followed by a an air comma.

For Example Adder (using one hand pretend as if you were pulling an idea out of the top of your head). The For Example Adder should always be followed by an air comma... "For example,... "

We believe one of the most important Adders is "because." When you are ready for your students to add a critical thinking component to Oral Writing, teach them the Because Clapper. To indicate that you want your kids to use "because" as their next Adder, clap your hands once. When students say the word "because" they clap their hands once, congratulating themselves. Many kindergarteners use "because" clappers at home!

Here are two problems that may develop with Oral Writing and easy solutions. First, when you are modeling Oral Writing, you may ask a child for an Adder and she is stumped. Teach your kids that whenever they need help, they should simply exclaim "Help me!" and throw up their arms. This is a cue for the entire class to call out suggestions for whatever Oral Writing task is troubling one of their peers. Or, if you sense a student needs help and has forgotten "Help me!" call out, "Help her!" and the rest of the class will immediately chime in. This prompt, "Help me!" creates a marvelous opportunity for the class to participate in Oral Writing. In addition, it establishes a no-failure atmosphere of mutual support. (Occasionally, you may pretend that you don't know the next step in a lesson and call out "Help me!"; your students will be only too eager to pitch in with assistance.)

A second problem that may develop with Oral Writing is that, as the student speaks, he gets off topic. The more Adders that you require, the more opportunity there will be for information that does not directly relate to the topic sentence. Thus, as the student speaks, slowly walk your fingers down from your wrist toward your elbow. With each Adder, let your fingers take another "step." The instant a student speaks an Adder that is off topic, leap your fingers off your arm, exclaim "Aieeee!" as if you were falling through the air and say, "Oh no! You fell off topic!" If all students are mirroring your finger walking, this will be an ongoing lesson in the simple, but crucial writing skill... every sentence in a paragraph must be on topic, directly linked to the first sentence.

After your students have mastered the Oral Writing routine, then the student who asks the question uses her fingers walking down her arm, as she listens to the Answerer create an answer.

When you are ready for your students to start speaking essays, put an essay frame like the following on the board. (This example would be used at the end of the day.)

Q. What did we learn today?
Today we learned three (things, facts, skills). First, _____.
Second, _____. Third, _____.

    The first (thing, fact, skill) we learned was _____. [add several Adders.]

    The second (thing, fact, skill) we learned was _____. [add several Adders.]

    The third (thing, fact, skill) we learned was _____. [add several Adders.]

    In conclusion, _____. [add several Adders.]

The main challenge with Oral Writing is that it initially involves only one student prompted by the teacher. Once the pattern is learned, as noted above, divide your class into ones and twos. The ones are the teachers; the twos are the students. The ones ask questions you have provided; the twos answer, self prompting with gestures. When you shout "Switch!" your class responds, "Switch" and the twos become the prompting teachers and the ones become the responding students.

Obviously, an excellent source for questions posed by you or your students would be writing prompts from state standards tests.

Now, where does the *Wacky Star Fun Button* fit in to Oral Writing? Almost everything we do in WBT, as noted by Heather Hansen, WBT Intern, is either a game or leads to a game. Oral Writing is a powerful learning activity but to deepen student involvement, we need to make Oral Writing fun.

In the front of your room, put a large red circle labeled *Wacky Star Fun Button*. When you "push" the button with your finger, your students get to make wacky noises until you "let go" of the button. You can use season appropriate wacky noises... Horrible Halloween Howls... Thanksgiving Turkey Gobble Calls... or simply wacky animal noises ,weird space alien exclamations, imaginary insect squawks. Kids love to make weird sounds! Use the Scoreboard to train your kids that they must stop making their wacky noises as soon as you take your finger off the button. Making wacky noises may be so hysterically entertaining that it could be difficult to quiet your kids. Thus, we suggest that you only push the *Wacky Star Fun Button* right before recess, lunch or at the end of the day.

As Oral Writing proceeds successfully in class, occasionally walk over to the *Wacky Star Fun Button* and make one line of a star. Little by little, during the day, when students are successfully employing Oral Writing continue to add small parts to your star. You can draw this out as long as you wish... several days if you so desire. When the star is completed, always right before students leave for recess, lunch or home, dramatically push the *Wacky Star Fun Button* and let your class briefly erupt in wacky noises. Oink! Bow wow! Baaa! Mooo! Meow! Caw! Caw!

Other variations might be to give a few student leaders their own *Wacky Star Fun Button* and direct them when to push it... or let an outstanding student come up to the front and briefly push the hysteria inducing button.

And so, what is the connection between the *Genius Ladder*, Oral Writing and *The Writing Game*?

Climbing the *Genius Ladder*, students create ever more sophisticated grammatical constructions which they verbally rehearse daily in Oral Writing ... and employ in actual writing in *The Writing Game*.

H. Ten Minute Writing: Because we believe writing is the crucial intellectual skill, we think every day should conclude with a writing exercise. As St. Augustine remarked, "I write to learn what I know." We favor two kinds of tasks:

- grade level writing prompts, similar to those on state tests
- summative writing: "What did you learn today?" "What are two skills you learned today?" "What are three subjects we covered today?"

You can make the above tasks as simple or complex as you wish. Include sentence and paragraph frames if students need more structure. For example, here are frames, from easy to challenging, that might be used for summative writing:

- Today I learned _____. (Add more sentences about what you learned.)
- Today I learned _____ and _____. (Add more sentences about the first thing you learned. Then add more sentences about the second thing you learned.)
- Today I learned two skills. The first skill was _____. (Add more sentences about the first skill.) The second skill was _____. (Add more sentences about the second skill.)
- Today we covered three subjects. The first subject was _____. (Add several sentences about the first subject). The second subject was _____. (Add several sentences about the second subject.) The third subject was _____. (Add several sentences about the subject.)
- Our day was divided into three parts. First, _____. Second, _____. Third, _____.
(Write a 3-5 sentence paragraph about the first part of today.)
(Write a 3-5 sentence paragraph about the second part of today.)
(Write a 3-5 sentence paragraph about the third part of today.)
(Write a three sentence concluding paragraph.)

As a motivator for outstanding focus during *10 Minute Writing*, use the *Wacky Star Fun Button*. Oh gosh! Maybe we get to make Weird Imaginary Animal Noises before we leave for home!

To assist students in writing carefully, use Red-Green Marker Dots.

Tell students you will be checking their work for one kind of error, for example, messiness. Walk around the room with a red marker and a green marker. Put a red mark by each student's messiest word and a green mark by their neatest word. As the days unfold, add to the features you will be marking on student papers. Here is a suggested list:

1. Name and date in upper right corner
2. Neatness
3. Word spacing
4. End marks
5. Consecutive sentences do not start with the same word.
6. No sentence starts with "and" or contains more than one "and."
7. Three sentence minimum per paragraph (can be adjusted for grade level)
8. Five sentence maximum per paragraph
9. Five words minimum per sentence. (eliminates many "blah" sentences... can be adjusted for grade level)
10. Twelve word maximum per sentence (eliminates many run-ons ... can be adjusted for grade level)

Note that almost any student at any level can be expected to correctly follow these rules. As the year unfolds, add more complex rules about misspellings, fragments and sentence construction that are more difficult to follow.

Two last proofreading suggestions. First, when you are proofreading for all 10 items, give each student a copy of the list above. When you mark a red dot on a student's paper, she puts an X beside the rule that was broken. Thus, as you walk around the classroom, the list of rules gives you a differentiated guide of the kinds and frequency of each student's errors.

Second, when you are ready to teach students to proofread their own papers, give each kid a paperclip. The paperclip is attached to the side of the student's paper, pointing at the first rule. Students proofread by tapping items on their paper that follow each rule (making corrections as necessary). When you are satisfied that your kids have checked for a rule, ask them to move the paperclip down to the next rule... and start tapping and checking!

I. Mind Soccer Posters: To generate anticipation, before you introduce Mind Soccer to your kids, slowly, over a period of several weeks, put up one or two Mind Soccer posters on your wall (available as free downloads at WholeBrainTeaching.com)

WHAT IS A WBT DAILY SCHEDULE?

After your students are settled, begin the day with a review of the classroom rules. Repeat this review as necessary; we suggest rule rehearsal may be appropriate after each recess and after lunch. As students gain familiarity, use student leaders from the Super Improvers Team for these recitations.

One of the first tasks every morning is checking for one, two, or three star homework (see WBT Homework Model below).

Review, for a few minutes, Power Pix questions, answers and gestures several times per day.

At some point in the morning, guide a discussion of the *Genius Ladder*.

A key part of the daily routine for every WBT Model Classroom is Prove It! We've adapted this game from Sixth St. Prep, in Victorville California, one of the top ranked elementary schools in California. Developed by former principal Linda Mikels, Prove It! is a key component in their remarkable test scores.

Students spend 20 minutes every morning playing Prove It! using sample questions from state tests, 10 minutes for math and 10 minutes for language arts. Using a computer projector, students employ test taking strategies (each school should decide which are best) to answer multiple choice questions. In addition to proving one answer is correct, students must prove the other answers are incorrect. With individual white boards, students write out their reasons (in their own shorthand ... it takes too long to write complete sentences for each answer) for identifying right and wrong answers. They compare their analysis with their neighbors and, at the teacher's request, hold up the results on their white boards. In essence, Prove It! gives students daily, intensive, critical thinking practice in answering the kinds of questions they will be faced with at the end of the year.

At least once per day, and usually more often, students should be setting personal records while playing one of WBT's speed games: SuperSpeed Numbers, SuperSpeed Letters and Phonics, SuperSpeed 100, SuperSpeed Math or Complexors (found in *The Writing Game*, a download under "Free Ebooks" at our website). Every student should have a log where they can easily track their progress while playing these games. Here are grade level suggestions:

K-1: SuperSpeed Numbers, SuperSpeed Letters and Phonics, Smoothy Bumper Planet

2nd-3rd: SuperSpeed 100 or SuperSpeed 1000, SuperSpeed Math, Complexors.

4th-6th: SuperSpeed 1000, SuperSpeed Math, Complexors

Secondary Language Arts: SuperSpeed 1000, Complexors
Secondary Math: SuperSpeed Math (including SuperSpeed Fractions)

Students will be strongly motivated to increase their basic skills in language arts and math as they see their scores in the WBT speed games steadily improving. Students who make significant improvement in the speed, should be recognized on the Student Super Improvers Team.

Every 5-10 minutes during the day, and more often if necessary, mark a positive or negative mark on the Scoreboard. Use the Ping Pong strategy described in the WBT Manual as necessary.

Use the 5 step Lesson Template described at the end of this document to introduce new material.

All through the day, use Teach-Okay whenever you communicate with your class. Keep your presentations, micro-lectures, in the 15-45 second range. Write Teach-Okay units into your lesson plans. Make a note to yourself where you should be using Mirror, Mirror Words, Hands and Eyes, and Switch.

Orally time all transition activities. See the WBT Manual for directions in how to quickly hand papers out and in, get students seated, lined up, etc.

In the first weeks, use more or less recess time as your Scoreboard reward. See the WBT Manual for additional motivators.

Several times a day, have your students review concepts on the Power Pix wall. Review can include question, answer, gestures, Oral Writing or a higher order thinking skill like comparing and contrasting two Power Pix.

All through the day, students practice Oral Writing for the thrill of having the *Wacky Star Fun Button* pushed.

HOW DO YOU EVALUATE CLASSROOM MANAGEMENT PROGRESS?

As described in the WBT Manual, at the end of the first week, divide your class into Alphas, Go-Alongs, Fence Sitters and Challenging Kids. Update your classroom management score weekly. Also, use the self scoring system described in the manual to keep tabs on your own behavior.

WHAT IS A WBT YEARLY SCHEDULE?

Start the Scoreboard in week one and the Super Improvers Team in week two. Use these two powerful motivators for as long as possible; Thanksgiving is a good target. Try to stay at the Scoreboard level for as long as possible; Thanksgiving is a good target. Then, after Thanksgiving, introduce the White Practice Cards. After 2-4 weeks, add the Purple Practice Cards and then, later, the Green Practice Cards if a few students need in-class guidance. After New Year's, move to Level 4, the Guff Counter; then as needed, add Level 5, the Independents, Level 6, the BullsEye Game and Level 7, the Agreement Bridge.

But remember... it's your class! Mix up the Levels if you believe it will help your kids. For example, to take care of persistent backtalk, you may want to introduce Level 4, the Guff Counter, a few weeks before Christmas. Don't worry. The WBT Police will not visit your classroom, though we may occasionally look in the window.

Use material from *The Writing Game*, *The Genius Ladder* and Oral Writing as soon as you begin writing instruction.

Begin using the SuperSpeed games in math and language arts daily after the second week of school. The reward for these games should be intrinsic. Simply encourage students to celebrate when they break personal records and record their success in their personal record log. If you wish, after Christmas, give students award certificates for their success (but no candy, stickers, or cheesy trinkets!).

WHAT IS THE WBT HOMEWORK MODEL?

There is considerable evidence that the amount of homework assigned has almost no correlation to the amount that students learn in elementary school, and very little correlation, in middle and high school. (See, *The Case Against Homework* by Sara Bennett and Nancy Kalis.) Nonetheless, at WBT we are not yet ready to abandon the homework ship; we want students to be motivated to do, at minimum, about half an hour of work every night building basic skills.

In essence, we think there are five core components of any successful homework package:

1. Free reading for at least 20 minutes
2. Increasing reading fluency with a reading speed exercise
3. Increasing math fluency with a math speed exercise
4. Recording results for 1-3 in a homework log
5. Recognizing significant improvements in reading and math on the Student Super Improvers Team.

Only 100 words, called sight words, make up 50% of all the words children read. The more quickly children master sight words, the more enjoyable their reading experience. To increase reading speed, kindergarteners should review *Biffytoons Minis* with their parents for about 5 minutes per evening. Higher grades can simply read the first 100 words of *SuperSpeed 1000* as quickly as possible and record their times in their homework log.

To increase math fluency, kindergarteners should spend time working with parents on *Smoothy Bumper Planet*. Higher grades should be assigned to play one of the games in SuperSpeed Math. Kids should time themselves to see how quickly they can complete one of the pages (teacher's choice) in addition, subtraction, multiplication, division, gnarlies or fractions.

Students love to set and break personal records and, with some help from their teacher, they can find enjoyable material for free reading. Thus, the homework assignment we suggested above will be far more pleasant than filling in worksheets!

Recognizing students who dramatically break personal records using the photo system as described in the Super Improvers Team section will provide many students with irresistible motivation to work hard at home on reading and math.

Our strategy for increasing homework completion, the Universal Homework Model (UHM), is simple. The completion rate of homework by students determines the number of minutes the class will play Mind Soccer on Fridays. Please take our word for it... Mind Soccer is so hysterically fun, kids will do almost anything to play... and it involves nothing but fast paced academic review!

In addition to using Mind Soccer as the reward, the key feature of UHM is that there are three levels of homework. Students choose their level. However, we can't use the term "levels" because that concept is part of our classroom management system. Thus, we'll use stars.

One Star Homework: As many times as you wish, try to improve your speed in reading the first 100 sight words in SuperSpeed 1000. Then, as many times as you wish, see how quickly you can orally complete an assigned page in SuperSpeed Math. Next, read for 20 minutes. In your homework log, record your best times for SuperSpeed 1000, SuperSpeed Math and the amount of time you spent reading. Ask your parents to sign your log.

Two Star Homework: Complete your homework log as above, have it signed by your parents; write your teacher a one page letter describing what you read.

Three Star Homework: Complete your homework log as above, write your teacher a one page "sloppy copy" letter describing what you read and then, in your neatest handwriting, create a masterpiece letter to your teacher describing what you read.

As the year unfolds, we suggest adding easy to check rules for the masterpiece letter: no paragraphs longer than five sentences or shorter than three, no sentences shorter than five words... etc. All the rules should be adjusted by grade level; we have no problem if the rules are so easy to check, that teachers simply thumb through the homework assignments.

Now, how would UHM work in class?

After the five classroom rules have been reviewed, the teacher asks the kids to stand who completed One Star homework. She counts the students and gives the class one point for each homework completion. Next, the kids stand who did Two Star homework and hold it over their head. Everyone applauds! The teacher counts the standing students and gives the class two points for each Two Star completion. Finally, the kids stand who did Three Star homework and hold it over their heads and WAVE it! Everyone claps and cheers! Oh, all the kids are so happy! The standing students bask in the glory of earning so many points for their whole class! The teacher counts the standing kids and gives the class three points for each completion. The score is added up and posted on the board.

To determine how long your kids get to play Mind Soccer on Friday, use this scale.

- 80% of total possible points for Three Star Homework = 3 minutes of Mind Soccer
- 60% of total possible points for Three Star Homework = 2 minutes of Mind Soccer
- 40% of total possible points for Three Star Homework = 1 minutes of Mind Soccer.

Thus, assume you have 30 students and 4 homework assignments in a week and everyone (!) does Three Star Homework. This would give your class a total of 360 possible points. Your scale, which you should put on the front board, would be:

360-288 = 3 minutes of Mind Soccer
287-216 = 2 minutes of Mind Soccer
215-144 = 1 minute of Mind Soccer
less than 144 = 1 minute less, last recess on Friday

The penalty in the last line, is optional.

The timing on Friday should be very strict... use a kitchen timer with a loud buzzer. Stop the instant the buzzer sounds; you want your kids begging to play longer. "Oh sorry! I hope we have lots of Three Star homeworks next week. Tell your neighbor how many Three Star homeworks you're going to do!"

As you can tell, the UHM system has quite a bit of fun and peer pressure built into it. Imagine what class feels like on Thursday at the end of the day.

The teacher looks at the homework score, quickly figures out how many points are needed to get three minutes of Mind Soccer for the next day. Oh no! Almost everyone has to do Three Star homework! Who is willing to volunteer??? For recognition (i.e. accountability) the teacher puts the names of these volunteers on the board. Some kids are so desperate for recognition, they ask "What is four star homework?!" Natural leaders and outsiders, exactly the two groups we want to reach, will be among the main volunteers to do extra homework to gain their peers' esteem.

To make homework completion even easier to evaluate, assign homework captains who check the homework log for each student, each day. Juan stood up for One Star homework; the captain checks and sees Juan was being honest and records 1 star in Monday's box on the log. At the end of the week, each student's homework, with the log on top, is stapled together and handed in to the instructor. Students who only completed One Star homework all week, would only turn in one page, the homework log.

The only problem we see in this system is easy to solve. You may have some students so motivated by the rewards of completing their homework that they fib about their personal records in SuperSpeed 1000 and SuperSpeed Math. Give a few student leaders stopwatches and ask them, occasionally, to time students to see if they are as capable at school, of matching records they claim to set at home.

When you note dramatic, legitimate improvements in the SuperSpeed games, reward students by recognition on the Student Super Improvers Team.

WHAT DO YOUR KIDS NEED?

Student supplies in a WBT Model Classroom are, thankfully, fairly cheap. You will need a class set of small whiteboards to use in Prove It! Student folders should contain the WBT materials every child will use, SuperSpeed games, mini-Biffytoons, pages from *The Writing Game*, a homework log, blank pages where students record their writing from the *Genius Ladder* and *The Writing Game*. Most importantly, every student folder should have a page where students record personal and team records that they set while playing SuperSpeed and Complexors in *The Writing Game*.

We've found that nothing motivates a class more and promotes more learning per minute than having students set and break records ... think of these speed games as a Mind Olympics in which all students have a daily chance to win, simply by beating their own previous best.

THE MODEL CLASSROOM CHECKLIST

Every room should (eventually) contain:
1. Five rules posters
2. Power Pix displays for math and language arts
3. Scoreboard
4. Super Improvers Team
5. *Genius Ladder*
6. Oral Writing diagram

7. *Wacky Star Fun Button*
8. Mind Soccer Posters
9. Class homework points

The daily schedule should (eventually) include:
1. Rules rehearsals (initially, first task in the morning, after lunch and after each recess)
2. Homework check and points totaling
3. Genius Ladder
4. Prove It!
5. Personal record setting and recording: SuperSpeed and Complexors
6. Oral writing (and the occasional activation of the *Wacky Star Fun Button*)
7. Frequent marks (initially at least 40 per day) on the Scoreboard
8. Timed transitions
9. Frequent review of the Power Pix wall
10. Units from *The Writing Game* (as needed)
11. End of the day *10 Minute Writing*

Your instruction should include:
1. The Big Seven: Class-yes, class rules, teach-okay, scoreboard, hands and eyes, mirror, switch
2. Teach-okay units in the 20-45 second range
3. Oral writing prompts
4. Five step lessons (see following section)
5. Recognition of student improvement on the Super Improvers Team
6. A merry grin

CHAPTER 31

BONUS CHAPTER:
The Five Step WBT Lesson Template

Recently, my colleagues and I at WBT put together a very useful addition to our teaching techniques, a five step lesson template. Here are the five steps:

Step 1 Question: Ask a question.

Step 2 Answer: Give the answer to the question, in kid friendly language, accompanied by a gesture.

Step 3 Expand: Expand the answer with examples, Brain Toys, diagrams, explanations.

Step 4 Test: Test for comprehension with the Yes-No Way, QT or other tests.

In the Yes-No Way test, the teacher asks a question. For example, "Is 'boy' a noun?" If the answer is "yes," students pump their fists and exclaim "yes!" If the answer is "no" students point their fingers at their foreheads and then extend their arms outward, exclaiming in disbelief, "no way!" The Yes-No Way test provides teachers with a rapid, visual overview of students' comprehension.

A second test used in our 5 step template is the Quick Test, abbreviated QT. The teacher says, "QT"; students respond, "Cutie!" and cover their eyes. The teacher makes true/false statements. For example, "A noun is a person, place or action word." If the answer is true, students silently give a thumbs up gesture. If the answer is false, students silently give a thumbs down gesture. QT provides a rapid, clear picture of individual student's understanding. If 90% of the class passes both tests, the teacher should go on to Step 5 below. If not, the teacher should cycle back to Step 3 above and reteach the concept with new material.

Step 5 Critical Thinking: The teacher gives students tasks that require they use what they have learned in a critical thinking context. A key component of these tasks often involves writing. Here are some typical assignments.

- Employ the concept in each of the sentence types on the *Genius Ladder*.
- Write a letter to the aliens on Planet Zork explaining the concept.
- Write several sentences that compare and contrast the current concept (for example, noun) with previous concepts (verb, adjective, preposition)
- Use the current concept in as many sentences as possible that also contain the word "because."

In addition students could explain the concept to their neighbor with a collection of Brain Toys.

For a video example of the Five Step Template, see Farrah Shipley's superb demo at: http://www.youtube.com/user/ChrisBiffle

WHAT ARE SOME SAMPLE FIVE STEP LESSONS?

Your First WBT Lesson

(This simple, entertaining lesson will teach the following: Rule 1, Rule 1 gesture, following directions quickly, Class-Yes, Mirror, Mighty Groan, Mighty Oh Yeah, Help me!, Yes-No Way, QT and critical thinking sentence frames!)

Rule 1

Step 1 Question: What is Rule 1?

Step 2 Answer: Rule 1 is "Follow directions quickly!" (Gesture: raise one finger and then waggle your hand rapidly forward through the air.)

Step 3 Explain: Give examples of what it means to follow directions quickly.

1. You say, "Rule 1" and your students, making the Rule 1 gesture, rapidly say, "Follow directions quickly!" and are sitting up straight with their hands folded.
2. You say, "Class!" Your students rapidly respond, "Yes!" and are sitting up straight with their hands folded.
   Repeat steps 1-2.
3. You say, "Mirror!" Your students rapidly respond, "Mirror!" and lift their hands, mirroring your gestures.

Repeat steps 1-3

4. You say, "Mighty Groan!" and your students rapidly lift their shoulders, groan and then are sitting up straight with their hands folded.
5. You say, "Mighty Oh Yeah!" and your students rapidly clap their hands and exclaim, "Oh Yeah!" and then are sitting up straight with their hands folded.

Repeat steps 1-5

6. You count to five and then , raising your hands, exclaim, "Help me!" and your students rapidly respond, "Six!" Repeat this routine for other numbers, the alphabet, etc.

Repeat steps 4-6

7. Teach your students that when you clap twice and say "Teach!", they rapidly clap twice, say "Okay!" and turn to their neighbors.

Repeat steps above as needed.

Step 4 Test: Students respond "Yes" or "No Way" (with emphatic gestures) to the following questions:

- Is Rule 1 follow directions slowly?
- Is Rule 1 follow directions kinda fast?
- Is Rule 1 follow directions quickly?
- If I say "Class!" do you say, "What?"
- If I say "Mirror!" do you say, "Mirror?"
- Is this the Rule 1 gesture? (make various gestures)

If the 90% of the class answers correctly, use the QT test with the following True/False statements.

- Rule 1 is follow directions quickly.
- If I clap twice and say "Teach!" you clap twice and say, "Okay!"
- When I, or anyone else, says "Help me!" you should give that person your help.
- We use Rule 1 in many classroom activities.
- When we give a Mighty Groan, we clap our hands.
- When we give a Mighty Oh Yeah, we clap our hands.

If at least 90% of your students passed the QT test then go on to step 5. If not, return and reteach Step 3 with new materials.

Step 5 Critical Thinking:

Complete these sentence frames, first by speaking, then by writing, as many times as possible:

- Using examples of Rule 1, complete each sentence type in the *Genius Ladder*.
- An example of following directions quickly would be _____.
- Rule 1 is fun because _____.
- If I was a teacher, I would (or would not) use Rule 1 because _____.
- Play Zork: Write a letter to the aliens on Planet Zork. Using examples they could understand, explain Rule 1.
- Use Sockless Hand Puppets, then the Air Blackboard, then Props, then Action Figures to explain Rule 1 to your neighbor.

At the end of the lesson, post a sheet of typing paper with the word "Rule 1" on the Power Pix wall (or, use the custom designed signs available in the store at WholeBrainTeaching.com).

Noun

Step 1 Question: What is a noun?

Step 2 Answer: A noun is a person, place or thing (for gestures, point to yourself for "person," sweep your arms around the room for "place," knock on a desk for "thing").

Step 3 Explain: Give other examples of nouns. Ask students to point to nouns in the room. Then, ask students to find nouns in a list of verbs, nouns and adjectives on the board. Ask them to explain why a word on the list is, or isn't ,a noun using "because" in their explanation.

Step 4 Test: Students respond "Yes" or "No Way" (with emphatic gestures) to the following questions:
- Is "boy" a noun?
- Is "run" a noun?
- Is "happy" a noun?
- Is "tree" a noun?
- Is "school" a noun?
- Is "eating" a noun?

If 90% of the class answers correctly, use the QT test with the following True/False statements.
- Every noun is a person, place or activity.
- Every noun is a person, thing or adjective.
- Every noun is a person, place or thing.
- "Desk" is a noun.
- "Running" is a noun.
- There are two nouns in the following sentence: "The boy went home."

If at least 90% of your students passed the QT test then go on to step 5. If not, return and reteach Step 3 with new materials.

Step 5 Critical Thinking: Students complete one or more of the following exercises:

- Given a noun, for example "dog," complete each sentence type in the *Genius Ladder*.
- Talk to your neighbor and compare and contrast verbs and nouns.
- Write simple sentences and underline each noun.
- Play Zork: Write a letter to the aliens on Planet Zork. Using examples they could understand, explain the Earthling word, "noun."
- Use Sockless Hand Puppets, then the Air Blackboard, then Props, then Action figures to explain nouns to your neighbor.

At the end of the lesson, post a sheet of typing paper with the word "noun" on the Power Pix wall.

Verb

Step 1 Question: What is a verb?

Step 2 Answer: A verb is an action word. (gesture: pump your arms as if you are running.)

Step 3 Expand: Provide examples of verbs. Ask students to give each other original examples of verbs. Tell students to find verbs in a list of verbs, nouns and adjectives on the board. Ask them to explain why a word on the board is, or isn't, a verb using "because" in their explanation.

Step 4 Test: Students respond "Yes" or "No Way" (with emphatic gestures) to the following questions:

- Is "running" a verb?
- Is "ate" a verb?
- Is "dog" a verb?
- Is "pencil" a verb?
- Is "wrote" a verb?
- Is "sleeping" a verb?

If 90% of the class responds correctly, use the QT test with the following True/False statements.

- Every verb is a person, place or thing.
- Verbs are action words.
- "Blue" is a verb.
- "to eat" is a verb.
- "Running" is a verb.
- There are two verbs in the sentence, "I ate beans at home."

If at least 90% of your students passed the QT test then go on to step 5. If not, return and reteach Step 3 with new materials.

Step 5 Critical Thinking: Students complete one or more of the following exercises.

- Given a subject and verb, for example "Pedro runs...", complete each of the sentence types in the *Genius Ladder*.
- Talk to your neighbor and compare and contrast verbs and nouns.
- Play Zork: Write a letter to the aliens on Planet Zork. Using examples they could understand, explain the Earthling word, "verb."
- Use Sockless Hand Puppets, then the Air Blackboard, then Props, then Action figures to explain verbs to your neighbor.

At the end of the lesson, post a sheet of typing paper with the word "verb" on the Power Pix wall.

Multiplying Fractions

Step 1 Question: How do we multiply fractions?

Step 2 Answer: We multiply fractions across and then we reduce the answer if possible. (Make an X by crossing your forearms when you say "multiply" and then wave one hand horizontally when you say "across;" pinch your fingers together when you say "reduce.")

Step 3 Expand: Work sample fraction multiplication problems on the board. Use "Help me!" as a cue for students to tell you the next step.

Have pairs of students work together, with one student being the "captain" and the other student being the "rookie." The captain tells the rookie what to do; the rookie follows the captain's instructions by writing and solving fraction multiplication problems. After several minutes, students switch roles.

Step 4 Test: Students respond "Yes" or "No Way" (with emphatic gestures) to the following questions:
- Is this the multiplying fractions gesture? (use several gestures)
- When multiplying fractions do we ever use addition?
- When multiplying fractions do we ever use subtraction?
- When multiplying fractions do we multiply numerators and denominators?
- Can every answer of a multiplying fractions problem be reduced?

If 90% of the class responds correctly, use the QT test with the following True/False statements.
- Multiplying fractions is the same as adding fractions.
- To reduce an answer, we must use division.
- The top number in a fraction is called the denominator.
- 1/3 times 1/3 is 1/6. (add other problems simple enough for students to do in their heads.)

If at least 90% of your students passed the QT test then go on to step 5. If not, return and reteach Step 3 with new materials.

Step 5 Critical Thinking: Students complete one or more of the following exercises.
- Write sentences that compare and contrast adding fractions and multiplying fractions.
- Write a paragraph that could be used in a textbook, describing how to multiply fractions.
- Write a letter to your cousin Doofus describing how to multiply fractions. Use simple examples and labeled diagrams that even Doofus could understand.
- Play Zork: Write an email to the aliens on Planet Zork. Using ex-

amples they could understand, explain the Earthling word, "fraction." Then, write another email explaining how to multiply fractions.

- Use Sockless Hand Puppets, then the Air Blackboard, then Props, then Action Figures to explain how to multiply fractions to your neighbor.

At the end of the lesson, the teacher posts a sheet of typing paper with the word "multiplying fractions" on the Power Pix wall.

Handing In Papers

Step 1 Question: How do we hand in papers?

Step 2 Answer: We hand in papers as quickly as possible to the paper captains; the paper captains stack the papers neatly on the teacher's desk. (Use gestures to demonstrate how quickly papers are handed in. Then tap on your desk indicating where papers should be stacked.)

Step 3 Expand: Let students practice the right and wrong way to hand in papers.

Step 4 Test: Using a practice stack of papers, time your class to see how quickly they can hand in papers. After several tries, put their best time on the board as the class record.

Step 5 Critical Thinking: Students complete one or more of the following exercises.
- Employing each sentence type in the *Genius Ladder*, describe the correct way to hand in papers.
- Ask students to evaluate the current plan for handing in papers. Then, give them time to write a new design for handing in papers. The new design should include a way to test the plan's effectiveness. Encourage suggestions that would make the procedure fun… students cheering, clapping, finger snapping, chanting.

At the end of the lesson, post a sheet of typing paper with the words "Handing in papers" on the Power Pix wall.

Note that almost any lesson can be put into these five steps. Virtually every state standard could be set up as a question which requires an answer, an expanded explanation, comprehension tests and critical thinking tasks.

Now, how would the five step template fit into the Teach-Okay pattern? Simple! Every step begins with "Class" and ends with "Teach!"

Look at the following diagram:

Say "Class!"	Step 1: Pose a Question	Clap Twice, Say "Teach!"
Say "Class!"	Step 2: Give Answer with Gesture(s)	Clap Twice, Say "Teach!"
Say "Class!"	Step 3: Expand the Answer	Clap Twice, Say "Teach!"
Say "Class!"	Step 4: Test for Comprehension	Clap Twice, Say "Teach!"
Say "Class!"	Step 5: Give Critical Thinking Tasks	Clap Twice, Say "Teach!"

Here are three important points. First, Step 3 is the primary teaching opportunity. Use as many Teach-Okay cycles as necessary to fully clarify the answer to the question. For example, if you are teaching the definition of "fraction," you might spend 10 minutes with 10-15 Teach-Okays before you are confident students are ready to move on to the tests in Step 4.

The second important point is that a writing task should be included in all the critical thinking exercises in Step 5. WBT classrooms are writing classrooms. The *Genius Ladder* can be used for almost any critical thinking task associated with the lesson template.

The third important point is that you will need to post a sign, usually on typing paper, on a classroom wall for each concept you have taught. Power Pix, available as free downloads at WholeBrainTeaching.com, are a good source of concept signs for over 200 state standards. Your concept wall then becomes a primary teaching tool. Several times a day, ask students to review the question, answer, gesture and examples for some or all the concepts you have covered.

CHAPTER 32

BONUS CHAPTER:
11 Day Writing Lesson Plan

Following is an eleven day writing lesson plan (though it may take many weeks to complete). The lessons provide large quantities of careful reading and critical thinking, in addition to developing writing skills.

The eleven lessons are: sentence, topic sentence, paragraph, conclusion, essay, adjective, conjunction, compound sentence, complex sentence, compound-complex sentence, mega-complex sentence. Students begin with the simplest skill, writing sentences, and finish by creating three paragraph essays containing fairly sophisticated sentence constructions. These eleven lessons are appropriate for 2nd-6th graders, but may be adapted to younger or older students. Exercises for differentiated small group work have been included. In general, the high and middle groups work independently, while the teacher guides the low group.

Occasionally the lessons use material from *Book X*; *Book X* is any text you wish to use to provide writing samples. Several lesson refers to *The Writing Game*, a free download at WholeBrainTeaching.com.

Day One: Sentence

Step 1 Question: What is a sentence?

Step 2 Answer: A sentence is a complete message. (Hold a thumb and forefinger to your ear, mimicking a phone.)

Step 3 Expand: Speak examples of sentences and fragments. Explain the Midnight Phone Call Test. "Imagine you are sound asleep and the phone rings. Rinnnng! You pick it up and someone says, 'Running and laughing on the beach.' Click! Was that a complete message?"

Explain that a sentence is a complete message that would make sense in the middle of the night. Mix up examples of sentences and fragments. Students, using the word "because," discuss the examples, explaining which would, or would not, pass the Midnight Phone Call test.

Further explain that from this point forward in the class, you want all your questions answered with complete sentences (Oral Writing). Give examples of the correct and incorrect way to answer questions.

- What is your favorite food?
  Incorrect: Pizza!
  Correct: My favorite food is pizza!
- What did you do yesterday?
  Incorrect: Played soccer.
  Correct: Yesterday I played soccer.
- Do you think it will rain today?
  Incorrect: No.
  Correct: I don't think it will rain today.

Summarize the points you have made about sentences.

Read aloud from *Book X*. Stop and ask, "What is this story about?" Or, "What just happened to the main character?" Or, "What do you think will happen next?"

Ask students to respond with complete sentences.

Step 4 Test
Yes/No Way
- Is this the gesture for a sentence? (make various gestures)
- Is every sentence a complete message?
- Is this a sentence: "I like grapes on my cereal."

- Is this a sentence: "Liking grapes on my cereal."
- Is this a sentence: "The pig's name is Wilbur."

If 90% of your students pass the test, go on to the Quick Test.

QT: Quick Test
- The test for a sentence is called the Midnight Phone Call Test.
- Whenever we answer a question in class, we must use a sentence.
- A sentence can have only three words.
- A sentence cannot have more than 10 words.
- A sentence is an incomplete message.
- A sentence is a complete message.

Step 5 Critical Thinking
- Using any one of a list of words on the board, write simple sentences.
- (Upper grade) Using any word on the board, complete the *Genius Ladder*.
- Play Zork: Write an email to the aliens on Planet Zork. Using examples they could understand, explain the Midnight Phone Call Test and why it is so useful in understanding sentences.
- Use Sockless Hand Puppets, then the Air Blackboard, then Props, then Action figures to explain sentences to your neighbor.

At the end of the lesson, post a sheet of typing paper with the word "Sentence" on the Power Pix wall.

Small Groups
A. High group: Students create their own list of words and write sentences that use the sentence types on the *Genius Ladder*.
B. Middle group: Students, working in pairs, write sentences about a new list of subjects created by the teacher.
C. Low group: Working with the teacher, students speak sentences and then complete the teacher's dictation prompts. For example, "I like cake because _____." "I have fun when I _____. " "My dog is _____. "

Day Two: Topic Sentence

Review key ideas about sentences from the previous day.

Step 1 Question: What is a topic sentence?

Step 2 Answer: A topic sentence states the one main subject of a paragraph. (Hold up one finger and shake it emphatically.)

Step 3 Expand: Explaining a topic sentence is one of the most difficult and important tasks in teaching writing.

Give examples of strong and weak topic sentences from a list on the board.

- Wilbur is a pig.
  (Point out that very little could be added to this weak topic sentence.)
- Wilbur has many exciting, adventures in *Book X*.
  (Point out that information about Wilbur's exciting adventures could be added to this strong topic sentence.)
- *Book X* is a white book with drawings and 113 pages.
  (Point out that very little could be added to this weak topic sentence.)
- *Book X* is an exciting story.
  (Point out that information about *Book X's* exciting events could be added to this strong topic sentence.)

Students talk about strong and weak topic sentences.

The teacher points out that a strong topic sentence covers more information, gives the big picture. A weak topic sentence covers less information, gives close-ups. It's easy to write more sentences about a strong topic sentence; it's hard to write more sentences about a weak topic sentence.

Read aloud from *Book X*. Stop occasionally and speak a sentence about what you read. Ask students to discuss why it was, or wasn't, a strong topic sentence.

Read aloud again and ask, "What is happening in the story now?"

Students respond with a complete sentence. Guide them in shaping their sentence into a strong topic sentence.

Read aloud and give a weak topic sentence. Ask students to change it into a strong topic sentence. Point out that this will be difficult.

Step 4 Test
Yes/No Way
- Is this the gesture for topic sentence? (Make various gestures)
- Can a topic sentence state the two main subjects of a paragraph?
- Does a strong topic sentence always have more words than a weak topic sentence?
- Does a strong topic sentence give the big picture?
- Is a topic sentence the same as a paragraph?
- Does a topic sentence state the one main subject of a paragraph?

QT: Quick Test
- A topic sentence is one of several sentences in a paragraph.
- A topic sentence states the main subject of a paragraph.
- A topic sentence must be longer than other sentences in a paragraph.
- A topic sentence can be shorter than other sentences in a paragraph.

Step 5 Critical thinking: Sentence frames (students write and complete sentences below in as many ways as possible):
- I like school because ___. (add several Adders)
- _____ is a very exciting movie. (add several Adders)
- The best thing about me is that I am _____. (add several Adders)
- There are three reasons why I like _____. (add several Adders)
- *Book X* will be about _____. (after seeing pictures from the book _____ add several Adders)

At the end of the lesson, post a sheet of typing paper with the words "topic sentence" on the Power Pix wall. Students share their sentences and discuss which are strong or weak.

Small Groups

A. High Group: Students write paragraphs using topic sentences from Step 5 above. Supporting sentences in the paragraph must include sentence types from the *Genius Ladder*.

B. Middle Group: Working in pairs, students write as many topic sentences as possible on any of following subjects: school, games, friends, home, the playground, movies, favorite toys, favorite candy.

C. Low Group: The teacher asks for ideas about topic sentences on a variety of subjects. Then, students are guided by the teacher as they work as a group to create topic sentences.

Day Three: Paragraph

Review key concepts about sentences and topic sentences from the previous two days. Students discuss what happened in *Book X*. Mentioning individual characters and events, the teacher asks questions like, "What happened at the start of the story? ... Why did the farmer want to get rid of Wilber?" Students answer the teacher's questions with complete sentences (followed by Adders, if requested by the teacher).

Step 1 Question: What is a paragraph?

Step 2 Answer: A paragraph is a group of sentences about a topic sentence. (Gesture: bring three fingers on one hand, representing sentences, toward the upraised, index finger on the other hand, representing a topic sentence)

Step 3 Expand Write 5 sentences, out of paragraph order, on the board. Three of them are related. One sentence is the topic sentence. Ask the following questions:

- Which sentence is the topic sentence?
- Which sentences are about the topic sentence?
- Why isn't this sentence about the topic sentence?
- How should we order the sentences that are part of the same paragraph?

Read aloud selections from *Book X*. Insert a random sentence. Ask students to explain why the sentence doesn't belong in the paragraph. Ask: "What is the subject of the paragraph? What is the subject of the sentence I just spoke?" Guide the discussion until students understand that all sentences in a paragraph in a story are about the same subject, usually what is happening.

Read aloud again from *Book X*. Insert random sentences; students hold up their hands when they hear the sentence you created. Ask students to explain why that sentence doesn't belong in the paragraph. Ask, "What is the subject of the paragraph? What is the subject of that sentence?" Continue with this exercise until students see, again, that all the sentences in a paragraph must be about the same subject.

Next, introduce the concept of the Adder. An Adder is a sentence that adds information to any previous sentence. (Thus, Adders form the bulk of student writing, adding information to topic sentences.)

The teacher demonstrates the Adder gesture, pointing her index fingers at each other and spinning them, as if saying "More!"

This diagram is placed on the board: Question -> Answer -> Adders.

Whenever the teacher asks a question, she may use the Adder gesture to prompt students to add more sentences to their answer. Thus, students are encouraged to speak paragraphs.

Step 4 Test

Yes-No Way

- Should every paragraph have a topic sentence?
- Can a paragraph have 10 sentences?
- Can a paragraph have 3 sentences?
- Can a paragraph have no sentences?
- Is this the gesture for paragraph?
- Is this the gesture for a topic sentence? (make various gestures)
- Is this the gesture for sentence? (make various gestures)
- Is this the gesture for an Adder? (make various gestures)

QT: Quick Test

- An Adder always comes before a topic sentence.

- Every paragraph has a topic sentence at the end.
- A topic sentence is the longest sentence in a paragraph.
- A topic sentence is the shortest sentence in a paragraph.
- A topic sentence states the main idea in a paragraph.
- A paragraph is a group of sentences about one topic sentence.

Step 5 Critical Thinking: Students use paragraph frames filling in the following as many times as possible.
- There are two reasons I like ___. First, ___. Second, ___.
- ___ is an exciting game to play. One reason why ___ is exciting is because ___. Another reason why ___ is exciting is because ___.
- One person I admire is ___. (Add several Adders explaining why you admire this person)

At the end of the lesson, post a sheet of typing paper with the word "paragraph" on the Power Pix wall.

Small Groups
A. High group: Students revise paragraphs created in Step 5 by adding sentence types from the *Genius Ladder*.
B. Middle Group: Students work in pairs to revise paragraphs from Step 5; every paragraph must contain five sentences. At least one sentence must be a Complex Extender from the *Genius Ladder*.
C. Low Group: Guided writing. The teacher and her group write paragraphs together beginning with topic sentence frames from previous day:
- I like school because _____.
- _____ is a very exciting movie.
- The best thing about me is that I am _____.
- _____ there are three reasons why I like _____.
- *Book X* will be about _____. (after seeing pictures from the book)

At the end of the lesson, post a sheet of typing paper with the word "paragraph" on the Power Pix wall.

Day Four: Conclusion

Review previous days' concepts using the Power Pix wall.

Step 1 Question: What is a conclusion?

Step 2 Answer: A conclusion briefly sums up what has been said. (Gesture: wave one hand over the other as if you're an umpire signaling "safe," the play is over. This is the same gesture as for the Concluder in Oral Writing.)

Step 3 Expand: Speak several sentences about what the class did that morning. Then say, "In conclusion," and sum up what you have said.

Follow the same pattern for describing information from *Book X*, what you want to do in the summer, your favorite game as a child, etc.

Put a list of topics on the board: the playground, dessert, video games, superheroes, a great book, movies, toys. Model how you can speak several sentences, using adders, about these topics and then sum up what you have said, with "In conclusion."

Read from *Book X*; speak several sentences summarizing what you have read and then finish your oral paragraph with "In conclusion." Read several more sections and ask students to repeat your example. Prompt your kids by using the adder gesture and then the conclusion gesture.

Point out that for variety, you can use "To sum up," in place of "In conclusion, "... model the use of "To sum up, " several times.

Step 4 Test
Yes/No Way
- Is this the conclusion gesture?
- Is this the topic sentence gesture?
- Is this the paragraph gesture?
- Does a conclusion sum up what has been said?
- Does the conclusion come at the start of a paragraph?
- Does the conclusion introduce what is going to be said?
- Does the conclusion sum up what has been said?

QT: Quick Test

- A conclusion can end a paragraph.
- A good conclusion briefly sums up what has been said.
- A conclusion can end with "to sum up."
- A conclusion can start with "to sum up."
- Another way of saying "In conclusion, " is "Next."

Step 5 Critical Thinking

Students complete the following paragraph frames first by speaking, then by writing.

Several important things happened in the story. First, _____. Second, _____. Third, _____. In conclusion, _____.

Book X is an exciting story. One reason it is exciting is because _____. Another reason it is exciting because _____. To sum up, _____.

Students follow these directions, completing the task as many times as possible in 10 minutes:

1. Write a topic sentence.
2. Write two sentences about the topic sentence.
3. Add a concluding sentence that begins, "In conclusion, ..."

At the end of the lesson, post a sheet of typing paper with the word "Conclusion" on the Power Pix wall.

Small Groups

A. High Group: Students individually write two paragraphs. The first paragraph must contain 5 sentences and is about *Book X* (or any topic on the board). The second paragraph begins with either "In conclusion, " or "To sum up," and must contain two sentences.

B. Middle Group: The students work in pairs to write a two paragraph essay using the pattern above from the High Group.

C. Low Group: The assignment is the same as with the Middle Group, but is guided by leading suggestions by teacher.

Day Five : Essay

The teacher reviews key concepts from the previous four days.

Step 1 Question: What is an essay?

Step 2 Answer: An essay is three or more paragraphs about one HUGE topic. (Gesture: spread your arms out as wide as possible to emphasize "huge".)

Step 3 Expand: Point out that there are many kinds of essay topic sentences, but you are going to start with one that is simple, a sentence that contains the word "and."

Refer to material from *The Writing Game*, available as a free download at WholeBrainTeaching.com, especially Puzzle 8 on page 64 to clarify how a simple essay can be built from a topic sentence containing "and."

Using any of the 40 topics at the bottom of page 64 of *The Writing Game*, walk students through the construction of three paragraph essays. The final sentence should begin, "In conclusion" or "To sum up,".

Step 4 Test

Yes-No Way

- Should every paragraph have a topic sentence?
- Should every paragraph have an essay topic sentence?
- Can an essay topic sentence contain the word "and"?
- Does an essay have to have at least three paragraphs?
- Is this the gesture for an essay? (make various gestures)
- Is this the gesture for topic sentence? (make various gestures)
- Is this the gesture for sentence? (make various gestures)
- Is this the gesture for an Adder? (make various gestures)
- Can an essay have one paragraph?

QT: Quick Test

- A essay topic sentence is about the one main subject of an essay.
- An essay topic sentence must go in the middle of a paragraph.

- The word "and" should go at the start of an essay topic sentence.
- The word "and" is the last word in an essay topic sentence.
- An essay is three or more paragraphs about one HUGE topic.
- An essay can be 10 paragraphs long.
- An essay describes several parts of one main subject.

Step 5 Critical Thinking: Students fill in the following essay frame as many times as possible in 10 minutes:

- I like [A] and [B]. [Write a sentence about A]. [Write a sentence about B].
  [Indent and write at least two sentences about A.]
  [Indent and write at least two sentences about B.]
  [Indent] In conclusion, _____.

At the end of the lesson, post a sheet of typing paper with the words "essay" on the Power Pix wall.

Small Groups

A. High Group: Students revise essays created in Step 5 by including two of the sentence types on the *Genius Ladder*.
B. Middle Group: Students work in pairs on the same task as the High Group.
C. Low Group: The teacher guides her group in writing three paragraph essays, using the essay model in Step 5 above.

At the end of the lesson, post a sheet of typing paper with the word "Essay" on the Power Pix wall.

Day Six: Adjective

The teacher reviews key concepts from the previous four days.

Step 1 Question: What is an adjective?

Step 2 Answer: An adjective adds information to a noun. (Gesture: make a fist, representing a noun; then, cover the fist with the other hand, representing an adjective adding information to the noun.)

Step 3 Expand: Make two columns on the board, the first on the students' right listing nouns and the other listing adjectives. Point out how the adjectives add information to the nouns. Ask students to create their own adjective, noun connections.

Refer to material from *The Writing Game* at WholeBrainTeaching.com, especially on page 24 to clarify how nouns and adjectives may be combined.

Explain that the Spicy Sentence on the *Genius Ladder* always contains an adjective. Give students examples of sentences that are "too spicy," that use too many adjectives or use adjectives inappropriately. Invite students to create sentences that are too spicy and then to revise them until they are "perfectly tasty."

Step 4 Test

Yes-No Way
- Should every sentence have an adjective?
- Is an adjective always linked to a noun?
- Is this the adjective gesture (make several gestures)?
- Does the phrase "blue boat" contain an adjective? (create other phrases and then sentences that do and do not contain adjectives)

QT: Quick Test
- The sentence "I like ripe apples" contains an adjective.
- In the sentence "I like ripe apples" apples is the adjective.
- In the sentence "I like ripe apples" I is the adjective.
- In the sentence "I like ripe apples" ripe is the adjective.

Create more sentences like the ones above.

Step 5 Critical Thinking: Using adjectives on the board, students complete every sentence type on the *Genius Ladder*.

At the end of the lesson, post a sheet of typing paper with the words "adjective" on the Power Pix wall.

Small Groups
A. High Group: Students write paragraphs using sentences from Step 5 above.

B. Middle Group: Students work in pairs on the same task as the High Group.

C. Low Group: The teacher guides her group in writing three sentence paragraphs using sentences from Step 5 above.

Day Seven: Conjunction

Review previous days lessons using the Power Pix wall.

Step 1 Question: What is a conjunction?

Step 2 Answer: A conjunction is a word that joins together other words in a sentence. (Gesture: make circles with the forefinger and thumb on each hand; link these circles together.) FANBOYS is a list of conjunctions (for, and, not, but, or, yet, so). (Gesture: as you say FANBOYS name each conjunction, counting them off on seven fingers.)

Step 3 Expand: Give examples of how conjunctions are used, placing special emphasis on the three that are employed most often in student writing: and, but, or.

List the FANBOYS on the board. Ask students to work with a partner, making sentences from the FANBOYS.

Review the Midnight Phone Call test as a way of distinguishing complete from incomplete messages (sentences).

Point out that conjunctions can be used in two ways: joining two complete messages together (independent clauses) or joining a complete message with an incomplete message (impendent clause with dependent clause).

For example:

TYPE A: I like bananas and John likes oranges. (two complete messages)

TYPE B: I like bananas and oranges. (complete and incomplete message)

Read from *Book X*, stopping occasionally to give students an opportunity to identify sentences that contain conjunctions and discuss if they are Type A or Type B. Read short sentences and invite students to expand them with conjunctions followed by complete or incomplete messages.

Step 4 Test
Yes/No Way
- Is this the sentence gesture?
- Is this the summary gesture?
- Is this the topic sentence gesture?
- Is this the paragraph gesture?
- Is this the prediction gesture?
- Is this the conjunction gesture?
- Can a conjunction only join two complete sentences together?
- Is "or" a conjunction?
- Is "if" a conjunction?
  (add other short words)

QT: Quick Test
- "The" is a conjunction.
- A conjunction can join two incomplete sentences together.
- "And" is a conjunction.
  (add other short words)
- A conjunction can join an incomplete message and a complete message together.
- A conjunction can join two complete messages together.

Step 5 Critical Thinking
Students write as many sentences using conjunctions as possible in five minutes.

At the end of the lesson, post a sheet of typing paper with the word "conjunctions" on the Power Pix wall.

Small Groups
A. High Group: Students individually write three sentence paragraphs on any topic on the board. The second sentence of every paragraph must contain a conjunction.

B. Middle Group: Same as High Group but students work in pairs.

C. Low Group: Same as Middle Group, but with guided discussion and leading suggestions by teacher.

Day Eight: Compound Sentence

Review previous days using the Power Pix wall.

Step 1 Question: What is a compound sentence?

Step 2 Answer: A compound sentence is two complete messages joined by a conjunction. (Hold up a "phone" to each ear, to show a compound sentence is made up of two complete sentences.)

Step 3 Expand: Review the Midnight Phone Call test as a way of distinguishing complete from incomplete messages (sentences).

Review the previous lesson. Give examples of how conjunctions are used to make compound sentences, placing special emphasis on the three conjunctions that are employed most often in student writing: and, but, or. List the FANBOYS on the board. Ask students to work with a partner, making compound sentences from the FANBOYS.

Reviewing the previous day's lesson, point out that conjunctions can be used in two ways: joining two complete messages together (a compound sentence) or joining a complete message with an incomplete message (not a compound sentence).

For example:

TYPE A: Yesterday, Joe went to the store to buy bananas and Sarah bought apples. (two complete messages = compound sentence) Point out that compound sentences must contain two subjects like "Joe" and "Sarah" above.

TYPE B: Yesterday, I went to the store and then to the movies. (not a compound sentence)

Read from *Book X*, stopping occasionally to give students an opportunity to identify sentences that contain conjunctions and discuss if they are Type A or Type B. Read short sentences and invite students to expand them with conjunctions followed by a complete message, thus creating a compound sentence.

Step 4 Test

Yes/No Way

- Is this the sentence gesture?
- Is this the summary gesture?
- Is this the topic sentence gesture?
- Is this the paragraph gesture?
- Is this the prediction gesture?
- Is this the conjunction gesture?
- Is this the compound sentence gesture?
- Can a conjunction only join two complete messages together?
- Does every compound sentence contain a conjunction?
- Does a compound sentence contain two complete messages?
- Does a compound sentence contain two complete messages with two different subjects?
- Can a compound sentence contain two, incomplete messages?

QT: Quick Test

(Students give a thumbs up if the sentence is compound and a thumbs down if the sentence isn't compound.)

- There are tether ball poles on the playground and a big area for jumping rope.
- Everyone should get a college education or go to work after leaving high school.
- After school, Juan likes to play football and Melanie likes to read graphic novels.
- The teacher gave most of the students high grades but Emily got a very low grade.
- Down in the basement is a giant, blue snail who likes to play softball while eating pickles.

Step 5 Critical Thinking

Students write as many compound sentences as possible in five minutes on any of the following topics: sports, school, video games, recess, food, deserts, summer, exercise, plants, animals, the zoo

At the end of the lesson, the teacher posts a sheet of typing paper with the word "compound sentence" on the Power Pix wall. Students share their sentences and discuss which are, and are not, compound sentences.

Small Groups

A. High Group: Students individually write three sentence paragraphs on any topic on the board. The first sentence of the first paragraph must contain "and." The second sentence of the second and third paragraph must contain any FANBOY except "and." The last sentence of the last paragraph, must begin "In conclusion," or "To sum up."

B. Middle Group: The students work in pairs to write paragraphs using the pattern above from the High Group.

C. Low Group: Same as Middle Group, but with leading suggestions by teacher.

Day Nine: Complex Sentence

Review previous days using the Power Pix wall.

Step 1 Question: What is a complex sentence?

Step 2 Answer: A complex sentence is sentence with a complete and an incomplete message. Complex sentences can use comma openers or comma splitters. (Pick up a "phone" and hold it to your ear, nodding to show that you received a complete message. Pick up a second phone and hold it far away from your other ear, shrugging to show you received an incomplete message.)

Step 3 Expand: Review the Midnight Phone Call test as a way of distinguishing complete from incomplete messages (sentences).

Use material from *The Writing Game*, pages 38-41 to expand your lesson on the two ways of constructing complex sentences.

Give examples of two kinds of complex sentences, comma opener and comma splitter.

Comma opener: Out in the woods, the bear ate a tasty berry.

Comma splitter: The bear, out in the woods, ate a tasty berry.

Comma opener: Quickly wiping his mouth, the bear looked for another berry.

Comma splitter: The bear, quickly wiping his mouth, looked for another berry.

Comma opener: Listening carefully, the bear heard someone coming.

Comma splitter: The bear, listening carefully, heard someone coming.

List prepositions on the board that can be used for comma openers and comma splitters: over, under, beside, through, before, behind, between, on, (etc.)

Students speak complex sentences to each other using prepositions in comma openers and comma splitters.

List adverbs on the board that can be used to begin comma openers and comma splitters: quickly, slowly, happily, neatly, sweetly, rapidly, easily, (or other "ly" words).

Students speak complex sentences to each other using adverbs in comma openers and comma splitters.

As students speak complex sentences to each other, they make a comma in the air, "air punctuation" and make the sound effect "zoop!"

Step 4 Test
Yes/No Way

- Is this the sentence gesture?
- Is this the summary gesture?
- Is this the topic sentence gesture?
- Is this the paragraph gesture?
- Is this the adjective gesture?
- Is this the conjunction gesture?
- Is this the compound sentence gesture?
- Is this the complex sentence gesture?
- Does a complex sentence contain an incomplete message?
- Must a complex sentence always contain a conjunction?
- Does a complex sentence contain two complete messages?
- Can a complex sentence contain two, incomplete messages?

QT: Quick Test

(Students give a thumbs up if the sentence is complex and a thumbs down if the sentence isn't complex.)

- According to the website, there are tether ball poles on the school's playground and a big area for jumping rope.
- Everyone should get a college education or go to work after leaving high school.
- Juan, a great athlete, likes to play football or baseball.
- Surprising everyone, the teacher gave all her students high grades.
- Down in the basement is a giant, blue snail who likes to play softball while eating pickles.

Step 5 Critical Thinking

List these and other topics on the board: sports, school, video games, recess, food, deserts, summer, exercise, plants, animals, the zoo

Students follow these directions:

1. Write a topic sentence on any subject on the board using the conjunction "and." For example, "There are lions and tigers in the zoo."
2. Write a complex sentence about the first part of the topic sentence. "Lions, sometimes called the 'kings of the jungle', are near extinction in many parts of Africa."

   Write a complex sentence about the second part of the topic sentence. "In the wild, tigers eat rabbits and other small animals."
3. Add a summary sentence that begins, "In conclusion, ..." or "To sum up, ..."

Ask students to create as many of these four sentence paragraphs as possible in 10 minutes.

At the end of the lesson, post a sheet of typing paper with the word "complex sentence" on the Power Pix wall.

Small Groups

A. High Group: Students individually write three sentence paragraphs on any topic on the board. The second sentence of every paragraph must be complex.

B. Middle Group: The students work in pairs to write paragraphs using the pattern above from the High Group.

C. Low Group: Same as Middle Group, but with leading suggestions by teacher.

Day Ten: Compound-Complex Sentence

Review previous days using the Power Pix wall.

Step 1 Question: What is a compound-complex sentence?

Step 2 Answer: A compound-complex sentence is sentence with TWO complete messages and an incomplete message. (Hold up two fingers to emphasize "two.")

Step 3 Expand: Review the Midnight Phone Call test as a way of distinguishing complete from incomplete messages (sentences).

Review the two kinds of complex sentences, comma openers and comma splitters.

Referring to the *Genius Ladder* on the board, give examples of the steps that would be used to create a compound-complex sentence.

Remind students that compound sentences must contain two subjects.

Add the following examples:

1. Write a complete message: *Batman is a great superhero.*

2. To form a compound sentence, add a conjunction and another complete message with a new subject: *Batman is a great superhero but Superman is stronger and more daring.*

3. To form a compound-complex sentence, add an incomplete message: *Batman, loved by the citizens of Gotham City, is a great superhero, but Superman is stronger and more daring.*

1. Walking is a great form of exercise.

2. Walking is a great form of exercise but some people prefer cycling.

3. Walking, *loved by many,* is a great form of exercise, but some people prefer cycling.

1. The Lakers will win the next NBA championship.

2. The Lakers will win the next NBA championship _and Kobe Bryant will be their most valuable player._

3. The Lakers will win the next NBA championship and, _of course,_ Kobe Bryant will be their most valuable player.

List prepositions on the board that can be used for comma openers and comma splitters: over, under, beside, through, before, behind, between, on, against (etc.)

Give students the task of writing compound-complex sentences that use prepositions in the dependent clause.

List adverbs on the board that can be used to begin comma openers and comma splitters: quickly, slowly, happily, neatly, sweetly, rapidly, easily, (or other "ly" words).

Give students the task of writing compound-complex sentences that use adverbs in the dependent clause.

Next read from _Book X_, stopping occasionally to give your students an opportunity to identify sentences that contain conjunctions and how they might be modified into compound-complex sentences.

Step 4 Test
Yes/No Way

- Is this the sentence gesture?
- Is this the summary gesture?
- Is this the topic sentence gesture?
- Is this the paragraph gesture?
- Is this the adjective gesture?
- Is this the conjunction gesture?
- Is this the compound sentence gesture?
- Is this the compound-complex sentence gesture?
- Does a compound-complex sentence contain a conjunction?
- Does a compound-complex sentence contain two complete messages?
- Does a compound-complex sentence contain a complete and an incomplete message?
- Can a compound-complex sentence contain two, incomplete messages?

Read the following sentences. If they are compound-complex, students respond "Yes!," otherwise they answer "No Way!"
- If I want to take a break, I go play basketball or I eat a bowl of cereal.
- If I want to take a break, I go play basketball or eat a bowl of cereal.
- If I want to take a break, I go play basketball but sometimes my brother needs my help on homework.
- Barking like crazy, the big dog chased the car and the car raced away.
- Barking like crazy, the big dog chased the car and then he ran home.
- While Mary sat on a chair, a big spider sat down beside her.
- While Mary sat on a chair, a big spider sat down beside her and spun a web.
- While Mary sat on a chair, a big spider sat down beside her and then, Mary ran away.

QT: Quick Test
- A compound-complex sentence must have a conjunction.
- A compound-complex sentence must have two complete messages.
- A compound-complex sentence must have an incomplete message, two complete messages and one conjunction.
- A compound-complex sentence is like a complex sentence because it contains an incomplete message.
- A compound-complex sentence is like a complex sentence because they both must contain conjunctions.

Step 5 Critical Thinking
List these and other topics on the board: sports, school, video games, recess, food, deserts, summer, exercise, plants, animals, the zoo

Students build compound-complex sentences as follows;
1. Write a simple sentence, a complete message.
2. Add a conjunction and another complete message with a new subject.
3. Add an incomplete message that is either a comma opener or a comma splitter.

At the end of the lesson, the teacher posts a sheet of typing paper with the word "compound-complex sentence" on the Power Pix wall.

Small Groups

A. High Group: Students individually write three sentence paragraphs on any topic on the board. The second sentence of every paragraph must contain a compound-complex sentence. The last paragraph must begin with "In conclusion, " or "To sum up, ".

B. Middle Group: The students work in pairs to write paragraphs using the pattern above from the High Group.

C. Low Group: Same as Middle Group, but with guided discussion by teacher.

Day Eleven: Mega-complex Sentence

Review previous days using the Power Pix wall.

Step 1 Question: What is a mega-complex sentence?

Step 2 Answer: A mega-complex sentence is any sentence that weaves at least two incomplete messages into a complete message!! (Make a sewing (weaving) motion with one hand then clap both hands to your cheeks in amazement at the wonder of a mega-complex sentence.)

Step 3 Expand: Review the Midnight Phone Call test as a way of distinguishing complete from incomplete messages (sentences).

Review the two kinds of complex sentences, comma openers and comma splitters.

Give examples of the three steps used to build a mega-complex sentence.

1. Write a complete message: *Soccer is the world's greatest sport.*

2. Add an incomplete message: *Soccer, a challenging game, is the world's greatest sport.*

3. To form a mega-complex sentence, add another incomplete message: *According to Maria, soccer, a challenging game, is the world's greatest sport.*

Here are several more examples.

1. The policeman looked in the car.
2. *Surrounded by a crowd*, the policeman looked in the car.
3. Surrounded by a crowd, the policeman, *nervously shaking*, looked in the car.

1. You should eat breakfast.
2. *Though you don't think so*, you should eat breakfast.
3. Though you don't think so, you, *even when you are in a hurry*, should eat breakfast.

1. The teacher looked around the classroom.
2. *As it rained outside*, the teacher looked around the classroom.
3. As it rained outside, the teacher, *smiling happily*, looked around the classroom.

List prepositions on the board that can be used for comma openers and comma splitters: over, under, beside, through, before, behind, between, on, against (etc.)

Students construct mega-complex sentences using prepositional phrases.

List adverbs on the board that can be used for comma openers and comma splitters: quickly, slowly, happily, neatly, sweetly, rapidly, easily, (or other "ly" words).

Students construct mega-complex sentences using adverbial phrases.

Using short sentences from *Book X*, help your students build mega-complex sentences.

Step 4 Test
Yes/No Way

- Is this the sentence gesture?
- Is this the summary gesture?
- Is this the topic sentence gesture?
- Is this the paragraph gesture?
- Is this the adjective gesture?
- Is this the conjunction gesture?
- Is this the compound sentence gesture?

- Is this the compound-complex gesture?
- Is this the mega-complex sentence gesture?
- Does a mega-complex sentence contain two incomplete messages?
- Can a mega-complex sentence contain a conjunction?
- Can a mega-complex sentence contain three incomplete messages and two conjunctions?

(Regardless of how your students answer this last question, write examples on the board of convoluted mega-complex sentences.)

For example:

While trying to finish the marathon, John, unfortunately, strained his calf and his ankle, though he pretended that he was fine.

In the dark forest, the giant snail, in complete silence, swallowed pickles and pears, while trying to decide between playing softball and tennis when suddenly a boy shouted, very loudly, "hello!"

QT: Quick Test

(Students give a thumbs up if the sentence is mega-complex and a thumbs down otherwise.)

- There are tether ball poles on the playground and a big area for jumping rope.
- There are tether ball poles on the playground and, so that everyone can have fun, a big area for jumping rope.
- According to the school website, there are tether ball poles on the playground and, so that everyone can have fun, a big area for jumping rope.
- Everyone should get a college education or go to work after leaving high school.
- Juan likes to play football but he loves playing baseball.
- Juan, an athletic boy, likes to play football but he, unlike the rest of his family, loves playing baseball.
- Though you don't believe me, down in the basement, right under your feet, is a giant, blue snail eating a pickle.

Step 5 Critical Thinking

List these and other topics on the board: sports, school, video games, recess, food, deserts, summer, exercise, plants, animals, the zoo

Students follow these directions:

1. Write a topic sentence on any subject on the board using the conjunction "and."
2. Write a sentence about the first part of the topic sentence that is a complex sentence.
   Write a sentence about the second part of the topic sentence that is a mega-complex sentence.
3. Add a summary sentence that begins, "In conclusion, ..." or "To sum up, ..."

Ask students to create as many of these four sentence paragraphs as possible in 10 minutes.

At the end of the lesson, post a sheet of typing paper with the word "mega-complex sentence" on the Power Pix wall.

Small Groups

A. High Group: Students individually write three paragraph essays on any topic on the board. The second sentence of every paragraph must contain a mega-complex sentence. The first sentence of the last paragraph begins with "In conclusion, " or "To sum up,".
B. Middle Group: The students work in pairs to write paragraphs using the pattern above from the High Group.
C. Low Group: Same as Middle Group, but with leading suggestions by teacher.

APPENDIX

Mind Sports

Mrs. Maestra found that the best way to keep her students engaged in playing the Scoreboard game, central to WBT's classroom management system, was to occasionally change the rewards they could earn. She motivated them with more or less homework, time allotted to recess, watching videos, listening to music, or chatting. However, the reward she, and her students, valued the most, was playing learning games, especially the three WBT Mind Sports: Mind Soccer, Mind Volleyball and Mind Basketball.

Each Mind Sport required almost no materials, could be played in as few as five minutes, and involved her students in a high spirited summary of large amounts of classroom material. In effect, Mrs. Maestra's kids worked hard at the Scoreboard to earn the right to review their lessons! Like so much else in WBT, this convinced Mrs. Maestra that she was in Teacher Heaven.

Each Mind Sport game is inspired by Fred Jones, one of the founders of modern classroom management theory, but is souped up with special Whole Brain Teaching features.

Mrs. Maestra set a time limit for how long a Mind Sport game lasted. If she started with just five minutes, the game was over so quickly that her students begged her to let them play again. This was exactly what she wanted... but she never played two games in a row on the same day. Mrs. Maestra's rule was that every game had to be earned with good classroom behavior.

When Mrs. Maestra decided it was time to reward her class with Mind Sports, she made a special square on the blackboard. At the end of every day, if there are more positive than negative marks on the Scoreboard, then Mrs. Maestra put a star in the square. When there were 10 stars, her class had earned the right to play a Mind Sport for five minutes.

Here are Mind Sport directions Mrs. Maestra received at a WBT conference:

MIND SOCCER

Purpose

Like soccer, Mind Soccer is played between two teams. The purpose of the game is to score goals. Goals are scored by quickly answering questions posed by the referee.

Rules

There is only one rule in Mind Soccer: Keep The Referee Happy. You're the Ref.

Equipment

A blackboard, an eraser and a set of short answer, often one word, review questions that you have created. You will be reading questions from this list; arrange them in groups from easiest to hardest.

The Set Up

Draw a horizontal line, about six feet long, near the bottom of your whiteboard. Mark off the line in 11 equidistant vertical marks. The horizontal line stands for a soccer field; each end of the line is a soccer goal; the vertical marks divide the field into units (like a football field). Place an eraser under the vertical mark in the middle of the field. The eraser is the soccer ball.

How To Play

1. Divide the class into two teams. We'll use boys against girls, but it could be right side of the class against left side, etc.
2. Set a kitchen timer to the amount of time the game will be played.
3. Designate one player to also serve as the scorekeeper.
4. Teams are given 10 seconds to elect a captain. If no captain is elected, the ref, you, picks one.
5. To start the game, the captains stand face to face at the front of the room. You pose one of your review questions and, just as in "Family Feud", the captains slap their hands down on a desk as quickly as possible if they know the answer. The captain who is quickest, gets

the chance to respond. If the captain is right, his/her team gets the ball. Otherwise, the opposing team's captain gets the ball.

6. Assume the girls' team wins control. Picking one player at a time or the team as a whole, ask review questions to the girls' team. If the player's answer is correct, loud, fast and with an energetic gesture, that counts as a "strong kick." Advance the ball, the eraser, almost a full hash mark down the field toward the boys' goal. If the answer is correct but too quiet or slow or doesn't have an energetic gesture, that is a "weak kick." Advance the ball a short distance toward the boys' goal. If the girls' answer is wrong, shout "Turnover!" and now the boys' team gets a chance to play. If you like a rowdy classroom, encourage teams to cheer when the ball is going their direction and groan when it isn't. Thus, whenever the ball moves, your class will be cheering and groaning. For a hysterical example of how Mind Soccer is played in class, see Chris Rekstad's video, "Mind Soccer," at http://www.youtube.com/watch?v=KAD9pHMbvS8.

7. Use the following to add excitement to Mind Soccer:

Steal! Whenever you, the referee, want to reverse the direction of the game, shout "Steal!" This means the other team has suddenly gotten control of the ball. Of course, you will shout "Steal!" whenever you want to generate an intense amount of excitement ... like when one team is very close to the goal and about to score.

Foul! Whenever one team or the other misbehaves in the slightest, complains about the ref's call, anything, you shout "Foul!" As the ref, you then have three choices. You can award control of the ball to the opposing team; you can move the ball up or down the field, penalizing one team or the other; or, most exciting, you can declare a Penalty Kick. (Encourage teams to cheer or groan as appropriate.)

Penalty Kick! Move the ball to the first hash mark in front of the opposition's goal. The attacking team chooses a kicker, usually the team captain. The defending team chooses a goalie, usually the team captain. Goalie and kicker face off in front of the room, like the initial kickoff. You state a question; the player who slaps a hand down first gets first try at the question. If the goalie is first and correct, the penalty kick is blocked. If the goalie is first and wrong, the penalty kick scores. If the captain is first and correct, the penalty kick scores. If the captain is first and wrong, the penalty kick is blocked. If a goal is scored, the scoring team shouts "Goooooooaaaaalll!!!" like Andres Cantor, the famous Mexican announcer.

Free Ball! Often in soccer, neither team is in control of the ball. When you shout "Free Ball!", anyone on either team can answer. Fire questions at your students; when one side gets several questions in a row correct, point at them and say, "You won the Free Ball!" Then start giving questions to individual players on the winning team.

Read The Ref's Mind Free Ball! For hilarious excitement, say, "I'm thinking of a key concept we covered. Free Ball! Read my mind!" Both teams shout answers at you, energetically covering enormous quantities of review material. Give them hints as you wish. Award control of the ball to the team that reads your mind, or, failing that, that has the most attempts at reading your mind.

Your Strategy

You will use a large number of review questions in Mind Soccer; thus, it is important to have a list so you can keep the game moving along quickly. Use any question, addition, subtraction, division, multiplication, state capitals, key concepts from science, names of characters in stories, anything.

Keep the ball moving up and down the field. Make the game as exciting as you wish by shouting Steal!, Penalty Kick!, Free Ball! or Read The Ref's Mind Free Ball! Never let one team get more than one goal ahead of the other. Many soccer games end in ties. Give the weakest players easier questions; stronger players get harder questions. If, like many Whole Brain Teachers, you believe in the importance of gestures that enhance learning, award answers that have a particularly appropriate, descriptive gesture a "very strong kick."

Continue playing until the timer goes off. Then resist students' entreaties to play again. The privilege to play Mind Soccer, like all Mind Sports, is earned by tallying positive marks on the Scoreboard.

MIND VOLLEYBALL

Purpose

Like volleyball, Mind Volleyball is played between two teams. The purpose of the game is to score points. Points are scored by quickly answering questions posed by the referee.

Rules

There is only one major rule in Mind Volleyball, *Keep the Ref Happy!* And you, of course, are the ref. When anyone argues with you or the opposing team... or even looks the slightest bit unhappy, you can award a point to the other team. This reduces hassles between you and the class or between opposing sides.

Equipment

All you'll need is a long list of typed questions and answers. Use math facts, states and capitals, vocabulary words and definitions... anything that you want your students to review.

How To Play

1. Divide your class into teams (boys vs. girls works wonderfully); one team sits on your right, the other team sits on your left. Leave a clear space, representing the net, between the two teams.
2. Set a kitchen timer to the amount of time the game will be played.
3. Designate one player to also serve as the scorekeeper.
4. One after the other, you ask three players on one side a different question. If they all are correct, the other side gets three questions. Keep going until one side answers incorrectly. This scores a point for the opposing team. Then begin with three questions for the team

that lost the point. *To keep the game close, ask easier questions to the team that is behind.* If anyone complains about anything, award the opposing team a point. Keep playing until the timer goes off.

Suggestions

Before you begin the game, give students a demo of how quickly you, the ref, can award points to one side or the other if you see, or hear, unsportsmanlike conduct. While the game is played, continue to use your authority as ref to keep squabbling under control.

Encourage teams to cheer whenever they score a point... or if neighboring teachers complain, show your students how to celebrate with a "quiet riot," patting finger tips together and "screaming" their loudest whisper!

If a winning team wants to know their prize, you say, "Next time we play, your side will get the first question." If they complain that this isn't a substantial enough reward, say "You just made the ref very unhappy. Next time we play, the other team gets the first question!"

MIND BASKETBALL

Purpose

Like basketball, Mind Basketball is played between two teams. The purpose of the game is to score baskets. Baskets are scored by quickly answering questions posed by the referee.

Rules

Just as in the other two Mind Sports, there is one major rule, *Keep the Ref Happy!* And you are the ref.

Unlike real basketball, baskets in Mind Basketball count from one to five points.

Lay-up: one point

Mid-Ranger Jumper: two points

Three Point Line: three points

Half Court: four points

Full Court: five points

Equipment

Create a long list of typed questions and answers arranged in five categories, from easiest to hardest. You'll need lots of questions in each category for Mind Basketball.

How To Play

1. Divide the class into two teams, with an aisle separating them. Write the five types of shots and scores for each on the whiteboard.
2. Set a kitchen timer to the amount of time the game will be played.
3. Designate one player who will also serve as the scorekeeper.
4. One member from each team comes forward for the jump ball. Keep posing questions until one player answers correctly before the other player. The winning player's team gets to start.
5. Point at a student and ask her to choose what kind of shot she wants, Lay-up, Mid-Range Jumper, Three Point Line, Half Court or Full Court. In essence, she is choosing the difficulty of her question... and the number of points she is trying to score. If the girl answers correctly, shout "basket!" Her team cheers, and the scorekeeper records the appropriate points. If she answers incorrectly, her team groans. In either case, the other team gets the next question. Keep tossing questions from one team to the other, until the timer goes off.

Suggestions

The closer any game is the more exciting. You can keep the score tight in Mind Basketball by introducing any, or all, of the following.

Shot Clock: Unlike real basketball, the ref, you, can start a shot clock at any point in the game. Simply call, "shot clock" after you pose a question and begin counting loudly from 5 down to 0. The player must answer before you get to zero. Keep using the shot clock whenever you wish, until the timer goes off.

Technical Foul: When a player does or says anything that makes the ref unhappy, you have the option of calling "technical foul!" Then, a member of the opposing team gets two easy questions and, "possession of the ball," i.e. the next question as well.

Defense: If you like a rowdy class, and we do, then allow the team that is not answering a question to make wacky faces at the player whose turn it is to score.

Time Out: Tell the teams what the subjects are for the next few baskets. Then allow them a time out for a minute or so to quietly review questions that you might toss at them.

Steal: To keep the game exciting, don't let either team get too far ahead. If one team is drubbing another, pose a question to the leading team, and then before a player has a chance to answer, shout "Steal!" Then pose the same question to a strong player on the other team.

Overtime: If you use your powers as a ref skillfully, you can arrange for a tie score when time expires. Set the clock for one or two minutes and then start firing questions at players, giving them very little time to answer. You know you've been successful if when the timer goes off, both teams beg you to let them play again.

Rehearsing Procedures

As you've seen, we believe in having our students rehearse rules and procedures... rather than scolding them when they forget how to behave. But how, exactly, should we rehearse?

Assume you are having trouble getting students to respond to your "Class!" with a crisp "Yes!" and some of your kids aren't responding at all. Imagine that!

Here is a script written by WBT board member, Andrea Schindler which provides an excellent example of WBT rehearsal.

> **SCRIPT: CLASS-YES REHEARSAL**
>
> **Teacher:** Claaaaaaasssss.
> **Students:** (Some students) Yeeeeeeesss.
> **Teacher:** Class! Class!
> **Students:** (Some students) Yes! Yes!
> **Teacher:** Classity class!
> **Students:** (Some students) Yessity yes!

If you've tried three times to get your students' attention and everyone isn't responding, your next step is to make a forwny mark on the Scoreboard. Exclaim, "Mighty Groan!" No matter how many students groan at this point, continue as follows:

> **Teacher:** I didn't have everybody participating with the Class-Yes. Would you like to try again?
> **Students:** Yes!
> **Teacher:** When I say Class! You say Yes! Class!
> **Students:** (Some students) Yes.
> **Teacher:** What's rule #1?
> **Students:** Follow directions quickly!
> **Teacher:** What was that? Follow directions slooooooowly???

Students: No! Follow directions quickly.

Teacher: Well when I say "Class" everybody must say "Yes!", but also you have to stop what you are doing and look at me as fast as you can. Like lightening speed fast! Can you be lightening speed fast?

Students: Yes!

Teacher: Tell your neighbor, "I'm lightening speed fast, are you lightning speed fast?"

Students: (They tell their neighbors.)

Teacher: Tell your neighbor, "I bet you're not as fast as me!"

Students: (They tell their neighbors.)

Teacher: Okay, let's see who is lightning speed fast. Practice being busy.

Students practice looking down or doing their work... you may have to model this.

Teacher: Claaaaassssss!

Students: Yeeeeessss!

Teacher: Class! Class!

Students: Yes! Yes!

Now point out several students who were really fast. ("I saw Sam was fast. Michael was fast and Sarah was fast! Their heads almost spun off they were so fast!") Mark a Smiley point on the Scoreboard and get a Mighty Oh Yeah. Continue:

Teacher: Buuuuuuuut I didn't have everybody being fast. (Mark a frowny point.) Give me a Mighty Groan.

Students: (They give a Mighty Groan.)

Teacher: Would you like to try again?

Students: Yes!

Teacher: Can you be as fast as Sam, Michael, and Sarah?

Students: Yes!

Teacher: Tell your neighbor, "I'm faster than Sam, Michael, and Sarah!"

Students: (They tell their neighbors.)

Teacher: Okay! Practice being busy! (Pause while students pretend they are busy.) Claaaaaaaasssss!

Students: Yeeeeeesss!

Teacher: OOOOOOhhhhh Class!

Students: OOOOOOhhhhh Yes!

Teacher: Great job, let me hear your "Mighty oh Yeah!" (Mark a Smiley point.)

This is a good example of an initial, extended rehearsal. Later rehearsals can be briefer. But here is the important point: if you want things done a certain way in your classroom, then it is better to rehearse what you want, rather than scold kids for not learning what you haven't taught them yet!

Notes to Parents

Note To Parents

YOUR CHILD NEEDS MORE PRACTICE

Your child is having problems at school with the rule circled above. Please have your student practice the gesture for the rule at home for as long as you feel necessary. For school records, I'll need this note signed and returned tomorrow. If you have any questions you can reach me at:

My son/daughter practiced the gesture at home for _____ minutes.

Student

_____

Parent

_____

Date _____

Note To Parents

YOUR CHILD IS DOING GREAT!

Your child is doing a great job with the rule circled above! I really appreciate your student's dedication, cooperation and consistent effort. Please give your child extra one on one time for the good work already accomplished. For school records, I'll need this note signed and returned tomorrow. If you have any questions you can reach me at:

The reward I gave my child was:

_____

Student

_____

Parent

_____

Date _____

Free Whole Brain Teaching E-Books

All of the following are free downloads at WholeBrainTeaching.com.

Biffytoons Manual
Teach young learners sight words with Biffytoons cartoons. This eBook is packed: 48 full color cartoons, 48 line drawings, 48 mini-cartoons and Biffytoons Bingo... a host of features introduce new readers to the most common words in English.

Industrial Strength Whole Brain Teaching
We designed this special, extra strength, version of Whole Brain Teaching for the most challenging K-12 classes. You'll be especially happy with *Industrial Strength Whole Brain Teaching* if you'd like to train your rebel students to be classroom leaders.

Kindergarten Power Pix
Over 170 pages and more than 70 full color signs! Everything you need to teach math and language arts State Standards to your little ones.

Mind Soccer!
The incredible K-12 Review Anything Game is perfect for use with Whole Brain Teaching's Scoreboard.

Power Student Olympics
Watch your students break 100's of personal records in reading, math, writing and art.

Practice Cards
A powerful addition to Whole Brain Teaching's Classroom Management System. Give your kids Positive Practice following the classroom rules.

SuperSpeed 100
New readers learn 100 of the most common sight words, while having a blast!

SuperSpeed 1000

Teach your class 1,000 of the most common sight words! Kids will *beg you* to let them play!

SuperSpeed Letters & Phonics

The easy way to teach beginning readers the alphabet and letter sounds; kids love this game.

SuperSpeed Math

Addition! Subtraction! Multiplication! Division! Students can't get enough of SuperSpeed Math.

SuperSpeed Numbers

A lively game for school or home that teaches the counting numbers 1-100. Works like a wonder.

Teaching Challenging Teens

Our 225 page classroom management guide is designed especially for middle school and high school.

The Agreement Bridge

The Agreement Bridge is Whole Brain Teaching's most powerful tool for helping troubled students. Teacher and student work together in a game that teaches, and rewards, collaborative problem solving. Bonus chapters include descriptions of how the game may be played with a group of students or between peer mentors and their classmates.

The Crazy Professor Reading Game

One of our first eBooks, *The Crazy Professor Reading Game* has also been one of our most popular. Used by thousands of K-12 teachers across the country, the Crazy Professor is designed to deepen students' reading comprehension of both fiction and nonfiction. In a gamelike format, your kids learn to paraphrase, translate ideas into gestures, skim read for key ideas, connect their reading to personal experiences, and much more!

Whole Brain Teachers Training Manual
Everything you need to be a Whole Brain Teacher trainer!

Whole Brain Teaching Case Studies
Over 60 true stories of Whole Brain Teaching in action!

Free Whole Brain Teaching Videos

The 22 Whole Brain Teaching (WBT) videos below were shot over a period of three years, beginning in Fall 1997 and finishing in Spring 2010. Viewed in chronological order, they show the development of our techniques from Power Teaching (our first name) to Whole Brain Teaching. As with any complex art, we learned as we went along.

All the videos below can be seen at:

http://www.youtube.com/user/ChrisBiffle

Intro to Whole Brain Teaching: Lessons 1-8
Each short video demonstrates a key component of WBT. Taken in order, the movies show what we believe is a logical sequence for introducing many of our strategies to classes from kindergarten through high school.

WBT Basics
Chris Biffle uses his philosophy classroom to demonstrate the Big Six (an early version of the Big Seven). Note that all of the techniques employed with young adults can also be found in our videos of elementary students.

How to Begin WBT Part 1 and 2
Our most recent video demonstrates how to begin the Big Seven using middle school students as a sample population. The Big Seven, fully described on our website WholeBrainTeaching.com, are: Class-Yes, the Five Classroom Rules, Teach-Okay, Scoreboard, Mirror, Hands and Eyes, Switch. The class in this video had practiced for about 25 minutes before beginning. With older kids, the Big Seven can be introduced fairly quickly, as demonstrated in the video. In K-3 classes, introduction of the Big Seven might be spread over several weeks.

WBT College Aristotle
Biffle demonstrates advanced techniques to combine individual and group learning in a WBT classroom.

Portrait of a New Teacher

The video provides an impressionistic overview of a new teacher, Andrea Schindler, using Whole Brain Teaching in its earliest stage of development. In seven minutes, you'll see a portrait of the birth of a remarkable teacher; Andrea is currently (2010) one of the most viewed and imitated kindergarten educators in the U.S.

WBT Kindergarten

Andrea Schindler, who began Whole Brain Teaching on her first day as an instructor, demonstrates several engaging WBT strategies with young learners. This video is among the most popular in the WBT series.

WBT 1st Grade

An excellent demonstration of low key, Whole Brain Teaching, If you like quiet, calm, intensely focused classes, and who doesn't?, these first graders provide excellent models.

WBT 6th Grade Math

One of the most viewed education videos on YouTube (over 100,000 at last count!), this sixth grade teacher combines remarkably effective pacing, humor and gestures to teach a complex subject, the order of operations. To show the range of WBT, contrast these highly trained, disciplined 6th graders to the rowdy, spontaneous 4th graders in the critical thinking video above

Crazy Professor

In one of our first videos, Chris Rekstad demonstrates an early version of The Crazy Professor Reading Game, designed to increase student reading comprehension for both fiction and nonfiction.

SuperSpeed 100

A classroom of special ed kids master 100 of the most common sight words using one our most popular free downloads at WholeBrainTeaching.com. SuperSpeed 100 is used from grades K-5; the key motivator is that students are setting and breaking personal records for reading speed.

Mind Soccer

This entertaining, often hilarious video, features WBT Co-Founder Chris Rekstad and his fourth grade, Yucaipa, California class. As you'll see, Mind Soccer provides a remarkably flexible (and comic!) format for reviewing course material. The game is so entertaining that kids will work hard, tallying marks on the Scoreboard, for the privilege of playing Mind Soccer. A whole class learning with as much energy as possible for the reward of reviewing what they have learned? You know what that is. Teacher Heaven.

Classroom Rules Signs

The following signs, designed by Saskia Biffle, are available in full color, in the Store menu at WholeBrainTeaching.com.

BIBLIOGRAPHY

There are a host of books on the brain, brain research and teaching. Here are eight of the best.

Freberg, Laura A., *Discovering Biological Psychology,* Wadsworth Publishing, 2009

Greene, Ross W. *Lost at School,* Scribner, 2009

Horstman, Judith, *The Scientific American Day in the Life of Your Brain,* Jossey-Bass, 2009

Jones, Fred, *Tools for Teaching,* Fredric H. Jones & Associates, 2007

Kagan, Spencer, *Collaborative Learning,* Kagan Cooperative Learning, 1994

Kotulak, Richard, *Inside the Brain,* Andrews McMeel Publishing, 1997

Medina, John, *Brain Rules,* Pear Press, 2008

Restak, Richard, *The New Brain,* Rodale Books, 2003

ABOUT THE AUTHOR

 CHRIS BIFFLE is the author of seven books (McGraw-Hill, HarperCollins) on critical thinking, reading and writing. He began his teaching career in 1967 by co-founding Children's House in Watsonville, California, one of the first daycare centers in the United States for the children of migrant workers. Over the last four decades, Chris has received grants from the U.S. Department of Education, the National Endowment for the Humanities, served on the Perseus Project when it was based at Harvard, and been featured on over 25 radio and television broadcasts. In 2004, Chris led the "Save Our Schools" 300 mile march on Sacramento protesting education budget cuts. He has been lead presenter at over 100 Whole Brain Teaching conferences, attended by 20,000 educators. Tens of thousands of instructors across the United States and around the world base their teaching methods on his free eBooks available at WholeBrainTeaching.com. Videos produced by Chris have received over 3,000,000 views on the internet.

Notes